Quirkology

QUIRKOLOGY

How We Discover the Big Truths in Small Things

RICHARD WISEMAN, PH. D.

BRISTOL PARK BOOKS / NEW YORK

First Bristol Park Books edition published in 2013

Bristol Park Books
252 W. 38th Street
NYC, NY 10018

Bristol Park Books is a registered trademark of Bristol Park Books, Inc.

Published by arrangement with Basic Books

Designed by Timm Bryson

ISBN: 978-0-88486-525-4

Printed in the United States of America

To Mum and Dad

What is the use of such a study? The criticism implied in this question has never bothered me, for any activity seems to me of value if it satisfies curiosity, stimulates ideas, and gives a new slant to our understanding of the social world.

—STANLEY MILGRAM,
THE INDIVIDUAL IN A SOCIAL WORLD

Contents

List of Figures ix

Prologue
The Mysterious Q-Test xi

Introduction
Exploring the Backwaters of the Human Brain 1

1 What Does Your Date of Birth *Really* Say About You?
The New Science of Chronopsychology 7

2 Trust Everyone, but Always Cut the Cards
The Psychology of Lying and Deception 45

3 BELIEVING SIX IMPOSSIBLE THINGS BEFORE BREAKFAST

Psychology Enters the Twilight Zone 89

4 MAKING YOUR MIND UP

The Strange Science of Decision Making 127

5 THE SCIENTIFIC SEARCH FOR THE WORLD'S FUNNIEST JOKE

Explorations into the Psychology of Humor 179

6 SINNER OR SAINT?

The Psychology of When We Help and When We Hinder 227

7 THE PACE OF LIFE AND OTHER QUIRKOLOGICAL ODDITIES

The Future of Quirkology 265

AFTERWORD

How to Pep Up the Dullest of Dinner Parties 275

ACKNOWLEDGMENTS 279

NOTES 283

INDEX 307

Figures

Graph 1: *Born Lucky results: The percentage of lucky people born in each month of the year.* 33

Figure 1: *Photographs showing either a genuine smile or a fake one.* 68

Figure 2: *Duchenne stimulates the face of his volunteer.* 73

Figure 3: *Close-up of the genuine and fake smiles.* 74

Figure 4: *Genuine and doctored photographs used in Kimberley Wade's false-memory experiment.* 78

Figure 5: *Composites of the last six Democratic and Republican presidents.* 156

Figure 6: *Composites of the last six Democratic and Republican presidents, excluding Bill Clinton and George Bush Jr.* 157

Figure 7: *Which image do you find more attractive?* 174

Figure 8: *A giant chicken crosses the road to help promote LaughLab.* 183

Figure 9: *A 3D scan showing the parts of the brain involved in finding jokes funny.* 201

Figure 10: *Another giant chicken reveals the world's funniest joke.* 223

Table 1: *The 32 countries in the "pace of life" experiment ranked by their speed of walking.* 271

Prologue

The Mysterious Q-Test

Before we begin, please take a few moments to complete the following exercise.

Using the first finger of your dominant hand, please trace the capital letter *Q* on your forehead.

There are two ways of completing the exercise. You can draw the letter *Q* with the tail of the *Q* toward your right eye like this:

In this case, *you* can read it, but someone facing you can't.

Or you can draw it with the tail of the *Q* toward your left eye.

In this case, someone *facing you* can read it, but you can't.

As we will discover later, the way in which you completed the task reveals a great deal about an important aspect of your life.

INTRODUCTION

Exploring the Backwaters of the Human Brain

I have long been fascinated by the quirky side of human behavior. When I was a psychology undergraduate, one of my very first experiments involved standing for hours in London's King's Cross railroad station looking for people meeting partners who had just gotten off a train. The moment they were locked in a passionate embrace, I would walk up to them, trigger a hidden stopwatch in my pocket, and ask, "Excuse me, do you mind taking part in a psychology experiment? How many seconds have passed since I just said the words 'excuse me'?" After querying around fifty such couples, I discovered that people greatly underestimate the passing of time when they are in love, or, as Albert Einstein once said, "Sit with a beautiful woman for an hour and it seems like a minute, sit on a hot stove for a minute and it seems like an hour—that's relativity."

An interest in the more unusual aspects of psychology has continued throughout my career. After finishing my undergraduate degree, I traveled north to the University of Edinburgh in Scotland and spent four years working on a doctorate examining the psychology of deception. Once that was completed, I accepted an academic position at the University of Hertfordshire, and set up my own research unit to examine unusual areas of psychology. I am not the first academic to be fascinated by this approach to examining behavior. Each generation of scientists has produced a small number of researchers who have investigated the strange and unusual.

The maverick Victorian scientist Sir Francis Galton might be considered the founding father of this approach because he devoted much of his life to the study of offbeat topics.[1] He objectively determined whether his colleagues' lectures were boring by surreptitiously measuring the level of fidgeting in their audiences, and he created a "Beauty Map" of Britain by walking along the main streets of major cities with a punch counter in his pocket, secretly recording whether the people he passed were good, medium, or bad looking (London was rated the best, Aberdeen the worst).

Galton's work on the effectiveness of prayer was more controversial.[2] He hypothesized that if prayer really worked, then members of the clergy—who obviously prayed longer and harder than most—should have a longer life expectancy than others. When his extensive analyses of hundreds of entries in biographical dictionaries revealed that the clergy actually tended to die *before* lawyers and doctors, the deeply religious Galton was forced to question the power of prayer.

Even the making of tea caught Galton's attention; he spent months scientifically determining the best way to brew the perfect cup of tea. He constructed a special thermometer that allowed him constantly to monitor the temperature of the water inside his teapot, and after much rigorous testing, Galton concluded that "the tea was full bodied, full tasted, and in no way bitter or flat . . . when the water in the teapot had remained between 180 degrees and 190 degrees Fahrenheit, and had stood eight minutes on the leaves."[3]

Satisfied with the thoroughness of his investigation, Galton proudly declared, "There is no other mystery in the teapot."

On the surface, Galton's investigations into boredom, beauty, prayer, and tea-making may appear to have nothing in common. But in fact they are all excellent and early examples of an approach to investigating human behavior that I have called "quirkology." Put simply, quirkology uses scientific methods to study the more curious aspects of everyday life. This approach to psychology has been pioneered by a few researchers over the past hundred years who have followed in Galton's footsteps and had the courage to explore the places mainstream scientists avoid. These brave academics have

- examined how many people it takes to start a Mexican wave in a football stadium;[4]
- charted the upper limits of visual memory by having people try to remember 10,000 photographs accurately;[5]
- identified the perceived personality characteristics of fruits and vegetables (lemons are seen as dislikable, onions as stupid, and mushrooms as social climbers);[6]
- secretly counted the number of people wearing their baseball caps the right way or back to front;[7]
- stood outside supermarkets with donation boxes quietly measuring how different types of requests for donations

determined the amount of money given (simply saying "Even a penny helps" almost doubled donations);[8]
- discovered that children's drawings of Santa Claus grow larger in the build-up to Christmas Day, and then shrink during January.[9]

For the past twenty years, I have carried out similarly strange investigations. I have examined the telltale signs that give away a liar, explored how our personalities are shaped by month of birth, uncovered the secret science behind speed dating and personal ads, and investigated what a sense of humor reveals about the innermost workings of the mind. The work has involved secretly observing people as they go about their daily business, conducting unusual experiments at art exhibitions and concerts, and even staging fake séances in allegedly haunted buildings. The studies have involved thousands of people all over the world.

This book details my adventures and experiments and also pays homage to unusual research carried out by the small band of dedicated academics that has kept the quirky flag flying for the past century. Each chapter reveals the secret psychology underlying a particular aspect of our lives, from deception to decision making, selfishness to superstition. Along the way, you will encounter some of my favorite pieces of strange but fascinating research: experiments that have, for instance, measured the amount of subsequent horn-honking when cars become stalled at traffic lights; examined why a disproportionate number of marine biologists are called Dr. Fish; secretly analyzed the type of people who take more than ten items through express lines in supermarkets; asked people to behead live rats with a kitchen knife; discovered whether suicide rates are related to the amount of country music played on national radio; and proved beyond all reasonable doubt that Friday the thirteenth is bad for your health.

Most of the research that you are about to encounter has, until now, been hidden away in obscure academic journals. The work is serious science, and much of it has important implications for the way in which we live our lives and structure our society. However, unlike the vast majority of psychological research, these studies have something quirky about them. Some use mainstream methods to investigate unusual topics. Others use unusual methods to investigate mainstream topics. All are aimed at discovering the big truths in small things.

Let the quirkology begin.

1 WHAT DOES YOUR DATE OF BIRTH *REALLY* SAY ABOUT YOU?

The New Science of Chronopsychology

Given that approximately 100 million Americans read their daily horoscopes, and about 6 million have paid professional astrologers to analyze their personalities,[1] it is easy to argue that many people believe there may be something to astrology. Even world leaders are not immune to the lure of the soothsaying stargazers. Both Ronald and Nancy Reagan were fond of consulting with the cosmos, and President Reagan allowed astrologers to influence the timing of international summits, presidential announcements, and the flight schedule of Air Force One.[2]

Although astrology is dismissed by many mainstream scientists, some dedicated researchers have seriously investigated the relationship between people's lives and their dates of birth. They have studied mass murderers, trawled through millions of U.S. tax returns, examined the birth dates of major athletes, had more than 20,000 people go online to assess their luck, and asked a four-year-old child to predict the movement of international stock markets.

Over the years, the work has sifted fact from fiction to reveal the many ways in which our date of birth *really* influences the way we think and behave.

Prophets and Profits

The British Association for the Advancement of Science (BAAS) was established in 1831 by the eminent Scottish scientist Sir David Brewster. The BAAS has several claims to fame. The term "dinosaur" was first used at one of its meetings in 1841, and at their 1860 annual gathering, the physicist Sir Oliver Lodge presented one of the first public demonstrations of wireless transmission. Also in 1860, they staged an infamous public debate about evolution between the biologist T. H. Huxley and the bishop of Oxford, Samuel Wilberforce (nicknamed "Soapy Sam" because of his slipperiness during ecclesiastical debates). Rumor has it that during the debate Wilberforce turned to Huxley and asked: "Is it on your grandfather's or grandmother's side that you claim descent from the apes?" Unfazed, Huxley quietly muttered, "The Lord hath delivered him into my hands," and then publicly declared that he would rather be descended from an ape than from a bishop.

Each year the BAAS organizes a wonderful, week-long, national celebration of science, and in 2001 they invited me to conduct an experiment as part of the proceedings. After receiving the invitation, I happened to discover a newspaper article describing the latest fad in stargazing: financial astrology. According to the article, some soothsayers were claiming that the date of a company's formation could predict its future financial performance. If true, this had enormous implications for investors all over the world, and so I decided to find out whether heavenly activity really could influence the bottom line.

The experiment involved three participants—a financial astrologer, an experienced investment analyst, and a young child. At the beginning of the test we gave them a notional £5,000 each and asked them to invest the money in the stock market as they thought best. Then, over the course of a week, we tracked their choices. Who would make the wisest investments?

Finding astrologers willing to take part in these types of studies is notoriously difficult. The vast majority do not want their claims put to the test, and those who are interested rarely agree to the conditions associated with a scientific experiment. However, after a few dozen telephone calls, we found a professional financial astrologer who accepted the challenge because she thought the project sounded like fun.

Our remaining two guinea pigs proved easier to recruit. A quick Internet search and a couple of telephone calls uncovered an experienced investment analyst who was also happy to participate. Finally, a friend of a friend said she would ask her daughter if she wanted to be our third and final participant. A bar of chocolate sealed the deal, and Tia, a four-year-old girl from southeast London with no investment experience, completed the team. When Barclay's Stockbrokers, one of Britain's leading investment firms, agreed to adjudicate the contest, we were set to go.

We allowed our three volunteers to invest their cash in any of the one hundred largest companies in the United Kingdom's Stock Exchange. After carefully examining the formation date of the companies, our financial astrologer promptly chose a variety of sectors, including communication and technology-based stock (Vodafone, Emap, Baltimore Tech, and Pearson). Our investor drew on his seven years of extensive experience and decided to invest mainly within the communications industry (Vodafone, Marconi, Cable & Wireless, and Prudential).

We wanted Tia's choices to be random, and she happily approved a cunning selection procedure involving a stepladder and a big pad of paper. At 11:55 A.M. on March 15, 2001, I found myself balancing precariously on the top of a six-foot stepladder in the marble foyer of Barclay's Stockbrokers. Tia, and a small audience of Britain's top investors were waiting patiently on the ground below. One of my hands gripped the ladder tightly; the other held one hundred small pieces of paper, each bearing the name of a company. As the clock struck noon, I threw the papers high into the air and Tia randomly grabbed four of them as they gently fluttered to the ground. She carefully handed the four pieces to her mother, who announced that her daughter would invest in a well-known bank (Bank of Scotland), a consortium of well-known drinks brands (Diageo), a financial services group (Old Mutual), and a leading supermarket chain (Sainsbury). The onlookers applauded, and Tia curtsied to her small but appreciative audience.

To be as fair as possible, we allowed our participants to change their investments a few days into our week-long experiment. When our financial astrologer again consulted the heavens, she swapped three of her choices; her final portfolio contained BOC, BAE Systems, Unilever, and Pearson. In one interview with journalists, she justified her decisions on the basis that these companies had a good planetary wind behind them.[3] Our expert investor chose to stick with his original selections. A second round of random paper dropping left Tia with Amvescap, Bass, Bank of Scotland, and the Halifax.

At the end of the week, we regrouped at Barclay's Stockbrokers and examined the results. It had proved an exceptionally turbulent week for the stock market, with billions of dollars wiped off the value of the world's leading companies. Strangely enough, neither of our experts had seen the crash coming. In line with this dramatic downward trend, all three of our participants had lost money. At the bottom of the pack came the financial astrologer, whose planetary prognostications resulted in a 10.1 percent loss. The expert investor came a close second with a 7.1 percent loss. At the head of the class was Tia, with a loss of just 4.6 percent.

Our investor didn't exactly display the kind of optimism commonly associated with his trade; indeed, he told journalists that he had confidently expected to finish last and had thought all along that Tia would win.[4] Our astrologer turned to the heavens to help explain her failure: She noted that had she known beforehand that Tia was a Cancerian she wouldn't have played against her.[5] Tia, who was remarkably modest about her win, said that she couldn't explain her winning ways and didn't even study science at nursery school.[6]

The *Sun* newspaper was rather taken with Tia's success and carried a full-page profile of her in its financial section, including her three top tips for those eager to play the market: "Money isn't everything—sweets are," "Go to bed early," and "Watch the growing market in kids' toys."[7] *The Tonight Show with Jay Leno* expressed an interest in having Tia on the program, and I suspect that she was the only guest to decline on grounds of homework.

A week is not a long time in the world of finance, and so we decided to continue the experiment for a year. It proved to be a difficult twelve months for global finance, with the market showing an overall drop of 16 percent. However, almost one year after our original experiment, we asked Barclay's Stockbrokers to reassess the value of the three portfolios. This time, the differences were even more dramatic. Our expert investor had a 46.2 percent loss on his original investment. The financial astrologer did somewhat better, but still suffered a 6.2 percent loss. Once again, Tia led the pack. In the face of a falling market, she had managed to make a 5.8 percent profit.[8]

I wasn't entirely surprised that our experts' predictions were less than impressive. This was not the first time that the wisdom of financial analysts had come under scrutiny and been found wanting. In a similar Swedish study, a national newspaper gave $1,250 each to five experienced investors and a chimpanzee named Ola. Ola made his choice by throwing darts at the names of companies listed on the Stockholm exchange. After a month, the newspaper compared the profits and losses made by each competitor: Ola had outperformed the financial wizards. Similarly, the *Wall Street Journal* regularly asks four investors to pick one stock apiece, and then uses Ola's random dart-throwing technique to select four others. After six months, the paper compares the returns on the stocks selected by the experts with those of the "dartboard" portfolio's picks. The darts are often more successful, and they almost always beat at least one or two of the experts.

My test of financial astrology was not the first scientific examination of the alleged relationship between heavenly activity and earthly events. Similar work goes back for decades and has involved a series of unusual experiments, including work carried out by one of Britain's most prolific psychologists.

HEAVENLY PREDICTIONS

Hans Eysenck was arguably one of the most influential thinkers of the twentieth century, and at the time of his death in 1997 he was the living psychologist most frequently cited in scientific journals and magazines. Famous for liking the phrase "If it cannot be measured, then it does not exist," Eysenck spent much of his career trying to quantify aspects of the human psyche (including poetry writing, sexual behavior, humor, and genius) that many believed to be beyond the grasp of science. He is, however, perhaps best known for his work on the analysis of human personality, and he developed some of the most widely used personality questionnaires in modern-day psychology.

To appreciate Eysenck's astrological investigation fully, it is necessary to understand his investigations into personality. Eysenck first had thousands of people complete questionnaires about themselves; he then analyzed the results using powerful statistical techniques designed to uncover the key dimensions on which people differed. The results revealed that the variations in people's personalities are not nearly as complex as they first appear. In fact, according to Eysenck, they vary on only a handful of fundamental dimensions, the two most important of which he labeled "extroversion" and "neuroticism." The Eysenck Personality Inventory, which contains about fifty statements, was designed to measure these traits. It asks people to indicate whether each statement describes them by circling either "Yes" or "No."

The first of Eysenck's personality dimensions, extroversion, is all about the level of energy with which people approach life. High on the scale are the "extroverts." These people tend to be impulsive, optimistic, and happy; they enjoy the company of others, strive for instant gratification, have a wide circle of friends and acquaintances, and are more likely than others to cheat on their partners. At the other end of the scale come the "introverts," who are far more considered, controlled, and reserved. Their social lives revolve around a relatively small number of close friends, and they prefer reading a good book to going out for a night on the town. Most people fall somewhere between these two extremes, and the Eysenck Personality Inventory measures people's level of extroversion/introversion by presenting them with statements such as "I am the life of the party" and "I feel comfortable around people."

The second dimension, neuroticism, concerns the degree to which a person is emotionally stable. High scorers tend to worry; they have low self-esteem, set themselves unrealistic targets and goals, and frequently experience feelings of hostility and envy. In contrast, low scorers are calmer: They are more relaxed and resilient in the face of failure, and they are skilled at using humor to reduce anxiety; sometimes they even thrive on stress. The Eysenck Personality Inventory measures people's level of neuroticism by using statements such as "I worry about things" and "I get stressed out easily."

According to ancient astrological lore, six of the twelve signs of the zodiac are traditionally associated with extroversion (Aries, Gemini, Leo, Libra, Sagittarius, and Aquarius) and six with introversion (Taurus, Cancer, Virgo, Scorpio, Capricorn, and Pisces). Similarly, people born under the three "earth" signs (Taurus, Virgo, and Capricorn) are seen as emotionally stable and practical; those associated with the three "water" signs (Cancer, Scorpio, and Pisces) should be far more neurotic.

To find out whether this really is true, Eysenck teamed up with a respected British astrologer named Jeff Mayo. A few years before,

Mayo had founded the Mayo School of Astrology and rapidly gained a large international following of students. About 2,000 of Mayo's clients and students were asked to report their birth dates and to complete the Eysenck Personality Inventory. Those skeptical about astrology expected the findings to reveal absolutely no relationship between participants' personalities and ancient astrological lore. In contrast, proponents of astrology were confident that the positions of the heavens at the time of birth would have a predicable impact on people's thinking and behavior.

Much to the surprise of the skeptics, the results were perfectly in line with astrological lore. Those born under the signs traditionally associated with extroversion did have slightly higher extroversion scores than others, and those born under the three water signs obtained higher neuroticism scores than those born under the earth signs.[9] The astrological journal *Phenomena* announced that these findings were "possibly the most important development for astrology in this century."[10]

But Eysenck became suspicious when he realized that the participants in his study already had a strong belief in astrology. Most people who have such beliefs are well aware of the types that astrology predicts they are *meant* to be, and he wondered whether this knowledge had undermined the study. Could his participants have skewed the results by thinking that they had the personalities they knew were associated with their star signs? Could psychology, rather than the position of the planets on his subjects' birthdays, have accounted for his remarkable results?

Eysenck conducted two additional studies to explore this idea. The first involved people who were far less likely to have heard about the personality characteristics associated with different star signs—a group of 1,000 children. This time, the results were dramatically different and didn't match the patterns predicted by astrological lore: The children's levels of extroversion and neuroticism were completely unrelated to their star signs. To make certain, Eysenck ran a second birth date/personality study with adults, but he also assessed what they knew about astrology. Those knowledgeable about the effect the planets should have on personality did conform to the pattern predicted by astrology. In contrast, those who professed no knowledge showed no patterning. The conclusion was clear. The positions of the planets at the moment of a person's birth had no magical effect on personality. Instead, many of the people who were well aware of the personality traits associated with their signs had developed into the people predicted by the astrologers.[11] When Eysenck presented these follow-up findings at a conference exploring science and astrology, his biographer noted that "there was a strong feeling among some of the astrologers that Eysenck had first beguiled them with his patronage, and then betrayed them by bringing forward some ugly facts."[12]

This is not the only time that researchers have found evidence that people become what others expect them to be. In the 1950s, the psychologist Gustav Jahoda studied the lives of the Ashanti people in central Ghana. According to tradition, every Ashanti child receives a spiritual name that is based on the day he or she is born, and each day is associated with a set of personality traits. Those born on a Monday are referred to as *Kwadwo* and are traditionally seen as quiet, retiring, and peaceful. Children born on a Wednesday are referred to as *Kwaku* and are expected to be badly behaved. Jahoda wanted to know whether this early labeling could have a long-term impact on the self-image, and lives, of Ashanti children. To find out, he examined the frequency with which people born on different days of the week appeared in juvenile court records. The results showed that the label given to children at birth affected their behavior, with significantly fewer *Kwadwos,* and more *Kwaku,* appearing in the records.[13]

Did Eysenck's results cause millions to alter their belief in heavenly influence? Apparently not. Instead, many proponents of astrology argued that the star signs merely provided a rough guide to a person's personality, and that real accuracy could be obtained only by carefully studying the precise moment that a person entered the world. The claim has received a great deal of attention from researchers around the globe.

TIME TWINS AND POGO THE CLOWN

The British researcher Geoffrey Dean is a soft-spoken, mild-mannered man who has dedicated his life to collecting, and collating, information that might allow him to assess the potential impact of the stars on human behavior. Since he is one of the few scientific researchers who used to earn his living as a professional astrologer, he is in a unique position to carry out the work.

In 2000, I was invited to speak at an international science conference in Australia, and I was delighted to discover that Geoffrey was on the same program. During his talk, Geoffrey described his latest and largest project: an investigation that he referred to as the "definitive test" of astrology. Like so many good ideas, this one was very simple. According to the claims of astrologers, the position of the planets at a person's moment of birth predicts his or her personality and the key events in that person's life. If this is true, people born at the same moment, and in the same place, should be almost identical to one another. In fact, they should, as Geoffrey noted, be "time twins."

There is some anecdotal evidence to support the idea. In the 1970s, astrological researchers trawled through a database of births and noted that some people born within a few days of one another lead surprisingly similar lives. For instance, the French champion bicycle racers Paul Chacque and Leon Lével were born on July 12 and 14, 1910. They were both highly successful in 1936: Chacque won the Bordeaux-Paris section of the Tour de France, and Lével won the two mountain sections of the same race. In March 1949, Lével died when he fractured his skull in an accident on the Parc des Princes track. In September of the same year, Chacque died from a similar injury on the same track.[14]

Intriguing though cases such as these are, they could simply be the result of chance, and so Geoffrey decided to carry out more systematic work into the alleged phenomenon. He managed to uncover a database containing the details of just over 2,000 people born in London between March 3 and 9, 1958. The database had been created by a group of researchers who studied people as they progressed through life, and it contained the results of intelligence tests and personality questionnaires administered at the ages of eleven, sixteen, and twenty-three. The precise time of birth for each person had been carefully recorded, with more than 70 percent of them being born within five minutes of one another. Geoffrey arranged the group in order of birth and moved down the list, calculating the degree of similarity between each pair of time twins. Once again, the skeptics and proponents made very different predictions about what he would find. The skeptics thought that there would be no relationship between the test results of each pair on the list; the astrologers expected to see the type of striking similarities found between the personalities of identical twins.

This time, the skeptics were right. Geoffrey found little evidence of similarity between his time twins. People born at five minutes past eleven on March 4, 1958, were no more similar to their time twin born moments later than another person born days later.[15]

Geoffrey has carried out many tests like this and the results have one thing in common—none support the claims of astrology.[16] As a result, he sometimes describes himself as "the most hated person in astrology." Modern-day astrologers see him as something of a turncoat—a man who has gone over to the dark side by publicly declaring his skepticism about the impact of the heavens on our lives.

Geoffrey's research tends to be methodologically similar to the work carried out by Hans Eysenck in that it usually involves examining large amounts of data in search of the patterns predicted by astrology. This is not, however, the only way to test the accuracy of planetary predictions. Other researchers have examined the claims made by individual astrologers. One of the most unusual, and striking, examples of this approach was reported by an American researcher in the late 1980s, in the provocatively titled article "Astrology on Death Row."[17]

The researchers first found out the birth time, date, and place of the notorious serial murderer John Gacy. Gacy was a sadistic killer who received twelve death sentences and twenty-one life terms for the torture and killing of thirty-three men and boys. Dressing up as *Pogo the Clown,* and performing at children's birthday parties in his spare time, Gacy may have given rise to the notion of the "evil" clown. One of the researchers visited five professional astrologers and presented Gacy's details as his own. The researcher explained to each astrologer that he was interested in working with young people and asked for a general personality reading and some career advice. The astrologers got it badly wrong. One encouraged the researcher to work with young people because he could "bring out their best qualities." Another analyzed the information provided and confidently predicted that the researcher's life would be "very, very, positive." A third said that he was "kind, gentle, and considerate of others' needs."

The work of Hans Eysenck, Geoffrey Dean, and others show that heavenly predictions often fall far short of the mark. In doing so, they leave us with a bigger mystery: Why do so many people believe in astrology?

Bertram Forer and the Nightclub Graphologist

In the late 1940s, Bertram Forer was busy devising novel ways of measuring personality. One evening he visited a nightclub, where he was approached by a graphologist who offered to determine his personality on the basis of his handwriting. Forer declined the offer, but the chance encounter made him wonder why so many people were impressed with astrologers and graphologists. Forer could have carried on with his normal academic research. But curiosity got the better of him, and he decided to conduct an experiment. Long after his mainstream work on personality had faded into obscurity, he would still be famous for this unusual study.

Forer had the students in his introductory psychology class complete a personality test.[18] One week later, each student was handed a sheet of paper and told that it contained a short description of his or her personality based on test scores. Forer asked the students to examine the descriptions carefully, assign them an accuracy rating by circling a number between 0 (poor) and 5 (perfect), and then raise their hands if they thought the test had done a good job of measuring their personalities.

Let's turn back the hands of time and restage the experiment. Here is part of a description that was handed to students in Forer's study. Read it through and see whether you think it a fairly accurate description of your own personality:

> You have a need for other people to like and admire you. You have a tendency to be critical of yourself. You have considerable unused capacity that you have not turned to your advantage. While you have some personality weaknesses you are generally able to compensate for them. Disciplined and self-controlled on the outside, you tend to be worrisome and insecure on the inside. At times you have serious doubts as to whether you have made the right decision or done the right thing. You prefer a certain amount of change and variety and become dissatisfied when hemmed in by restrictions and limitations. You pride yourself as an independent thinker, and do not accept others' statements without satisfactory proof. But you have found it unwise to be too frank in revealing yourself to others. At times you are extroverted, affable, and sociable, while at other times you are introverted, wary, and reserved. Some of your aspirations tend to be rather unrealistic.

Forer's students read the description, made their ratings, and, one by one, raised their hands. After a few moments, he was surprised to see that virtually all the students had their hands up. Why was Forer so amazed?

As is sometimes the case with psychology experiments, Forer had not been entirely honest with his guinea pigs. The personality description he had handed them was not based on their test scores. Instead, it came from a newsstand astrology book that he had picked up a few days before. More important, *every student had received exactly the same personality description*—similar to the one that you read a few moments ago.

Forer had simply gone through the astrology book, selected about ten or so sentences from different astrological readings, and pasted them together to make one description. Even though they were all given the same personality description, 87 percent of students had circled either the number 4 or 5 on the rating scale, indicating that they were extremely impressed with the accuracy of what they had read. The reading Forer created has become world famous and has been used in thousands of psychology experiments and television shows.

Forer's results solved the mystery that had been bugging him since his chance meeting with the graphologist. To be *seen* as accurate, astrology and graphology do not have to *be* accurate. Instead, you simply give people a general statement about personality and their brains will trick them into believing that it is insightful and individual.

Immediately after conducting his study, Forer told his students that they had all received the same personality description, explained that the exercise had been "an object lesson to demonstrate the tendency to be overly impressed by vague statements," and pointed out the "similarities between the demonstration and the activities of charlatans." Apparently, most of Forer's students were not upset about being exposed as a tad gullible. Many of them bestowed on the psychology experiment the greatest honor that a student can give: They asked Forer for a copy of the personality description so that they could play the same trick on their friends. Most psychologists would have left it there, but Forer devised one last twist in a final attempt to inflict further humiliation on his long-suffering class.

Forer wondered whether his students would want to see themselves as astute, streetwise, and smart. If so, would their acceptance of vague personality statements have presented a challenge to this aspect of their self-identity? Moreover, rather than go through the painful process of seeing themselves as they really are, would they take the easy option of simply denying to themselves that they were taken in by the demonstration?

Three weeks later, Forer told his class that he had inadvertently erased their names from the rating sheets and asked them to jot down honestly the ratings they had assigned the original description. He had not lost the names at all, and so he was able to compare the ratings the students had originally given the description with the ratings they subsequently claimed they had given it. Half the students who had *originally* indicated that they thought the description was "perfect" (assigning it the maximum score of 5) subsequently claimed that they had given it a lower rating. It seems that the most gullible people would rather fool themselves than face up to their gullibility.

ENTER PHINEAS TAYLOR BARNUM

In the 1950s, the psychologist Paul Meehl christened Forer's original finding the "Barnum Effect," after the American showman Phineas Taylor Barnum, who once famously said that any good circus should have something for everyone.[19] Years of research have shown that almost everyone is susceptible to the Barnum Effect—men and women, young and old, believers in astrology and skeptics alike, students, and even human resources managers.[20]

One of the most interesting follow-up studies was conducted by the French researcher Michel Gauquelin.[21] Gauquelin sent the birth details of Dr. Marcel Petiot, a notorious French mass murderer, to a firm that used high-tech computers to generate allegedly accurate horoscopes. During World War II, Petiot told his victims that he was able to help them escape from Nazi-occupied France, but instead administered a lethal injection and watched them slowly die. Petiot, who later pleaded guilty to nineteen murders, was guillotined in 1946. The computerized horoscope managed to miss all the grisly aspects of Petiot's life and instead generated the same type of bland Barnum statements that had been used to such great effect by Forer, including:

> His adaptable and pliant character expresses itself through skill and efficiency; his dynamism finds support in a tendency towards order, control, balance. He is an organized and organizing person socially, materially and intellectually. He may appear as someone who submits to social norms, fond of propriety and endowed with a moral sense which is comforting—that of a worthy, right-thinking, middle-class citizen.

Although Petiot was executed in 1946, the horoscope predicted that between 1970 and 1972 he would experience "a tendency to make commitments regarding his romantic life."

Inspired, Gauquelin then offered free, computer-generated horoscopes through an advertisement he placed in a well-known newspaper. More than 150 people from all over France responded, and Gauquelin sent each one the reading based on the birth details of Petiot. He also asked them to rate the degree to which the horoscope presented an accurate description of their personalities. Ninety-four percent of recipients said that it was accurate. One person wrote to Gauquelin, noting: "The work done by this machine is marvellous . . . I would go so far as to say extraordinary." Another wrote, "It is absolutely bewildering that an electronic machine is able to probe people's character and future." Some people were so impressed that they offered to pay Gauquelin for a more detailed analysis.

So why are so many people taken in by these types of readings?

People endorse many of the statements because they are true for the vast majority of the population. After all, who hasn't had serious doubts about an important decision, would deny wanting other people to admire them, or doesn't strive for a sense of security? Even specific-sounding statements can be true of a surprisingly large percentage of the population. A few years ago, Susan Blackmore, a psychologist and a colleague of mine, conducted a survey in which she asked approximately 6,000 people about the sorts of seemingly specific statements that crop up in psychic readings, such as, "You have someone in your family named Jack."[22] She discovered that about a third of her subjects had a scar on the left knee, another third owned a tape or CD of Handel's *Water Music,* a fifth had a "Jack" in the family, and about one in ten had spent the previous night dreaming about someone they hadn't seen for years. It seems that many Barnum statements appear accurate because most people tend to think and behave in surprisingly predictable ways.

Then there is the "flattery effect." Most people are more than willing to believe anything that puts them in a positive light, and thus they endorse statements suggesting that they have a great deal of unused capacity or are independent thinkers. This effect explains why half the population is especially accepting of astrology. The twelve signs of the zodiac are traditionally split into the six "positive" signs (Aries, Gemini, Leo, Libra, Sagittarius, and Aquarius) and six "negative" signs (Taurus, Cancer, Virgo, Scorpio, Capricorn, and Pisces). The traits associated with the positive signs tend to be more favorable than those associated with the negative signs. Those born into Libra are traditionally seen as the type of people who seek peace and beauty, but Taureans are viewed as more materialistic and easily upset. Margaret Hamilton, a psychologist from the University of Wisconsin, asked her subjects to give their dates of birth and to rate the degree to which they believed in astrology on a seven-point scale. As predicted by the "flattery effect," those born under "positive" signs were significantly more likely to believe in astrology than those born under "negative" signs.[23]

The work of Forer, and those who have followed in his footsteps, demonstrates how horoscopes have fooled millions of people over thousands of years. Astrologers can produce any old rubbish and, providing it is sufficiently vague and flattering, most people will tick the "highly accurate" box. So, given that the scientific evidence in favor of astrology is less than overwhelming, it would be tempting to conclude that there is no real science associated with a person's date of birth.

Tempting, but wrong.

THE SCIENTIFIC STUDY OF TIME AND MIND

Chronopsychology is a new, and still relatively obscure, scientific discipline devoted to the study of time and mind. Much of the work in this area is concerned with circadian rhythms, shift work, and jet lag.

In 1962, the French caver and geologist Michel Siffre decided to track the movement of a glacier through an underground ice cave; to do so, he would have to live below ground for two months.[24] Rather than simply sit there taking measurements and twiddling his thumbs, Siffre made the most of his subterranean isolation by carrying out a unique experiment on the psychology of time. He decided not to take a clock with him into the cave, and so forced himself to rely entirely on his own body clock to decide when to fall asleep and when to be awake. His only link to the outside world was a telephone that provided a direct line to a team of researchers above ground. Siffre called the team whenever he went to sleep and woke up, and from time to time during his waking hours. Each time, the experimenters above ground did not give him any indication of the real time. Deprived of daylight for more than sixty days in his small nylon tent 375 feet below ground, Siffre's ability to judge time became radically distorted. Toward the end of the experiment, he would telephone the surface, convinced that only an hour had gone by since his previous call—whereas in reality several hours had elapsed. When he emerged from the cave after two months, Siffre was convinced that the experiment had been terminated early, and that it was only in its thirty-fourth day. The experiment provided a striking illustration of how daylight helps our internal clocks to keep accurate time.

Other chronopsychological research has examined ways of minimizing the effects of perhaps the most common and annoying form of disruption faced by the modern-day body clock: jet lag. One of the more unusual and controversial studies in this area was carried out in the late 1990s by Scott Campbell and Patricia Murphy of

Cornell University, and it involved shining lights on the back of people's knees.[25] Previous work had shown that shining light into a person's eyes fools the brain into speeding up or slowing down the subject's biological clock, and so can help overcome the effects of jet lag. Campbell and Murphy wondered whether people might detect similar signals from other parts of their bodies. Since the back of the knee contains a large number of blood vessels very close to the surface of the skin, they decided to test their hypothesis by applying light to the region using specially designed halogen lamps. In a small-scale study, they found evidence that light applied to the back of the knee matched the biological clock–altering ability of light shone directly into the eyes.

So what is the link between the ideas underpinning astrology and this fascinating scientific area of study? Not all chronopsychology is about spending months in caves and shining light on the backs of people's knees. In another branch of this obscure discipline, scientists have examined the subtle influences that people's birthdays may exert over the way in which they think and behave.

The concept behind this unusual branch of behavioral science is beautifully illustrated by the work of the Dutch psychologist Ad Dudink.[26] After analyzing the birthdays of approximately 3,000 English professional football players, Dudink found that twice as many were born between September and November as were born between June and August. It seemed that date of birth predicted people's sporting success. Some may have viewed the result as compelling evidence for astrology, arguing that the planetary positions associated with Virgo, Libra, Scorpio, and Sagittarius play a key role in creating successful athletes. There is, however, a more interesting and down-to-earth explanation for Dudink's curious finding.

At the time of his analysis in the early 1990s, budding English footballers were eligible to play professionally only if they were at least seventeen years old when the season started, which was in August. Potential players born between September and November would therefore have been about ten months older, and more physically mature, than those born between June and August. These extra few months proved to be a real bonus when it came to the strength, endurance, and speed needed to play football, with the result that those born between September and November were more likely to be picked to play at a professional level.

Years of research have revealed an overwhelming amount of evidence for the effect in many sporting arenas. Regardless of when a sporting season starts, there is an excess of athletes whose month of birth falls in the first few months of that season. From American Major League baseball to British county cricket, Canadian ice hockey to Brazilian soccer, the month of birth of athletes is related to their sporting success.[27]

Such chronopsychological effects are not limited to the lives of professional athletes; they also influence a factor that plays a key role in everyone's life: luck.

BORN LUCKY?

Are you lucky or unlucky? Why do some people always seem to be in the right place at the right time, but others attract little but bad fortune? Can people change their luck? About ten years ago, I decided to answer these types of intriguing questions by conducting research into the psychology of luck. As a result, I have worked with about 1,000 exceptionally lucky and unlucky people drawn from all walks of life.[28]

The differences between the lives of lucky and unlucky people are as consistent as they are remarkable. Lucky people seem to attract nothing but good fortune, fall on their feet, and appear to have an uncanny ability to live charmed lives. Unlucky people are the opposite. Their lives tend to be a catalog of failure and despair, and they are convinced that their misfortunes are not of their own making.

One of the unluckiest people in my study is Susan, a thirty-four-year-old nurse. Susan is exceptionally unlucky in love. She once arranged to meet a man on a blind date, but her potential beau broke both his legs in a motorcycle accident on the way to their meeting. Her next date walked into a glass door and broke his nose. A few years later, when she had found someone to marry, the church in which they intended to hold the wedding was burned down by arsonists just before the big day. Susan has also experienced an amazing catalog of accidents. In one especially bad run of luck, she reported having eight car accidents during one fifty-mile journey.

I wondered whether good and bad fortune really was chance, or whether psychology accounted for these dramatically different lives, and so I designed a series of studies to investigate. In one especially memorable study, I gave volunteers copies of a newspaper and asked them to tell me how many photographs were inside. What I didn't tell them was that halfway through the newspaper I had placed an unexpected opportunity. This "opportunity" took up half the page and announced, in huge type, "Win £100 by Telling the Experimenter You Have Seen This." The unlucky people tended to be so focused on the counting of the photographs that they failed to notice the opportunity. In contrast, the lucky people were more relaxed, saw the bigger picture, and so spotted a chance to win £100. It was a simple demonstration of how lucky people can create their good fortune by making the most of an unexpected opportunity.

The results revealed that the volunteers were making much of their good and bad luck by the way they were thinking and behaving. The lucky people were optimistic, energetic, and open to new opportunities and experiences. In contrast, the unlucky people were more withdrawn, clumsy, anxious about life, and unwilling to make the most of the opportunities that came their way.

Some of my most recent work in the area has taken a chronopsychological turn and explores whether there is any truth to the old adage that some people are born lucky.[29] The project had its roots in a curious e-mail that I received in 2004 from Jayanti Chotai, a researcher at the University Hospital in Umeå, Sweden.

Much of Jayanti's work examines the relationship between date of birth and various aspects of psychological and physical well-being. In one of his studies, Jayanti had asked a group of about 2,000 people to complete a questionnaire measuring the degree to which they described themselves as sensation seekers, and then looked to see whether there was a relationship between their questionnaire scores and their birth months.[30] Novelty and sensation seeking are fundamental aspects of our personalities. Very high sensation seekers can't stand watching movies that they have seen before, enjoy being around unpredictable people, and are attracted to dangerous sports such as mountain climbing or bungee–rope jumping. In contrast, very low sensation seekers like to see the same movies again and again, enjoy the comfortable familiarity of old friends, and don't like visiting places that they haven't been to before. Jayanti's results suggested that sensation seekers tended to be born in the summer, but those more comfortable with the familiar were likely to be born in the winter. Jayanti's e-mail explained that he had read about my work on the link between personality and luck and he wondered whether some people really were born lucky. It was an intriguing idea, and the two of us decided to team up and discover whether there was any truth to the expression.

Jayanti's previous work had suggested that the relationship between birth month and personality was real, but small. To detect very small effects, we knew we needed to design an experiment involving thousands of people. We also knew that proposition wasn't going to be easy. Getting even a few hundred students to participate in research is often problematic, and we needed thousands of people from all walks of life to take part if we were to have any chance of finding what we were looking for. Luckily, help was at hand.

The Edinburgh International Science Festival in Scotland is one of the oldest science festivals in the world, and the largest in Europe. By making the experiment part of the festival, we would stand a good chance of attracting the large numbers of people we needed. The festival organizers gave us the green light, and we set up a simple Web site where people could enter their birth dates and then answer a standard questionnaire that I had devised to assess their levels of luck.

Carrying out large-scale public experiments is always an unpredictable affair. Unlike laboratory research, you have only one opportunity to get it right, and you never know whether people will give up their time to participate. However, our study attracted the public's imagination and quickly spread around the globe. Within hours of going live, we had hundreds of people using the site. By the end of the festival, we had collected data from more than 40,000 people.

The results were remarkable. Jayanti had found that those with summer births were the risk takers. Our results revealed that those born in the summer (March to August) also rated themselves as luckier than those born in the winter (September to February). The resulting levels of luckiness across the twelve months showed an undulating pattern that peaked in May and was at its lowest in October (see graph 1). Only June failed to fit the pattern—something that we put down to a statistical blip.

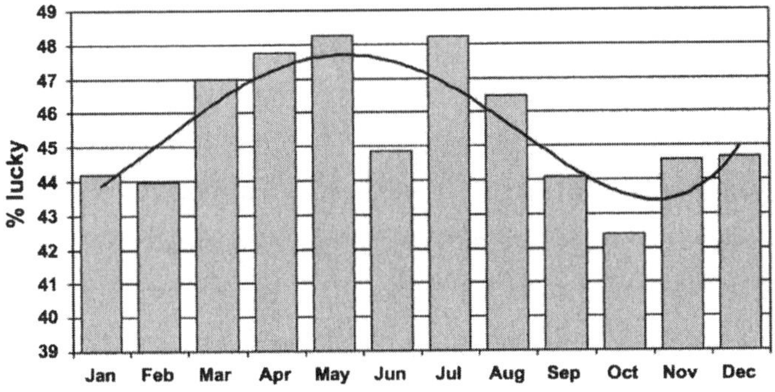

Graph 1 Born Lucky Results: The Percentage of Lucky People Born in Each Month of the Year.

There are lots of possible explanations for an effect such as this. Many revolve around the notion that the ambient temperature is lower in winter than in summer. Perhaps because babies born in winter enter a harsher environment than those born in the summer, they remain closer to their caregivers and so are less adventurous and lucky in life. Or perhaps women who give birth in late winter have had access to different foods than those who give birth in the summer, and this affects the personality of their offspring. Whatever the explanation, the effect is theoretically fascinating, and it suggests that the temperature around the time of birth has a long-term effect on the development of personality.

But before accepting any of the temperature-related explanations, it is important to rule out other possible mechanisms. Maybe the effect has nothing to do with temperature, but instead concerns some other factor that varies during the year. Proponents of astrology might argue that heavenly activity affects personality and that the alignment of the planets and stars during the summer months somehow gives rise to a luckier life.

The only way of assessing the competing explanations would be to repeat the study in a place where there is a different relationship between temperature and the months of the year. If the temperature-related explanations were correct, then the warmer months should still be associated with lucky births. If the astrological explanations were right, then May, June, July, and so forth should emerge as the lucky months.

People living in the earth's Southern and Northern Hemispheres experience almost the opposite relationship between temperature and month. In the Northern Hemisphere, it is hot in June and cold in December. In the Southern Hemisphere this pattern is reversed, and so June is a winter month and December is gloriously hot. Because of this, I decided to compare the temperature-related and astrological interpretations of the "born lucky" effect, by restaging the experiment on the other side of the world.

The city of Dunedin is situated on the southeastern coast of New Zealand's South Island, and is home to a biennial science festival. In 2006, I received an e-mail from the organizers of the festival. They had heard about the need to repeat the Born Lucky experiment in the Southern Hemisphere, and they wondered whether I should like to carry out the study again at their festival. I was soon on a plane to New Zealand.

The national media in New Zealand and Australia reported the Born Lucky 2 experiment, and this publicity helped attract people to another specially designed Web site. Within a few days, more than 2,000 people had provided their birth months and rated their degrees of luck. The results supported a temperature-related explanation for the effect. Those born in the summer months of the Southern Hemisphere (September to February) considered themselves significantly luckier than those born in winter (March to August). Again, an undulating pattern emerged across the twelve months, but this time it peaked in December and was at its lowest in April.

Experiments such as the Born Lucky studies suggest that the month in which people are born exerts a small, but real, influence over the way in which they behave. But other research has investigated exactly the opposite effect, namely, how people's behavior influences the alleged birth date of themselves and others.

THE CHRONOPSYCHOLOGY OF TAX EVASION AND LYING CLERGY

The U.S. tax system is set up in such a way that a family whose child is born on December 31 receives tax benefits for the previous twelve months, whereas a child born on January 1 doesn't. Because of this, there is considerable financial motivation for parents expecting a child around the end of the year to ensure that the baby is born before midnight on December 31. Although parents are unable to predict accurately the exact date of a natural birth, they are able to manipulate the child's date of birth by asking for an induced labor or a Caesarian section.

Would parents really manipulate their child's date of birth simply to obtain tax benefits? To find out, Stacy Dickert-Conlin, from Syracuse University, and Amitabh Chandra, from the University of Kentucky, analyzed U.S. birth records between 1979 and 1993.[31] Focusing on the final seven days of December and the first seven of January, they found a sudden and significant peak in the number of births at the end of December in all but one of the years.

The professors then dug deeper into the data to find out whether this unusual pattern really was caused by parents trying to increase their benefits. They carefully analyzed the individual family circumstances of nearly two hundred births that took place in either the week before, or the week after, January 1. For each birth they came up with two figures—the tax benefits associated with a December birth and the benefits associated with a January birth. The results revealed that the families of babies born in the last week of December had significantly more to gain financially from a December birth than the families of babies born in the first week of January. This was the clincher: compelling statistical evidence that parents were manipulating the birth dates of their offspring for financial gain.

There is, of course, a much easier way of manipulating your date of birth. A way that escapes the need for an induced labor, or a Caesarian section. Lie.

The actress Lucille Ball once famously said that the secret of staying young is to "live honestly, eat slowly, and lie about your age." She should know. Ball's actual date of birth was August 6, 1911, but through much of her career she claimed to have been born in 1914. Ball is far from being the only Hollywood legend to have lied about her age. Nancy Reagan made herself two years younger than she actually was, and she even published an incorrect date of birth in her autobiography. The Hollywood comedienne Gracie Allen was so secretive about her age that even her husband, her fellow performer George Burns, didn't know her real date of birth. Various sources claim that Allen was born on July 26 in 1894, 1895, 1897, 1902, or 1906. Throughout her life, Allen claimed that her birth certificate was destroyed in the 1906 San Francisco earthquake, even though the earthquake occurred a few months *before* her alleged birthday. When asked about the discrepancy, Allen allegedly remarked, "Well, it was an awfully big earthquake."

It is not difficult to figure out the psychology behind such minor manipulations. In a society that places great value on the beauty of youth, it isn't surprising that so many people wish to appear younger than they are. But would eminent, and allegedly upstanding, members of society be equally devious about even the *day* on which they were born?

To find out, Albert Harrison, a professor from the University of California, Davis, and his colleagues carefully worked their way through more than 9,000 biographical entries in several volumes of *Who's Who* and *Who Was Who,* counting the number of people born either directly on, or three days on either side of, the best-known dates in the American calendar: Independence Day (July 4), Christmas Day (December 25), and New Year's Day (January 1).[32] By chance alone, there should be roughly the same percentage of eminent people born on an auspicious day as on any one of the three days on either side of that date. However, something strange was going on. Statistically more people were born on Independence Day, Christmas Day, or New Year's Day than on one of the three days on either side of these dates. The likelihood of this distribution by chance is hundreds to one, suggesting that some eminent individuals were misreporting their birth dates to biographers in order to associate themselves with a day of national importance.

Harrison believes that the effect is caused by an unusual psychological phenomenon called "Basking in Reflected Glory" or, as many researchers refer to it, the "BIRG" effect. BIRG is a commonplace occurrence. We often hear people proudly announcing that they went to the same school as a well-known celebrity, or were one of the first to see an Oscar-winning film ("Guess who I had in the back of my cab yesterday?"). It even affects our everyday language. Psychologists secretly studying conversations on college campuses noticed big differences in a student's comments when his or her football team either won or lost a match. People were keen to associate themselves with their team's victory ("*We* won"), and just as eager to distance themselves from defeat ("*They* lost"). Harrison believes that the rich and famous were prepared to misreport their birthdays so that they could bask in the reflected glory of well-known days of the year. This interpretation of the data is supported by anecdotal evidence. The world-famous jazz musician Louis Armstrong claimed to have been born on July 4. However, the music historian Tad Jones examined Armstrong's birth records and discovered that he was actually born on August 4. Harrison's results suggest that this is not the only time a celebrity has blown his own trumpet.

To further investigate the BIRG effect within *Who's Who* and *Who Was Who,* Harrison and his team focused their attention on the occupation that was most clearly associated with one of the dates—the clergy and Christmas. Working back through their data, they classified each member of the clergy into one of two groups.

"Eminent clergy" were those who listed their rank as bishop or above; "noneminent clergy" consisted of everyone else. By chance alone, one would expect roughly the same percentage of both groups to be born on Christmas Day. In fact, significantly more eminent than noneminent clergy claimed to share a birthday with Christ, perhaps supporting the idea that the higher you go in the clergy, the more you feel the need to move closer to Jesus.

Perhaps we are being a little harsh on the eminent folk involved in Harrison's analysis. In much the same way as some parents change a child's date of birth to save a few dollars, others may have been so eager to see their children excel in life that they deliberately misreported infants' birth dates to make the events seem more auspicious. Modern-day hospital births make such misreporting problematic, but in days gone by, parents reported their children's births verbally to local registry offices, making such deception much easier. The mother of the eminent mystery writer Georges Simenon confessed to this type of manipulation, reporting her son's birthday as being a day earlier than Friday, February 13, 1903, because she considered the thirteenth to be "too hard a fate for her sweet newborn baby." If this interpretation of the results is valid, then it would be wrong to conclude that high-ranking clergy are more likely to lie than low clergy. Instead, the evidence would suggest that it is the *parents* of high-ranking clergy who are especially deceptive. Perhaps this represents one of the few instances in which there is empirical evidence to support the biblical notion that the sins of the fathers are visited upon their sons.

Some researchers now believe that parental lying may help account for a mystery that has baffled scientists for decades: a mystery that has come to be known as the "Mars Effect."

THE MARS EFFECT

In addition to sending out horoscopes based around the birth date of a mass murderer to innocent members of the public, Michel Gauquelin tested many aspects of astrology. According to astrological lore, being born when certain planets are high in the sky is a good omen, suggesting that the individual concerned will be eminent in his or her chosen career. In the 1950s, Gauquelin tested this notion by plotting the star charts of 16,000 people listed in a leading nineteenth-century French biographical dictionary. To his amazement, he discovered that certain planets were more likely to be above the horizon at the time of his chosen subjects' births. For more than fifty years this evidence, which has come to be known as the Mars Effect, puzzled even the most skeptical of thinkers. One researcher remarked that "it is probably not putting it too strongly to say that everything hangs on it," and Hans Eysenck noted that if the "results are ever shown to be spurious then, relatively speaking, the positive evidence that remains for astrology is weak."[33] Then, in 2002, Geoffrey Dean, the researcher who carried out the "time twins" experiment, undertook a remarkable piece of scientific detective work.[34]

During the nineteenth century, many in the French upper classes held a strong belief in astrology and had ready access to popular almanacs that showed the exact position of the planets throughout each day. In addition, parents reported the times and dates of their children's births verbally to local registry offices; the information was not officially and accurately recorded by doctors and midwives. Dean uncovered evidence to suggest that some parents deliberately misreported the dates of their children's births to make the events seem astrologically "auspicious." Such parents could have then subsequently provided their children with the schooling, and other resources, required to turn these alleged "heavenly predictions" into self-fulfilling prophecies. In short, Dean's work suggests that the Mars Effect may have little to do with astrology and much more to do with a quirky piece of social history.

So far, I have been exploring how, and why, people manipulate their own and their children's birth dates. An even stranger aspect of chronopsychology, however, has examined a more morbid topic: the relationship between the date of birth and the time of death.

CHRONOPSYCHOLOGY AND THE GRIM REAPER

David Phillips, a sociologist at the University of California, San Diego, is fascinated by death. Unlike many medical researchers, who are concerned with why people die, Phillips is more concerned with when. Specifically, he is interested in whether people are able to postpone death until after a moment of important emotional significance. He has devoted his career to the topic, starting in 1970, when he published a doctoral dissertation with the curious title "Dying as a Form of Social Behavior."

Phillips is intrigued by the notion that people can exert enough control over their bodies to delay their demise for a small, but vital, period of time. Just long enough, it seems, to allow them to enjoy an important national or personal event. There is certainly some anecdotal evidence to support the notion. Charles Schulz, the multimillionaire cartoonist and creator of the "Peanuts" strip, died on the eve of the publication of his last comic strip. The final cartoon contained a farewell letter signed by Schulz. Also, no fewer than three

American presidents, John Adams, Thomas Jefferson, and James Monroe, all died on July 4, thus raising the intriguing possibility that they held on long enough to ensure an auspicious date of death.

In one piece of research, Phillips examined whether people are more likely to die directly after a national holiday. There seemed little point in looking at mortality rates immediately before and after Christmas because any significant rise in reported deaths could have been caused by the fact that the temperature tends to decrease throughout December. Rather than try to convince entire nations to celebrate Christmas in randomly determined months, Phillips searched for another national festival that took place at a different time each year. That is when he found the Chinese Harvest Moon Festival. In this highly traditional celebration, a festival that moves around the calendar from year to year, the senior woman of the household directs her daughters in the preparation of an elaborate meal. An examination of Chinese death records around the event showed that the death rate dipped by 35 percent in the week before the festival and peaked by the same amount in the week after.[35]

One of Phillips's largest studies investigated whether date of birth influenced date of death.[36] Analyzing almost 3 million California death certificates between 1969 and 1990, Phillips reported that a woman is more likely to die during the week after her birthday than at any other time of the year. In contrast, a man is more likely to die during the week *before* his birthday. Phillips argued that this may be because women look forward to birthdays as times of celebration, whereas men are more likely to use birthdays to take stock of their lives; in doing so, they realize how little they have achieved in life, become stressed, and therefore increase their chances of dying. According to Phillips, these findings are not a result of seasonal fluctuations, of people misreporting the information on their relatives' death certificates, of putting off life-threatening surgery, or of committing suicide. Instead, he argues that the data supports the notion that some people are capable of "willing" themselves to live longer, or of cutting short their lives.

The idea is highly controversial, and it has attracted a great deal of debate.[37] Some researchers have been able to replicate the types of patterns found by Phillips and his team; others have failed to find such results or have attacked the methods used to conduct the work. Nevertheless, the idea that psychological factors influence physical well-being is supported by work showing a relationship between people's optimism and their health. For instance, in 1996, a team of researchers investigated the link between healthy thinking and longevity among 2,000 Finnish men. The team classified participants into three groups: a "pessimistic" group, whose members expected the future to be bleak; an "optimistic" group, whose members had much higher expectations about the future; and a "neutral" group, whose members held expectations that were neither especially positive nor especially negative. They then monitored the groups over six years and found that the men in the "pessimistic" group were far more likely to die from cancer, cardiovascular disease, and accidents than those in the "neutral" group. In contrast, those in the "optimistic" group exhibited a far lower mortality rate than those in the other two groups.[38]

Phillips is not the only researcher to investigate the strange factors that may influence the precise moment people meet the grim reaper. A paper published in the *Review of Economics and Statistics* in 2003 explored whether tax liability influenced a person's date of death,[39] combining Phillips's groundbreaking approach to death with the possibility that parents might manipulate their children's birth dates to obtain tax incentives. In this paper, Wojciech Kopczuk, from the University of British Columbia, and Joel Slemrod, from the University of Michigan, wondered whether people might die at a moment that is financially most beneficial to those left behind.

To discover whether this was the case, they analyzed the pattern in reported deaths around the time of significant changes to the U.S. tax system. There had been thirteen major changes to the tax laws since the introduction of the tax system in 1916, eight of them resulting in increases in the rate of tax and five resulting in decreases. The changes came into effect approximately a week after they were announced in the media. Analyzing the reported number of deaths in the two weeks before and after each change, the researchers found evidence of an *increase* in the death rate just *before* a rise in the tax rate came into effect, and a *decrease* in the death rate just *after* a drop in the tax rate. This suggests, as indicated in the title of their paper, that some people may indeed be "Dying to Save Taxes."

This is not, however, the only interpretation of their data. Deaths are often reported by relatives who are likely to inherit the deceased's estate, and thus have a vested interest in reducing their tax liability. Consequently, the effect may be evidence that people have misreported the day their wealthy loved one actually died or, in the worst-case scenario, was murdered.

2 Trust Everyone, but Always Cut the Cards

The Psychology of Lying and Deception

When I was eight years old, I saw something that changed my life.

My grandfather handed me a marker pen and asked me to write my initials on a coin. He carefully placed the coin on his palm and closed his hand. After gently blowing on his fingers, he opened his hand. The coin had mysteriously vanished. Next, he reached into his pocket and took out a small tin box that was sealed with several rubber bands. My grandfather handed me this strange-looking package and asked me to remove the bands and open the box. The box contained a small red–velvet bag. I carefully removed it, peeked inside, and couldn't believe my eyes. The bag contained the initialled coin.

My grandfather's magic trick spawned a fascination with conjuring that has lasted all my life. In my teens, I became one of the youngest members of a world-famous magic club, The Magic Circle. In my twenties, I worked as a professional magician, performing card tricks at some of London's most fashionable West End restaurants. Once in a while, I even made an initialled coin disappear and reappear in a little cloth bag sealed in a small tin box. Deceiving people twice a night sparked a strong sense of curiosity about why people are fooled. That interest was the catalyst for a psychology degree and, some twenty years later, I still haven't shaken my fascination with the psychology of deception.

Over the years, I have investigated the telltale signs that give away a liar, examined how fake smiles differ from genuine grins, and discovered how people can be fooled into believing that they have experienced events that didn't actually happen. I have unraveled the truth about deception.

We begin our journey into the shady world of skullduggery by examining an unusual body of work concerned with the evolutionary origins of deceit. It is a strange story involving a group of trunk-swinging elephants, talking apes, and children taking prohibited peeks at their favorite toys.

Jumbo Deception, Talking Apes, and Lying Children

A few years ago, the animal researcher Maxine Morris spotted some curious behavior while observing a group of Asian elephants at Washington Park Zoo in Indiana.[1] At feeding time, each elephant was given a big bundle of hay. Morris noticed that a couple of the elephants tended to eat their own hay quickly, sidle up to their slower-eating companions, and then start swinging their trunks from side to side in a seemingly aimless way. To the uninformed, it appeared that these elephants were just passing the time of day. However, Morris's repeated observations suggested that this apparently innocent behavior masked a duplicitous intent. Once the trunk-swinging elephants were sufficiently close to another elephant, they would suddenly grab some of the uneaten hay and quickly gobble it up. Elephants are notoriously nearsighted, and so the slow-eating elephants were often completely unaware of the theft.

It is tempting to view these "trunk-swinging—hay-stealing" episodes as evidence of a carefully planned and executed deception. A kind of jumbo version of *Ocean's Eleven.* But that may be little more than wishful thinking. In the same way that we talk to our computers and cars as if they were people, so we have a tendency to humanize the behavior of our four-legged friends. The seemingly deceitful elephants may simply have carried out the "trunk-swinging—hay-stealing" combination once by chance, found that they liked the resulting excess of hay, and repeated the pattern without really thinking about it. The only way to know for certain would be to discover what was actually going on inside an elephant's head. The bad news is that elephants are in no position to describe their innermost thoughts and feelings. The good news is that some researchers believe that this type of research has been successful not with elephants but with one of our closest evolutionary ancestors.

In the 1970s, talking gorillas were all the rage. As part of a large-scale research program exploring interspecies communication, Francine Patterson, a developmental psychologist from Stanford University, attempted to teach two lowland gorillas called Michael and Koko a simplified version of American Sign Language.[2] According to Patterson, the great apes were capable of holding meaningful conversations and could even reflect upon profound topics, such as love and death. Many aspects of the gorillas' inner lives appeared remarkably similar to our own. Michael, for instance, liked watching *Sesame Street;* Koko preferred *Mister Rogers' Neighborhood.* In 1998, Koko made a guest appearance on her favorite show, helping teach children that "there is more to a person than what you see on the outside." Michael likes painting and has produced many artworks, including self-portraits and several still-life representations. His work has proved remarkably popular with humans and has been shown at various exhibitions.

Koko is also no stranger to public attention. She has appeared in several films, and was the inspiration behind Amy, the talking ape in Michael Crichton's best-seller *Congo.* Koko also features in a promotional video on her Web site (using her communicative skills to appeal for donations) and, in 1998, took part in the first interspecies Web chat. The opening lines of the conversation between the interviewer, Koko, and Patterson illustrate some of the difficulties associated with trying to understand gorilla small talk:[3]

Interviewer: I'll start taking questions from the audience now, our first question is: "Koko, are you going to have a baby in the future?"

Koko: Pink.

Patterson: We've had earlier discussion about colors today.

Koko: Listen, Koko loves eat.

Interviewer: Me too!

Patterson: What about a baby? She's thinking . . .

Koko: *(Unattention)*

Patterson: She covered her face with her hands . . . which means it's not happening, basically, or it hasn't happened yet.

Despite difficulties, Michael and Koko's trainers believe they have uncovered instances wherein their two hairy colleagues were a tad economical with the truth.[4] In one example, Koko broke a toy cat and then signed to indicate that the breakage had been caused by one of her trainers. In another episode, Michael ripped a jacket belonging to a trainer and, when asked who was responsible for the incident, signed "Koko." When the trainer expressed skepticism about his answer, Michael appeared to change his mind and indicated that Patterson was actually to blame. When the trainer pressed the issue again, Michael finally looked sheepish (which isn't easy for a gorilla) and then confessed all. Whereas the instances of alleged deception among elephants were based purely upon observation, the apes' apparent linguistic skills seem to provide much more compelling evidence of intentional deceit.

The possibility of talking and lying apes has generated fierce debate among researchers. Proponents claim that Michael and Koko are clearly able to express their innermost thoughts and emotions, and that the behavior portrayed during the "Who ripped the jacket?"/"It was her" episodes are clear evidence of deception. In response, critics argue that the trainers are too eager to read meaning into the gorillas' random actions, and that when it comes to lying the great apes might simply be repeating behaviors that had got them out of trouble before. As with the hay-stealing elephants, it is almost impossible to know for certain.

Because of the difficulties of trying to decide whether elephants and gorillas really are capable of lying, other researchers have explored the development of deception in the next best thing: children. Some of the most interesting studies of children who cheat have involved asking youngsters not to take a peek at their favorite toys.[5] During these experiments a child is led into a laboratory and asked to face one of the walls. The experimenter then explains that he is going to set up an elaborate toy a few feet behind the child. After setting up the toy, the experimenter explains that he has to leave the laboratory and asks the child *not* to turn around and peek at the toy. The child is secretly filmed by hidden cameras for a few minutes, and then the experimenter returns and asks the child whether he or she peeked. Almost all three-year-olds do, and then half of them lie about it to the experimenter. By the time the children have reached the age of five, all of them peek and all of them lie. The results provide compelling evidence that lying starts to emerge the moment we learn to speak. Perhaps surprisingly, when parents watch the films of their children denying that they peeked at the toy, they are unable to detect whether their darling offspring are lying or telling the truth.

Adhering to the old theatrical adage of never working with children or animals, my own research into lying has focused on adult deceit.

The Language of Lying

Lies have changed the course of world history. Adolf Hitler's lies to Prime Minister Neville Chamberlain of Britain when the two met just before the outbreak of war in September 1938 are famous. Hitler was secretly preparing to invade Czechoslovakia, and he was therefore eager to prevent the Czechs from assembling a retaliatory force. The Führer assured Chamberlain that he had no intention of attacking Czechoslovakia, and the British leader believed him. A few days after the meeting, Chamberlain wrote to his sister and noted that he believed Hitler to be "a man who could be relied upon when he had given his word." Chamberlain was so convinced of Hitler's honesty that he urged the Czechs not to mobilize their troops, fearing that such a move might be viewed as an act of aggression by the Germans. The subsequent German attack quickly overwhelmed the ill-prepared Czechoslovakian forces and led to the start of World War II. The world might now be a very different place had Chamberlain been able to detect Hitler's lies during their fateful meeting.[6]

World leaders are not the only people who lie, and are lied to. Deception affects every one of us. A few years ago, I carried out a national survey into lying in collaboration with the *Daily Telegraph*.[7] Only 8 percent of respondents claimed never to have lied, and I suspect that most of these people couldn't bring themselves to tell the truth even in an anonymous survey. Other researchers have asked people to keep a detailed diary of every conversation that they have, and of all of the lies that they tell, over a two-week period. The results suggest that most people tell about two important lies each day, that a third of conversations involve some form of deception, that four in five lies remain undetected, that more than 80 percent of people have lied to secure a job (with most saying that they thought employers expected candidates to be dishonest about background and experience), and that more than 60 percent of adults have cheated on their partners at least once.[8]

Are you a good liar? Most people think that they are, but the truth is there are big differences in how well we can pull the wool over the eyes of others. There is, however, a very simple test that you can take to help determine your ability to lie. In fact, you have already taken it.[9]

At the start of the book I asked you to trace the letter *Q* (for quirkology) on your forehead. If you didn't do it then, please do it now. Using the first finger of your dominant hand, simply draw a capital letter *Q* on your forehead. Some people draw the letter *Q* in such a way that they themselves can read it; that is, they place the tail of the *Q* on the right-hand side of the forehead. Others draw the letter in a way that can be read by someone facing them, with the tail of the *Q* on the left side of the forehead. This quick test provides a rough measure of a concept known as "self-monitoring." High self-monitors tend to draw the letter *Q* in a way in which it could be seen by someone facing them—with the tail facing to the left. Low self-monitors tend to draw the letter *Q* in a way in which it could be read by themselves—with the tail facing to the right. What has this all to do with lying? High self-monitors tend to be concerned with how other people see them. They are happy being the center of attention, can easily adapt their behavior to suit the situation in which they find themselves, and are skilled at manipulating how others see them. As a result, they tend to be good at lying. In contrast, low self-monitors come across as being the "same person" in different situations. Their behavior is guided more by their inner feelings and values, and they are less aware of their impact on those around them. They also tend to lie less in life, and therefore are not as skilled at deceit as high self-monitors.

I have presented this fun test to groups of people for many years. Over time, I have noticed that a small number of people, upon hearing what the test is all about, quickly convince themselves that they traced the letter *Q* in the opposite direction to the way they actually drew it. These people are able to ignore the evidence right in front of them; they twist the facts to fit the type of person they want to be. As a result, the test provides a rough indicator of how good you are at deceiving both yourself and others.

The vast majority of psychological investigation into deception has not focused on the types of people who are good and bad liars. Instead, it has concentrated on the art and science of lie detection. Can people detect deceit? What are the telltale signs that give away a lie? Is it possible to teach people to become better lie detectors?

Soon after I took up my position at the University of Hertfordshire in 1994, I received a curious e-mail that had been sent out to academics across Britain. The e-mail explained that, as part of a week-long national celebration of science, resources were available for a large-scale experiment in which members of the public could participate. The experiment would reach an audience of millions because it would be conducted live on one of the BBC's flagship science programs, *Tomorrow's World.* The e-mail ended by asking academics to submit ideas for the experiment. I thought that it would be interesting to test the lie-detection skills of the entire country, and so I suggested asking several politicians to lie or to tell the truth on the program and have the public try to identify the lies. That way, I argued, it would be possible to determine scientifically which political party had the best liars. A few weeks later I was delighted to discover that my proposal had been chosen, and I started to fine-tune the study.

After numerous telephone calls, the situation became clear: Politicians were unwilling to participate, allegedly because they were terrible liars (none of us believed them). We looked for a prestigious alternative and invited a legendary television political interviewer, Sir Robin Day, to be our guinea pig. Sir Robin was to the BBC what Walter Cronkite was to CBS. His penetrating and abrasive style of interviewing politicians had made him one of the most trusted figures on British television, and had earned him the title of "Grand Inquisitor." We were delighted when Sir Robin accepted our challenge.

The design of the experiment was simple. I would interview Sir Robin twice, and in each interview I would ask him to describe his favorite film. In one interview he would say nothing but the truth, and in the other he would produce a complete pack of lies. We would then show both interviews on television and see whether the public could detect which interview contained the lies.

The BBC assigned a talented young director named Simon Singh to the project. Simon went on to write several best-selling science books, including *Fermat's Last Theorem* and *The Code Book.* The two of us have worked on various projects together over the years, but we first met to film Sir Robin's "truth" and "lying" interviews in the lobby of a large London hotel. Just after we finished setting up the camera, the door swung open and in walked Sir Robin. His trademark thick-rimmed glasses and colorful bow tie made him instantly recognizable. As he sat down in front of the camera, he seemed slightly nervous that he was about to receive questions rather than ask them. I began the first of the two interviews, asking him to describe his favorite film. He explained that he had a great love for *Gone With the Wind:*

So, Sir Robin, what's your favorite film?

Gone with the Wind.

And why's that?

Oh, it's, it, it's a classic, great characters; great film star—Clark Gable; a great actress—Vivien Leigh. Very moving.

And who's your favorite character in it?

Oh, Gable.

And how many times have you seen it?

Um . . . *(pause)* I think about half a dozen.

And when was the first time that you saw it?

When it first came out. I think that it was in 1939.

Once he had finished, I repeated the questions and he described being a big fan of *Some Like It Hot:*

So, Sir Robin, what's your favorite film?

Ah . . . *(pause)* er, *Some Like It Hot.*

And why do you like that?

Oh, because it gets funnier every time that I see it. There are all sorts of bits in it which I love. And I like them more each time that I see it.

Who's your favorite character in it?

Oh, Tony Curtis I think. He's so pretty . . . *(short pause)* and he's so witty, and he mimics Cary Grant so well, and he's very funny the way he tries to resist being seduced by Marilyn Monroe.

And when was the first time that you saw it?

I think when it came out, and I forget when that was.

Which do you think is the lie?

The full experiment took place a few weeks later on a live edition of *Tomorrow's World.* At the beginning of the program we played the two interviews and asked viewers to decide which they thought was the lie and then to register their votes by telephoning one of two numbers. It was the first time that anything like this had been attempted, and Simon and I had absolutely no idea whether people would make a telephone call in the name of science. We needn't have worried. Within minutes we had received more than 30,000 calls.

When the lines closed, we quickly set about analyzing our results. Fifty-two percent of viewers thought that Sir Robin had been lying about *Gone with the Wind,* and 48 percent voted for *Some Like It Hot.* We then showed viewers a short film clip of me asking Sir Robin whether he really liked *Gone with the Wind.* His reply was short and to the point: "Good heavens, no! It's the most crashing bore. I fall asleep every time I see it." At the end of the program we announced the findings and explained that when it came to detecting deceit, the public's skills were little better than chance.[10]

It could be argued that Sir Robin was an extremely skilled liar and that in everyday life people are much better at detecting deception. To investigate this possibility, one would have to carry out lots of experiments; many different types of people who lie and tell the truth about a huge range of issues would have to participate. It would be a mammoth task, but for the last thirty years or so, this is exactly what the members of a small band of highly dedicated psychologists have been doing.[11] They have had people visit art exhibitions and lie about their favorite paintings, steal money from a wallet and then deny the theft, endorse products they dislike intensely, and watch films depicting amputations while trying to convince others that they are looking at a relaxing beach scene. The research has studied the lying behavior of salespeople, shoppers, students, drug addicts, and criminals. Some of my work in this area has involved showing people videotapes of instances in which people have made high-profile public appeals for information about a murder, only later to confess and be convicted of the crime themselves.

The results have been remarkably consistent: When it comes to lie detection, the public might as well simply toss a coin. It doesn't matter whether you are male or female, young or old, few people are able to detect deception with any degree of reliability. The results suggest that we can't even tell when our partners are being economical with the truth.[12] In a series of experiments exploring romantic deception, one member of a long-term couple was presented with a series of slides containing images of a highly attractive person of the opposite sex and asked to try to convince his/her partner that he/she found the attractive person unattractive. The findings suggest that most people in long-term relationships are dreadful at telling when their partners are lying. Some researchers believe that many long-term couples have remained together precisely because they cannot spot one another's lies.

Perhaps the public shouldn't worry too much about their inability to detect lies. They are, after all, in good company. Paul Ekman, a psychologist from the University of California, San Francisco, showed videotapes of liars and truth-tellers to various groups of experts, including polygraph operators, robbery investigators, judges, and psychiatrists, and asked them to try to identify the lies.[13] All tried their best. None of the groups performed better than chance.

So why are people so bad at detecting deceit? The answer lies in the work of psychologists such as Charles Bond, a professor from Texas Christian University.[14] Bond has conducted surveys into the sorts of behaviors that people associate with lying. Unlike some psychological research, his work doesn't involve asking a few hundred American university students to check off boxes on a form. Instead, he has asked thousands of people from more than sixty countries to describe how they go about telling whether someone is lying. People's answers are remarkably consistent. From Algeria to Argentina, Germany to Ghana, Pakistan to Paraguay, almost everyone thinks that liars tend to avert their eyes, nervously wave their hands around, and shift about in their seats.

There is, however, one small problem. Researchers have spent hours upon hours carefully comparing films of liars and truth-tellers. Trained observers sit in front of a computer and watch digitized videos again and again. On each showing, the observers look out for a particular behavior, such as a smile, a blink, or a hand movement. Each time they see what they are looking for, they press a button and the computer records their responses. Each minute of footage takes about an hour to analyze, but the resulting data allows researchers to compare the behavior associated with a lie and the truth, and thus uncover even the subtlest of differences. The results are clear. Liars are just as likely to look you in the eye as truth-tellers, they don't move their hands around nervously, and they don't shift about in their seats (if anything, they are a little more static than truth-tellers). People fail to detect lies because they are basing their opinions on behaviors that are not actually associated with deception.

So, what are the signals that really give away a liar? To answer the question, researchers have searched for reliable differences between the behavior of liars and truth-tellers. The answer, it seems, is in the words we use and the way in which we say them.[15] When it comes to lying, the more information you give away, the greater are the chances that some of it will come back to haunt you. As a result, liars tend to say less, and to provide fewer details, than truth-tellers. Look back at the transcripts of the interviews with Sir Robin. His lie about *Gone with the Wind* contains about forty words, whereas the truth about *Some Like It Hot* is nearly twice as long. Now take a look at the level of detail in the two interviews. In the first interview, he presents a very general description of the film, merely stating that it is a classic with great characters. When he tells us the truth, however, he provides far more detail, describing a scene in which actor Tony Curtis tries to resist being seduced by Marilyn Monroe.

When it comes to the language of lying, this is just the beginning. Liars often try to distance themselves psychologically from their falsehoods, and so they tend to include fewer references to themselves, and their feelings, in their stories. Again, Sir Robin's testimony provides a striking illustration of the effect. When he lies, Sir Robin mentions the word "I" just twice, whereas when he tells the truth he says "I" seven times. In his entire interview about *Gone with the Wind*, Sir Robin only once mentions how the film makes him feel ("Very *moving . . .* "), compared to the several references to his feelings when he talks about *Some Like It Hot* ("It gets *funnier* every time that I see it . . . "; "There are all sorts of bits . . . I *love . . .* "; "[Curtis is] so *pretty . . .* so *witty . . .* ").

Then there is the issue of forgetting. Imagine someone asking you a series of questions about what you did last week. It is probable that you wouldn't be able to remember many of the trivial details and, being the honest person you are, would admit to your memory lapse. Liars tend not to do this. When it comes to relatively unimportant information, they seem to develop superpowered memories and often recall the smallest of details. In contrast, truth-tellers know that they have forgotten certain details and are happy to admit it. Sir Robin's interviews illustrate the point. There is only one instance when he admits that he cannot remember a detail, and it is when he tells us the truth about not being able to recall the first time he saw his favorite film, *Some Like It Hot.*

Research has yet to confirm exactly why body language is often so misleading and the language of lying so revealing. One theory is that because eye contact and hand movements are easy to control, liars can use these signals to convey whatever impressions they want. In contrast, trying to control the words we use, and the way we say them, is much harder; for this reason, a person's use of language becomes a far more reliable guide to the truth.

Whatever the theory, the simple fact is that the real clues to deceit are in the words that people use. So do people become much better lie detectors when they listen to a liar, or even just read the transcript of a liar's comments? I have to own up to a little falsehood of my own. I didn't tell you the whole truth about the experiment with Sir Robin. Like all good deceivers, I didn't actually lie to you, I just left out some important information.

Leslie Nielsen, Ketchup, and Sour Cream

The television experiment was just one small part of a much bigger study. On the same day the BBC program was aired, we also played just the soundtrack of the two interviews on a national radio station. Roger Highfield, the science editor, also arranged for the transcripts to be printed in the *Daily Telegraph.* Each time, listeners and readers were asked to guess which interview they thought contained the lies and to register their opinions by telephoning one of two numbers. Thousands of people were kind enough to participate. Although the lie-detecting abilities of the television viewers were no better than chance, the newspaper readers were correct 64 percent of the time, and the radio listeners scored an impressive 73 percent accuracy rate. When it comes to detecting lies, people are better off listening than looking.

The experiment with Sir Robin is far from being the only study to illustrate that people's lie-detecting abilities are increased by encouraging them to listen rather than to look. One of the more unusual pieces of research in the area was done by Glenn Littlepage and Tony Pineault from Middle Tennessee State University.[16] These researchers carried out their study using one of the best-known, and longest-running, game shows on American television. *To Tell the Truth* involved three contestants each claiming to be the same person. This trio was interrogated by four celebrity panelists who tried their best to uncover who was genuine and who was bluffing. After they had made their decisions, the host asked the truth-teller to stand up and reveal all. This show became a part of American popular culture, and it formed the basis for the opening sequence of the film *Catch Me If You Can.*

Littlepage and Pineault taped various editions of the show. In one of the episodes, three women claimed they were experts on the Middle Ages; in another, three men said that they had been asked by the People's Republic of China to discover the remains of a prehistoric "Peking Man." The researchers then showed the clips to groups of people. One group watched the show as normal, hearing both the sound and seeing the images. Another group heard only the soundtrack of the shows; a third saw only the images. The results demonstrated the importance of the language of lying. Those who saw just the images were terrible at spotting the bluffing contestants, whereas those who heard just the soundtrack were surprisingly skilled at working out who was about to be revealed as the truth-teller.

It is time to test your new lie-detection skills. A few years ago, a science show called *The Daily Planet,* which aired on the Canadian Discovery Channel, asked me to help conduct another national lie-detection experiment. They persuaded one of my childhood heroes, the Hollywood actor and comedian Leslie Nielsen (star of *Airplane, Naked Gun,* and *Police Squad!*), to be our guinea pig. Nielsen was interviewed twice by the show's host, Jay Ingram. In each interview, Nielsen was asked about his favorite food. As with the Sir Robin experiment, one of the answers was a complete pack of lies and the other was the honest truth. Can you spot the lie this time?

Interview 1

What is your favorite food?

What is my favorite food? What is my favorite food? And I can take my pick out of absolutely anything? Hmm . . . boy, that's a toughie, I tell you. It really depends. I guess . . . my favorite food is ketchup.

Ketchup! Why do you like ketchup so much?

I don't know. I think I am one of those people who is capable of putting ketchup on absolutely anything, or everything, whichever way you want to look at it. Yes, ketchup.

I am thinking really mainly about something that is a holdover from the time when I was a little boy. You know, how you go looking for it—you say, "Hey, Mommy, give me a piece of bread and jam." And I remember the time when my mother, she said, "We don't have any jam, Leslie, we don't have any jam." I said, "But, but, but." And she said, "I'll give you something." And she had a piece of bread and butter, and she put ketchup on it. And smoothed it over and so on. I'm addicted to it, and, I know I would catch myself, when I was . . . if I was feeling good around the house, no matter what it is, and I got hungry, I would head for the refrigerator and get out a piece of bread and butter and put ketchup on it. It made me feel even better.

Interview 2

So, Leslie Nielsen, what is your favorite food?

It's becoming a favorite for me . . . it's at the head of my list . . . I'm really only going by what comes into my mind first. And . . . you know, sour cream.

You take a dollop of sour cream and you put it on guacamole, for example, or . . . I think it is because I have got into a Mexican tinge here, and I can remember my mother, for example, when I was a kid, she would eat a tomato sandwich with mayonnaise on it. Well mayonnaise, later on, it looked like sour cream, it would be the last thing in the world that I would want to touch.

And . . . errr . . . so I really stayed away from it, but today . . . it's a very unusual flavor, and you can get it more or less low fat, which I am very careful and cautious

> about, and it is a new taste for me, but it is something that I am growing very rapidly to like very much—sour cream.

As you might already have guessed, Leslie loves ketchup and hates sour cream. The transcripts contain the linguistic patterns that are typical of lying and truth telling. First, the lie is far shorter than the truth—Leslie used about 220 words when he spoke about ketchup and roughly 150 when he described his "love" of sour cream. The transcripts also contain evidence of the "psychological distancing" associated with lying. When Leslie tells the truth, he uses the word "I" seventeen times, compared to just nine times when he lies. Also, the truth contains a fairly detailed description of the type of childhood experience that he associates with ketchup, with several descriptions of his emotions ("I'm *addicted* to it . . . "; "If I was *feeling good . . .* "; and "It made me *feel even better . . .* "). In contrast, Leslie's lie is far more factual (about how you can use it, that it has an unusual flavor, and it is low fat), and contains only a single and slightly strange reference, right at the very end of the interview, to how it makes him feel ("It is something that I am growing very rapidly to like very much . . . ").

Once you know the telltale signs associated with the language of a lie, detecting deceit becomes much easier. The most reliable signs of lying are in people's voices and in their unconscious choices of language: the lack of key details in their descriptions; the increase in pauses and hesitations; the way liars distance themselves from their deceit by avoiding self-references such as "I"; the failure to describe their feelings; and the way liars seem to remember minute information that truth-tellers forget. Learn to listen for the secret signals and the thin veil of deception is lifted. Suddenly you see what people really think and feel, and the world becomes a very different place. Honestly. Trust me on this one.

THE *MONA LISA,* FRESHLY GUILLOTINED HEADS, AND THE SCHOOL SISTERS OF NOTRE DAME

Do the results of the studies conducted with Sir Robin Day and Leslie Nielsen mean there are no telltale signs of deception that can be detected in people's body language and facial expressions? Not exactly. In fact, there are ways of spotting deception by using your eyes rather than your ears; you just have to know exactly what you are looking for. Let's consider one of the most common, and frequently faked, forms of nonverbal behavior: the human smile.

We all smile, but few of us have any insight into the complex psychology underlying this seemingly simple behavior. Do you smile because *you* are happy, or to let *other people* know that you are happy? This apparently straightforward question has generated fierce debate among researchers. Some have argued that the smile is driven almost entirely by an inner feeling of happiness; others have claimed that it is a social signal designed to let those around you know how you feel. To help settle the issue, Robert Kraut and Robert Johnston, professors from Cornell University, decided to compare the amount people smiled when they were happy but alone with when they were equally happy but with others.[17] After much deliberation, they hit upon the perfect place to conduct their study: a bowling alley. They realized that when bowlers rolled their balls down the lane and got a good score, they tended to be alone and happy. When they turned and faced their fellow bowlers, however, they would be just as happy but now they were interacting with others.

Over the course of several studies, Kraut and his colleagues secretly observed more than 2,000 bowls. Each time, the researchers carefully documented the course of events, including the bowlers' facial expressions, their scores, and whether they were facing the bowling lane or their friends. In one part of the study, the team quietly muttered the information into a dictaphone (avoiding possible suspicion by using code words for each factor) to ensure that their measurements were accurately recorded. Their findings revealed that only 4 percent of bowlers smiled when they obtained a good score, but they were facing away from their colleagues. However, when the bowlers turned around and looked at their friends, 42 percent of them had a huge smile pasted across their faces. Strong evidence that we don't smile simply because we are happy, but rather to let others know that we are happy.

Like all social signals, smiling is open to fakery. People often smile to give the impression that they are happy when, deep down, they feel less than joyous. But is a fake smile identical to a genuine smile, or are there telltale facial signals that separate the two expressions? It is an issue that has taxed researchers for more than a hundred years, and one that lay at the heart of an unusual experiment that I recently conducted in an art gallery.

In the previous chapter, I described how the directors of the New Zealand Science Festival were kind enough to let me undertake the second part of the Born Lucky experiment. Before leaving, I suggested to the festival organizers that we stage a second study that would help unmask the secrets of the fake smile. The idea was simple. I wanted people to see several pairs of photographs.[18] Each pair would contain two images of the same person smiling. One of the smiles would be genuine and the other fake, and the public would be asked to spot the genuine grins. A careful comparison of the photographs would reveal whether there were any telltale signs that give away a fake smile, and an analysis of results would determine whether people were able to utilize these signals. After some discussion, we hit upon the idea of staging the study as an exhibition in an art gallery. The Dunedin Public Art Gallery kindly agreed to host the event, ensuring that our unusual art-science exhibition would brush shoulders with works by Turner, Gainsborough, and Monet.

For my smiling experiment, I needed to create a way of having people produce both a genuine and a fake smile. Researchers have used a diverse range of techniques to provoke such facial expressions in the laboratory. In the 1930s, the psychologist Carney Landis wanted to photograph people's faces as they experienced a range of emotions, and so his researchers asked volunteers to listen to a jazz record, read the Bible, and flick through some pornographic images (Landis reports that "the experimenter was careful not to laugh or appear self-conscious during this last situation").[19] Two other situations were designed to provoke more extreme reactions. In one, volunteers were asked to place their hands in a pail of water containing three live frogs. After the volunteers had reacted, they were urged to continue feeling around in the water. The experimenter then ran a high voltage through the water, giving the subjects a considerable electric shock. However, Landis's pièce de résistance involved his final, and ethically most questionable, task. Here participants were handed a live white rat and a butcher's knife, and asked to behead the rat. Around 70 percent of the volunteers carried out the task after "more or less urging," and in the remaining cases the experimenter beheaded the rat himself.

Landis reports that 52 percent of people smiled during the beheading, compared to 74 percent receiving the electric shock. Most of the volunteers were adults, but the group did include a thirteen-year-old boy who was a patient at the University Hospital because he was emotionally unstable and had high blood pressure ("So, son, what happened at the hospital today?").

In my smiling study, I asked each of our volunteers to bring along a poodle and a large knife. Just kidding. Actually, we opted for two tasks that were a little less controversial. Each person was asked to come along with a friend. Whenever the friend made the volunteer laugh, we took a photograph of the genuine smile. We then asked volunteers to imagine that they had just met someone they disliked and had to fake a polite smile. Two of the resulting images are shown in figure 1. This pair of photographs, and nine other pairs, formed the basis for the exhibition.

Fig. 1 Photographs showing either a genuine smile or a fake one.

I am not the first academic to examine the science of smiling in an art gallery. In 2003, Margaret Livingstone, a Harvard neuroscientist, attempted to solve scientifically the mystery of perhaps the most famous smile in art.[20] The *Mona Lisa* was created by Leonardo da Vinci in the 1500s, and the painting has perplexed art historians for hundreds of years. Much of the debate has revolved around the nature of the subject's enigmatic facial expression: Some scholars argue that the painting clearly shows a smiling face, but others claim that the expression is one of great sadness. In 1852, a young French artist threw himself from the fourth-floor window of his Paris hotel after writing these words: "For years I have grappled desperately with her smile. Now I prefer to die." Livingstone took a somewhat more constructive approach to the issue.

People had noticed that Mona Lisa's smile was far more apparent to viewers when they looked at her eyes, and that it appeared to vanish when they looked directly at her mouth. This was a key part of the enigmatic nature of the painting, but people couldn't figure out how Leonardo had created the strange effect. Livingstone discovered that the illusion was due to the fact that the human eye sees the world in two very different ways. When you look at something directly, the light falls on a central part of the retina called the fovea. This part of the eye is excellent at seeing relatively bright objects, such as those in direct sunlight. In contrast, when you see something out of the corner of your eye, the light falls on the peripheral part of the retina, which is much better at seeing in semi-darkness. Livingstone found that Leonardo's picture is using the two parts of the retina to fool the eye. Analyses showed that the artist had cleverly used the shadows from the cheekbones to make the subject's mouth much darker than the rest of her face. As a result, the subject's smile appears more obvious when people look at her eyes because they are seeing it in their peripheral vision. When people look directly at her mouth, they are seeing the dark area of the painting more clearly with the fovea, and so the smile looks far less pronounced.

Livingstone was not the first scientist to be intrigued with the mystery of the human smile. Two hundred years earlier, a small band of European scientists conducted a series of strange studies on the same topic.

In the early nineteenth century, researchers were fascinated by how electricity might be used to gain important anatomical and physiological insights. Some of this work involved the rather gruesome, and often public, stimulation of fresh corpses. Perhaps the most famous exponent of this technique was the Italian scientist Giovanni Aldini.[21] Aldini specialized in bringing murderers back to life. In one well-publicized example of his work, Aldini traveled to London to reanimate a murderer named George Foster. Foster had been found guilty of killing his wife and child by drowning them in a canal and had been sentenced to hang on January 18, 1803. Shortly after his death, Foster's body was taken to a nearby house, where Aldini applied various voltages to his body under the watchful eye of eminent British scientists. The court calendar (subsequently appearing, rather appropriately, in an edited collection of papers by a Mr. G. T. Crook) reported the results:[22]

> On the first application of the process to the face, the jaws of the deceased criminal began to quiver, and the adjoining muscles were horribly contorted, and one eye was actually opened. In the subsequent part of the process the

> right hand was raised and clenched, and the legs and thighs were set in motion. It appeared to the uninformed part of the by-standers as if the wretched man was on the eve of being restored to life.

The description then went on to rule out the possibility of resurrection on the grounds that during Foster's execution "several of his friends who were under the scaffold had violently pulled his legs, in order to put a more speedy termination to his suffering"; it also noted that even if Aldini's demonstration had brought Foster back to life, he would have been hanged a second time because the law demanded that such criminals be "hanged until they were dead." The calendar also describes how one of the onlookers, a Mr. Pass, the beadle of the Surgeons' Company, was so shocked by the demonstration that he died of fright soon after his return home, thus making Foster one of the very few murderers to kill another victim *after* his own death.

Aldini was not the only scientist to experiment with the effects of electrical stimulation upon the muscles of the body. A few years later, a group of Scottish scientists carried out a similar demonstration with another murderer, contorting the man's face into "fearful action" and setting his fingers in motion such that "the corpse seemed to point to different spectators." Again, the resulting scene proved too much for many onlookers, with one man fainting and several leaving the room in disgust.[23]

In addition to laying the foundations for much modern-day work into the effects of medical electrical stimulation, this research resulted in two significant contributions to popular culture. The use of electricity apparently to resurrect the dead helped inspire Mary

Shelley to write *Frankenstein.* Also, the word "corpsing"—a term actors use when they suddenly laugh while trying to be serious—originates in the inappropriate grins exhibited on the lifeless heads.

Aldini's work also inspired a French scientist named Guillaume Duchenne de Boulogne to develop a more sophisticated system for investigating which muscles are involved in different facial expressions. Rather than work with recently executed murderers, Duchenne decided to take the more civilized approach of photographing living subjects as electricity was applied directly to their faces. After much searching, he found a participant who was willing to put up with the constant, and rather painful, stimulation of his face. In his book *The Mechanism of Human Facial Expression,*[24] published in 1862, Duchenne presents a less than flattering description of his guinea pig: "The individual I chose as my principal subject for the experiments . . . was an old toothless man, with a thin face, whose features, without being absolutely ugly, approached ordinary triviality, and whose facial expression was in perfect agreement with his inoffensive character and his restricted intelligence."

In addition, the man had another desirable attribute: almost total facial anesthesia. This meant that Duchenne could "stimulate his individual muscles with as much precision and accuracy as if [he] were working with a still irritable cadaver" (see fig. 2).

After snapping hundreds of photographs, Duchenne uncovered the secret of the fake smile. When electricity was applied to the cheeks of the face, the large muscles on each side of the mouth—known as the "zygomatic major"—pulled the corners of the lip upward to create a grin. Duchenne then compared this smile with the one produced when he told his thin-faced participant a joke. The genuine smiles included not only the zygomatic major but also the orbicularis oculi muscles that run right around each eye. In a

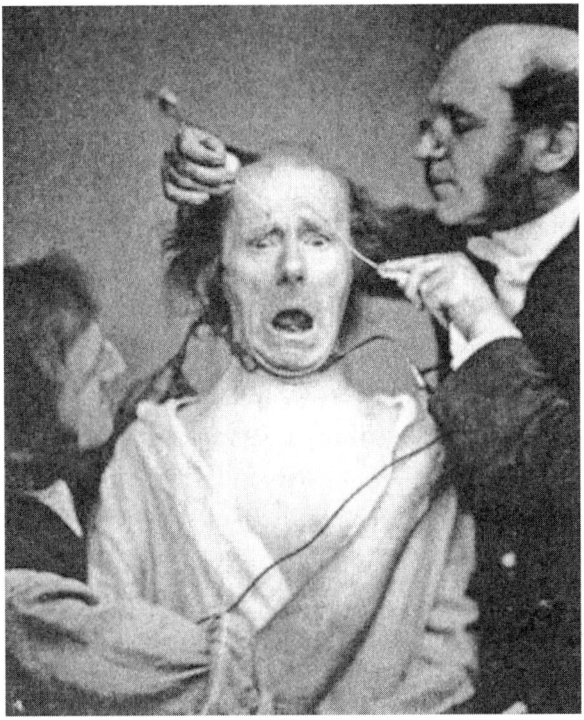

Fig. 2 Duchenne stimulates the face of his volunteer.

genuine smile, these muscles tighten, pulling the eyebrows down and the cheeks up, producing tiny crinkles around the corners of the eyes. Duchenne discovered that the tightening of the eye muscles lay outside of voluntary control; it was "only put into play by the sweet emotions of the soul."

Duchenne's work has been confirmed by more recent research,[25] and our twenty-first-century images of genuine and false smiles showed exactly the same effect. Take another look at the two photographs in figure 1. The image on the right shows a fake smile in which the zygomatic major muscles are pulling up the corners of the mouth. Researchers have recently christened this the "Pan American" smile, after the fake grin often produced by flight attendants working for the now-defunct airline. The left-hand picture shows a genuine smile in which both the zygomatic major muscles and the orbicularis oculi muscles around the eyes are involved. Here, the upward movement of the cheek has produced more striking contour lines at the sides of the nose and around the bottom and sides of the eyes. Also, the eyebrows, and the skin below the eyebrows, have moved down toward the eyes, making them slightly narrower and creating a "bagging" directly above the eyes. These subtle changes are easier to see in the enlargements of the photographs in figure 3 (the genuine smile is shown in the top image, and the fake in the bottom).

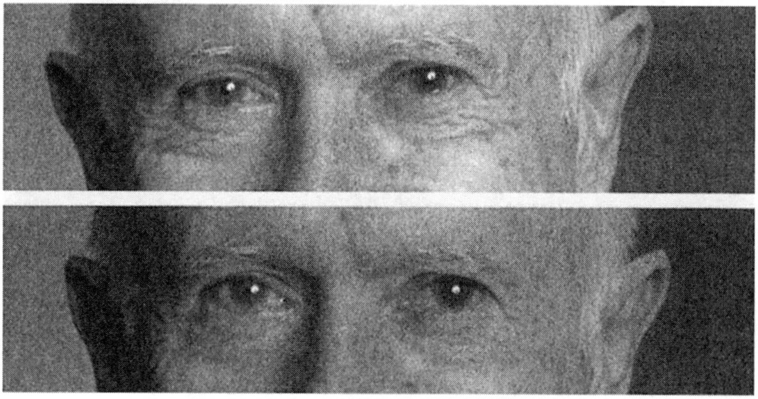

Fig. 3 Close-up of the genuine and fake smiles.

Hundreds of people visited the Dunedin Public Art Gallery during the festival and were happy to take part in the experiment. Participants were given a questionnaire, asked to look at each pair of photographs, and instructed to indicate which of them they believed showed the genuine smile. The results revealed that many people couldn't tell the fake from the genuine smiles, and even those who thought they were especially sensitive to the emotions of others scored little better than chance. Had they known exactly what to look for, however, the telltale clue was right in front of their noses (and just to the sides of the noses of the people in the photographs).

The people participating in the study were not especially skilled at spotting a genuine smile. The ability to differentiate between the two, however, using the type of system developed by Duchenne, has provided psychologists with a unique insight into the relationship between emotion and everyday life, to the point that researchers have recently started to look at the way small, and seemingly irrelevant, aspects of a person's behavior in early life may provide a useful insight into his or her long-term success and happiness.

The idea is beautifully illustrated by a study involving two hundred nuns carried out by Deborah Danner, a psychologist at the University of Kentucky.[26] Before joining an American nunnery known as the School Sisters of Notre Dame, each nun is required to write an autobiographical account of her life. In the early 1990s, Danner analyzed 180 autobiographies written by nuns who had joined the order in the mid-1970s, counting the frequency with which words describing positive emotions, such as "joy," "love," and "content," appeared. Remarkably, nuns who described experiencing a large number of positive emotions lived as much as ten years longer than the others.

Similar work suggests that the presence of the Duchenne smile in early adulthood provides a deep insight into people's lives. In the late 1950s, about 150 senior students at Mills College (a private women's college in Oakland, California) agreed to allow scientists to conduct a long-term study of their lives. During the next fifty years, these women provided researchers with ongoing reports about their health, marriages, family lives, careers, and happiness. A few years ago, Dacher Keltner and LeeAnne Harker, from the University of California at Berkeley, looked at the photographs of the women that had been taken for the college yearbook when they were in their early twenties.[27] Nearly all the women were smiling. However, when the researchers carefully examined the images, they noticed that about half of the photographs showed a Pan Am smile and half a genuine Duchenne smile. They then went back to the information that had been provided by the women throughout their lives, and they discovered something remarkable. Compared to the women with the Pan Am smiles, those displaying the Duchenne smiles were significantly more likely to be married, to stay married, to be happier, and to enjoy better health throughout their lives.

Lifelong success and happiness can be predicted by the simple crinkling around the sides of the eyes that first caught Duchenne's attention more than a century ago. Interestingly, Duchenne realized the importance of his discovery long before his fellow scientists. Summing up his feelings about his research at the end of his career, Duchenne noted: "You cannot exaggerate the significance of the fake smile. The expression which can be both a simple smile of politeness, or act as a cover to treason. The smile that plays upon just the lips when our soul is sad."

"Never Mind, Son, We'll Ride It Down Together."

When it comes to everyday deception, the language of lying and fake smiles is just the beginning of the story.

In the mid-1970s, psychologists started to take a serious look at the malleability of memory. In a classic series of experiments conducted by Elizabeth Loftus and her colleagues, participants were shown slides depicting a car accident.[28] Everyone saw a red Datsun driving along a road, turning at a junction, and then hitting a pedestrian. After seeing the slides, participants were fed misleading information in a very sneaky way. In reality, the slide of the road junction had contained a stop sign. However, the experimenters wanted to deceive participants subtly by suggesting that they had seen a different sign, and so asked them to name the color of the car that drove through the yield sign. Later on, the participants were shown a slide of the junction showing either a stop sign or a yield sign and asked to say which they had seen before. The majority were sure they had originally seen a yield sign at the junction. The study led to a whole raft of similar experiments in which people were persuaded to recall hammers as screwdrivers, *Vogue* magazine as *Mademoiselle* magazine, a clean-shaven man as having a moustache, and Mickey Mouse as Minnie Mouse.

Subsequent research revealed that the same idea can also be used to deceive people into "remembering" events that haven't actually happened. One recent study, conducted by Kimberley Wade from the Victoria University of Wellington and her colleagues, demonstrated the power of the effect.[29] Wade asked twenty people to persuade a family member to participate in an experiment that was allegedly concerned with why people reminisce about childhood events. The experimenters also asked their recruiters to supply them secretly with a photograph of this person as a young child. The experimenters then used this image to create a fake photograph depicting a childhood trip in a hot-air balloon. One of the original photographs, and the resulting manipulated image, is shown in figure 4. Finally, the experimenters asked their recruiters to supply three other photographs showing the person taking part in genuine childhood events, such as a birthday party, a visit to the beach, or day trip to the zoo.

Fig. 4 Genuine and doctored photographs used in Kimberley Wade's false-memory experiment.

The participants were interviewed three times over the course of two weeks. During each interview, they were shown the three genuine photographs and the fake one and were encouraged to describe as much about each experience as possible. In the first interview, almost everyone was able to remember details of the genuine events, but about a third also said that they remembered the nonexistent balloon trip, which some actually described in considerable detail. The experimenters asked all the participants to go away and think more about the experiences. By the third and final interview, half the participants remembered the fictitious balloon trip, and many described the event in some detail. One participant who, at an initial interview, correctly denied having been in a hot-air balloon, ended up producing the following account of the nonexistent event: "I'm pretty certain it occurred when I was in form one at the local school there . . . basically for $10 or something you could go up in a hot-air balloon and go up about twenty-odd meters . . . it would have been a Saturday and . . . I'm pretty certain that Mum is down on the ground taking a photo."

Wade's work is just one of a long line of experiments showing that people can be manipulated into recalling events that simply didn't happen. In another set of studies, participants were persuaded to provide detailed accounts of how, as children, they visited Disneyland and met someone dressed in a Bugs Bunny costume (Bugs is not a Disney character, and so would not have been in Disneyland).[30] The well-known "shopping mall" study had experimenters interview the parents of potential participants and ask them whether their offspring had ever become lost in a shopping mall as children.[31] After carefully selecting a group of people who had not experienced this event, the experimenters managed to persuade a large percentage of them to provide a detailed account of this traumatic, but nonexistent, experience. Related research has convinced people that they once experienced an overnight hospitalization for a high fever with a possible ear infection, accidentally spilled a punch bowl over the parents of the bride at a wedding reception, had to evacuate a grocery store because the sprinkler system was set off, and caused a car to roll into another vehicle by releasing its brake.[32]

The work shows that our memories are far more malleable than we would like to believe. Once an authority figure suggests that we have experienced an event, most of us find it difficult to deny it and we start to fill in the gaps from imagination. After a while, it becomes almost impossible to separate fact from fiction, and we start to believe the lie. The effect is so powerful that sometimes it doesn't even require the voice of authority to fool us. Sometimes we are perfectly capable of fooling ourselves.

In December 1983, President Ronald Reagan addressed the Congressional Medal of Honor Society. He decided to relate an alleged real-life story that he had told many times before. Reagan described how, during World War II, a B-17 bomber badly damaged by antiaircraft fire was limping its way home across the English Channel. The gun turret that hung beneath the plane had been hit; the gunner inside was injured and the door of the turret had jammed shut. When the plane started to lose altitude, the commander ordered his men to bail out. The gunner was trapped in the turret and knew he was going to go down with the plane. The last man to jump out of the plane later described how he saw his commander sitting next to the turret and telling the terrified gunner: "Never mind, son, we'll ride it down together."

Reagan explained how this remarkable act of courage had resulted in the commander's being posthumously awarded the Congressional Medal of Honor, and ended this part of his emotional speech by noting how the United States had been right to award its highest honor "to a man who would sacrifice his life simply to bring comfort to a boy who had to die." It is a wonderful story, and it suffers from only one small problem: It never happened. After checking the citations of all 434 Congressional Medals of Honor awarded during World War II, journalists could find no mention of the episode or anything like it. Eventually, a member of the public pointed out that the story was a near-perfect fit to events portrayed in the popular wartime film *A Wing and a Prayer.* In the climactic scene of the film, a radio operator informs the pilot that the plane is badly damaged, and that he is injured and cannot move. The pilot replies, "I haven't got the altitude, Mike. We'll take this ride together."

The deceptive effects of suggestion are not confined to world leaders who remember fiction as fact. The same techniques are frequently used by professional deceivers to persuade people that they have experienced the impossible.

REMEMBERING THE IMPOSSIBLE

Magicians are honest deceivers. Unlike most liars, they are completely open about their intentions to cheat. Despite this, they still have to convince an audience that objects can disappear into thin air, that women can be sawn in half, and that the future can be predicted with uncanny accuracy.

For more than a hundred years, a handful of psychologists have investigated the secret psychology used by magicians to fool their audiences. In the 1890s, the American psychologist Joseph Jastrow teamed up with two world-famous illusionists to discover whether the hand really is quicker than the eye. Jastrow is one of my academic heroes. In one of the first experiments into subliminal perception, this amazing character analyzed the dreams of blind people and figured out the psychology behind the Ouija board. Unfortunately, Jastrow also suffered from mental illness: One Chicago newspaper reported the onset of his illness with the headline "Famous Mind Doctor Loses His Own."

To investigate the psychology of magic, Jastrow collaborated with two illusionists named Alexander Herrmann and Harry Kellar.[33] Herrmann and Kellar were among the most famous magicians of their day and were locked in a constant rivalry throughout most of their professional lives. If one made a donkey disappear, the other would make an elephant vanish. If one made a woman levitate above the stage, the other would have his assistant float a few feet higher. If one plucked a fan of cards from thin air, the other would perform the same feat blindfolded. Jastrow invited these two great performers to his University of Wisconsin laboratory and had them participate in a range of tests measuring their reaction time, speed of movement, and accuracy of finger motion. Jastrow's results revealed little out of the ordinary, roughly matching those of a control group of nonmagicians collected a few years before.

But Jastrow scientifically demonstrated what most magicians already knew. Magic has little to do with fast movements. Instead, conjurors use a range of psychological weapons to fool their audiences. Suggestion plays a key role in the process. In the same way that people can be made to believe that they once went on a nonexistent trip in a hot-air balloon, or became lost in a shopping mall, so magicians have to be able to manipulate people's perception of a performance.

The concept can be illustrated with a simple laboratory-based experiment that I recently conducted into mind over matter.[34] I showed a group of my students a videotape in which a magician apparently used the power of his mind (actually sleight of hand) to bend a metal key. He then placed the key on the table, stood back, and said, "Look, it's amazing, the key is still bending." Afterward, all the students were interviewed about what they had seen. More than half were convinced that they had seen the key continuing to bend as it lay on the table, and they had no idea how the magician could have achieved such an impressive trick: a dramatic illustration of how an expert deceiver can draw upon years of experience to deliver a sentence with such confidence that people believe they see the impossible happening before their very eyes.

Psychology in the Séance Room

Perhaps my most memorable set of studies examined the role of suggestion in the séance room.[35] Much of this work was carried out with a friend of mine, Andy Nyman. Andy is a skilled actor and magician who helps create material for Derren Brown, the highly successful British television illusionist. I first met Andy many years ago at a conference on magic, and we discovered that we were both interested in the techniques used by fraudulent mediums in the nineteenth century to fake ghostly phenomena in the séance room. We were curious about whether the hundred-year-old techniques would fool a modern-day audience, and so we decided to stage a series of unusual experiments.

The plan was simple. We would invite groups of people to attend a theatrical reconstruction of a Victorian séance, and use various techniques, including suggestion, to fake spirit activity. We would then ask them to tell us what they had experienced so that we could assess whether they had been fooled by our attempts at deception. But first we needed a spooky-looking venue. We came across the House of Detention—a dark, dank, disused, underground Victorian prison in the heart of London. It was perfect. The owners kindly allowed us to rent this uninviting venue for a week, and we staged two fake shows per evening, with twenty-five people attending each séance.

When people arrived they were asked to complete a short questionnaire asking them whether they believed in the existence of genuine paranormal phenomena. I then led the group through the maze of underground prison corridors, briefly relating the history of the Victorian séance. Eventually they were taken along a narrow ventilation shaft into a large room at the heart of the prison. Here Andy introduced himself to the group and explained that he would be playing the part of the medium for the evening. With the room lit by a single candle, he asked everyone to join him around a large table in the center of the room.

For the next twenty minutes, Andy told the group a fictitious ghost story about the murder of a nonexistent Victorian music-hall singer named Marie Ambrose. According to Andy's carefully crafted script, Marie had lived close to the prison, and her ghost had often been seen in the building. Andy then passed around various objects that were allegedly associated with her life, including a maraca, a hand bell, and a wicker ball. In reality, I had bought the objects from a local junk shop a few days before the shows. All the objects, and the table around which everyone was seated, had small spots of luminous paint on them so that the group would be able to see them in the dark. Andy placed the objects on the table, asked everyone to join hands, and extinguished the candle. The room was plunged into darkness, but the objects on the table had a slightly luminous glow. Andy slowly started to summon the nonexistent spirit of Marie Ambrose.

The group was first asked to concentrate on the wicker ball. After a few minutes, it rose a few feet into the air, moved around the séance room, and gently returned to the table. Next, they turned their attention to the maraca, which, on a good night, slowly rolled across the table. These apparently ghostly phenomena were the result of the types of simple trickery that had been used by fake mediums at the turn of the century. It soon became obvious to us that they were still capable of having an impact on a modern-day audience. We filmed many of the séances with an infrared camera, and the tapes showed that some people around the table gasped, some screamed, and many sat shaking in stony silence.

Then came the most important part of the evening: the suggestion. Andy asked Marie to make her presence known by moving the heavy table. The table remained stationary, but Andy suggested that it was levitating, using comments such as: "That's good, Marie," "Lift the table higher," and "The table is moving now." Andy then released the nonexistent spirit of Marie back into the ether, the lights were turned on, and everyone was thanked for coming to the show.

Two weeks later, our guinea pigs were sent a questionnaire about their experiences during the show. We first asked people whether they thought that any of the events they had witnessed were paranormal. Forty percent of people who had expressed a prior belief in the paranormal thought that the phenomena were the result of genuine ghostly activity, compared with only about 3 percent of disbelievers. We then examined whether the suggestion had been effective. The results were startling. More than a third described how they had seen the table levitate. Again, participants' prior belief or disbelief in the paranormal played a key role, with half of disbelievers correctly stating that the table didn't move versus just a third of believers. Our questionnaire also asked people whether they had had any unusual experiences during the séance. It seemed that the atmosphere we had created caused people to experience a whole range of spooky effects, with one in five reporting cold shivers, a strong sense of energy flowing through them, and a mysterious presence in the room.

The message was clear. In the same way that simple suggestion can be used to fool people into recalling illusory childhood events, so it can also make a significant proportion of people experience the impossible.

A few years after the séance show, I teamed up with a television company to explore whether the same sort of techniques could be used to create a belief in New Age mumbo-jumbo, and even persuade people to part with their hard-earned cash. Before the study started, we visited a local hardware shop and bought two objects—a brass curtain ring worth fifty pence and a chrome light-pull for two pounds. The manager of a large shopping center in Hertfordshire allowed us to carry out the study in the middle of his mall.

This initial phase of the experiment was designed to establish a baseline. We stopped people, asked them to place the brass ring or light-pull in their hands, and tell us whether they felt anything odd. Perhaps not surprisingly, no one reported a thing. It was time to introduce some suggestion. I explained to the next set of passersby that I was a psychologist, that I had designed two objects to make people feel slightly unusual, and was now road-testing the designs. Again, people placed the objects in their hands. This time the reaction was quite different. Whereas before we had encountered nothing but blank faces, now the suggestion began to play with their minds. People started to report all sorts of slightly odd effects. Some said that the objects made them feel relaxed. Others said that they caused a slight tingling sensation. Often they would get an effect with one object and not the other, and they were keen to know the difference between the two. When I asked how much they would be prepared to pay for the objects, people estimated between five and eight pounds.

So far we had employed only verbal suggestion. Now it was time to add some visual elements into the mix. I donned a white laboratory coat and bought two cheap boxes for the curtain ring and light-pull. I approached a variety of shoppers and, once again, people were kind enough to help out. I explained that I was looking for honest feedback on the two devices, which were designed to elicit some strange feelings. This time the reactions were even more extreme. One person said that the brass curtain ring made him feel high. Another said that the chrome light-pull made him feel as if his hands were magnetic and attracted toward one another. Another said that she felt as if there were electricity running through her hands. It was a dramatic demonstration of how easily suggestion can be used to part the gullible from their cash. How much were people now prepared to pay for the fifty-pence brass ring or two-pound light-pull?

The estimates ranged between fifteen and twenty-five pounds.

3 Believing Six Impossible Things Before Breakfast

Psychology Enters the Twilight Zone

The Savoy Hotel in London is famous for fine dining, attentive service, grand interiors, and, of course, a three-foot-high wooden black cat called Kaspar. In 1898, a British businessman named Woolf Joel booked a table for fourteen at the hotel. Unfortunately, one of his guests cancelled at the last moment, leaving him with just thirteen diners. Deciding to ignore the old wives' tale that says it is unlucky to have thirteen people around a table, Woolf pressed ahead with the meal. Three weeks later, Woolf returned to South Africa, where he was shot dead in a highly publicized murder.

For decades after the incident, the Savoy didn't allow parties of thirteen to dine at the hotel; rather than run the risk of having another murder on their hands, management went so far as to have a member of staff join any such group. In the 1920s, the hotel asked the designer Basil Lonides to produce a sculpture to replace their human good luck charm, and he created Kaspar. Since then, this beautiful Art Deco cat has been joining wealthy parties of thirteen for dinner. At each meal he attends, he is fitted with a napkin, given a full place setting, and served the same food as his table mates. Apparently, he was a firm favorite with Winston Churchill, who helped secure his return when he was kidnapped during World War II by a group of high-spirited officers dining at the hotel.

Superstitious and magical thinking pervade our lives. Not surprisingly, the topic has attracted more than its fair share of strange and unusual research. The work has involved the extensive interviewing of real-estate agents, observing fisherman in remote regions of New Guinea, playing "pass the parcel" across an entire country, secretly introducing low-frequency sound waves into classical music concerts, and having a group of people attempt to walk across sixty feet of red-hot coals. The results have revealed why much of society believes in the impossible, why strange coincidences are surprisingly likely, and why people experience ghostly goings-on in allegedly haunted buildings.

Superstitious Minds

Dr. Samuel Johnson always tried to court good fortune by leaving his house right foot first and avoiding stepping on cracks in the pavement. Adolf Hitler believed in the magical powers of the number seven. President Woodrow Wilson believed the number thirteen had consistently brought luck into his life, noting that there were thirteen letters in his name, and during his thirteenth year at Princeton University he became their thirteenth president.[1] His Royal Highness Prince Philip apparently taps on his polo helmet seven times before a game. The Swiss tennis ace Martina Hingis allegedly avoids stepping on the court lines between points. The basketball star Chuck Persons admitted to feeling nervous before a game unless he had eaten two KitKats or two Snickers bars, or one KitKat and one Snickers bar.[2] Even the Nobel Prize–winning physicist Niels Bohr is rumored to have placed a horseshoe over his door (although here the evidence is debatable; when asked whether he thought it really brought him good luck, Bohr replied "No, but I am told it works whether you believe in it or not . . . ").

Irrationality is not restricted to princes, politicians, and physicists. According to a recent Gallup poll, 53 percent of Americans are at least a little superstitious, and an additional 25 percent admitted to being somewhat or very superstitious.[3] Another survey revealed that 72 percent of the public said that they possessed at least one good luck charm.[4] The results of my own 2003 superstition survey, conducted in collaboration with the British Association for the Advancement of Science, revealed the same high levels of belief in modern-day Britain: Approximately 80 percent of Britons routinely touch wood, 64 percent cross their fingers, and 49 percent avoid walking under ladders.[5] Even some of the brightest students in the United States engage in this type of behavior. Harvard undergraduates routinely touch the foot of the statue of John Harvard for good luck before going into their exams, and those at the Massachusetts Institute of Technology rub the nose of a brass image of the inventor George Eastman. Over the years, both Harvard's foot and Eastman's nose have developed considerable superstition-induced shines.

Although the consequences of many traditional beliefs, such as touching wood or carrying a lucky charm, are relatively harmless, the effects of other superstitious ideas have far more serious implications.

In early 1993, researchers wanted to discover whether it really was unlucky to live in a house numbered thirteen.[6] They placed advertisements in more than thirty local newspapers, asking people living in "number thirteen" houses to get in touch and rate whether their good fortune had decreased after moving to such a house. Five hundred replied, with approximately one in ten reporting that they had experienced more bad luck as a result of moving to the unlucky number. The researchers then wondered whether the belief might affect house prices and so conducted a national survey of real-estate agents about the issue. A surprising 40 percent said that buyers were often resistant to buying property numbered thirteen, and that this often resulted in sellers having to lower the price of the properties.

At other times, the effects can be a matter of life or death. In chapter 1, we met David Phillips, the sociologist who investigated whether people's birth dates influenced time of death. In an article published in the *British Medical Journal,* Phillips reported a link between superstition and the precise moment of passing away.[7] In Mandarin, Cantonese, and Japanese, the words for "death" and "four" are pronounced in almost exactly the same way. Because of this, the number 4 is seen as unlucky in Chinese and Japanese cultures. Many Chinese hospitals do not have a fourth floor, and some Japanese people are nervous about travelling on the fourth day of the month. The link also stretches to California, where new businesses are offered a choice of the last four digits in their telephone numbers. Phillips noticed that Chinese and Japanese restaurants contain about a third fewer instances of the number 4 than expected, a pattern absent in restaurants describing themselves as American. All this led Phillips to wonder whether the superstitious stress induced on the fourth day of each month played an important role in health. Could it be linked, for example, to the onset of a heart attack?

To assess the possible effects of these beliefs on health, Phillips and his team analyzed the records of more than 47 million people who had died in the United States between 1973 and 1998. They compared the day of death of Chinese and Japanese Americans with white Americans, discovering that in the Chinese and Japanese populations, cardiac deaths were 7 percent higher on the fourth day of each month than on any other day. This figure jumped to 13 percent when the investigators focused on chronic heart deaths. The mortality data from white Americans contained no peaks. The work is controversial, and has been questioned by other researchers.[8] Nevertheless, Phillips and his team are confident that something strange is happening, and they named the alleged effect after Charles Baskerville, a character in the Arthur Conan Doyle story *The Hound of the Baskervilles,* who suffers a fatal heart attack from extreme psychological stress.

It is one thing for superstitious people to inadvertently kill themselves, but quite another when their beliefs directly affect other people's lives. Thomas Scanlon and colleagues looked at traffic flow, shopping centers, and emergency hospital admissions that occurred on Friday the thirteenth. They discovered significantly less traffic flow, over a two-year period, on sections of London's orbital M25 motorway on Friday the thirteenth compared to Friday the sixth, suggesting that nervous drivers may be staying indoors.[9] They then examined various types of hospital admission on the two dates, including poisoning, injuries caused by venomous animals, self-harm, and traffic-related accidents. Of these, only the traffic accident grouping showed a significant effect, with more accidents on Friday the thirteenth than Friday the sixth.

The effect is far from trivial, with an increase of 52 percent on the fateful day. However, Scanlon and his colleagues had access only to admissions from one hospital, so the numbers were relatively small, and thus it was possible that their findings were simply due to chance. In a significantly larger but equally controversial study, the Finnish research Simo Näyhä examined similar records between 1971 and 1997 for the whole of Finland.[10] During this time there were 324 Friday the thirteenths and 1,339 "control" Fridays. The results supported the previous research, especially for women. Of the deaths for men, only 5 percent could be attributed to the unlucky day, but for women the figure was 38 percent. Both sets of researchers attributed the rise in accident rates to drivers' feelings of nervousness on the most inauspicious of unlucky days. The message is clear: Superstition kills.

The Year of the Fire-Horse

Superstitious beliefs can also exert a significant effect on entire societies. According to the ancient Sino-Japanese almanac, each year is labeled on the basis of two elements: one of twelve animals (such as a sheep, a monkey, or a chicken) and ten heavenly symbols (such as earth, metal, or water). The year of the Fire-Horse occurs just once every sixty years, which is perhaps just as well, because it symbolizes little but bad fortune. According to legend, women born in this year will have a fiery temperament, making them highly undesirable wives. Although this notion stretches back into the mists of time, it is kept alive in modern-day Japan through a popular Kabuki drama based on the story of Yaoya Oshichi. According to the story, in 1682 Oshichi fell in love with a young priest and thought it best to start a small fire to help cement their love. Unfortunately, she was born in the year of the Fire-Horse, and the fire spread out of control and eventually destroyed almost the whole of Tokyo.

The last year of the Fire-Horse was 1966, and the Japanese researcher Kanae Kaku decided to use the opportunity to examine whether superstitious thinking had an effect on the population of Japan.[11] The answer was a resounding, and astounding, yes. The year 1966 saw a 25 percent decrease in the Japanese birthrate (corresponding to almost half a million fewer babies born during the year), and an increase of more than 20,000 induced abortions. Subsequently, Kaku found similar drops in the 1966 birthrates for Japanese people living in California and Hawaii.[12]

Curious, Kaku dug deeper into the data, and discovered something even more remarkable.[13] According to legend, females born during the year of the Fire-Horse will lead especially unlucky, and ill-fated, lives. In 1966, there was no easy method for determining the sex of a child prior to birth, and thus the only way to ensure a dearth of female offspring would involve infanticide. Would parents actually be prepared to kill their female babies simply because of an age-old superstitious belief? Kaku examined the neonatal mortality rates from accidents, poisoning, and an external cause of violence between 1961 and 1967. The results were chilling. In 1966, the mortality rates for newborn girls, but not boys, were significantly higher than in the surrounding years. These patterns caused Kaku to conclude that Japanese girls were indeed being "sacrificed to a folk superstition" during the year of the Fire-Horse.

Kenji Hira and his team, researchers from Kyoto University, assessed the financial costs of another type of Japanese superstition.[14] Before 1873, Japan utilized a six-day lunar calendar, the days being designated Sensho, Tomobiki, Senpu, Butsumetsu, Taian, and Shakku. Even today, Taian is traditionally seen as a lucky day and Butsumetsu as an unlucky day. Because of this, many hospital patients wish to be discharged on Taian. Figures from three years of recent hospital admissions revealed that many patients were indeed arranging to ensure this outcome. The researchers estimated that this superstitious behavior cost Japan millions of dollars each year. In Ireland, too, there is a superstitious belief about hospitals: If you leave a place on a Saturday, you are unlikely to be away for long ("Saturday flit, short sit"). An analysis of 77,000 Irish maternity records over four years revealed that about 35 percent fewer patients than expected were discharged on Saturdays, but increases of 23 percent and 17 percent in discharges were observed on Fridays and Sundays, respectively.[15]

The message is clear. Superstitious beliefs are not just about the harmless touching of wood or the crossing of fingers. Instead, they can affect house prices, the number of people injured and killed in traffic accidents, abortion rates, monthly death statistics, and they can even force hospitals to waste significant amounts of funding on unnecessary patient care. Given the important implications of superstition, it perhaps isn't surprising that many researchers have examined just why it is that so many people allow irrational ideas to affect the way they think and behave.

Lotteries, Lunacy, and the Thirteen Club

Proponents of superstition argue that there must be something to these beliefs because they have survived the test of time. They have a point. Lucky charms, amulets, and talismans have been found in virtually all civilizations throughout recorded history. Touching wood dates back to pagan rituals that were designed to elicit the help of benign and powerful tree gods. When a ladder is propped up against a wall it forms a natural triangle, which was seen as symbolic of the Holy Trinity, and to walk under the ladder was seen as breaking the Trinity. The number thirteen is seen as unlucky because there were thirteen people at Christ's last supper.[16]

Skeptics view this type of historical data not as evidence of the validity of superstition but as a depressingly deep-seated irrationality, noting that scientific tests of superstition have consistently obtained negative findings. They, too, have a point. The alleged relationship between superstitious behavior and national lotteries is a good example. Each week, millions of people around the world buy lottery tickets in the hope of changing their lives for the better. The winning numbers are drawn at random, and so there should be no way of predicting the outcome of the lottery. But that doesn't stop people from trying all sorts of magical rituals to increase their chances of being successful. Some people choose the same "lucky" numbers every week. Others base their choices on their birthdays, their children's ages, or their addresses. A few have even developed more obscure rituals, including writing each of the numbers on pieces of paper, spreading them across the floor, letting the cat into the room, and choosing those touched by the cat.

When the National Lottery was first launched in Britain, I worked with fellow psychologists, Peter Harris and Matthew Smith, to put these rituals to the test.[17] In a large-scale experiment conducted with a BBC television program called *Out of This World,* we asked 1,000 lottery players to send us their numbers prior to a draw, to indicate whether they thought themselves lucky or unlucky, and to describe the method they had used to make their selection. The lottery forms were returned remarkably quickly. In all, we received replies from seven hundred people who, among them, intended to buy about 2,000 lottery tickets. After Matthew and I had entered everyone's choice of numbers into a giant spreadsheet the day before the draw, we realized that we had collected some extraordinary information. If lucky people really do pick more winning lottery numbers than unlucky people, then the numbers that were being chosen by the lucky people, but not by the unlucky ones, would be more likely to be winning numbers. It hadn't occurred to us before, but if the theory was right, some of the data we had collected for our experiment could make us millionaires.

Matthew and I debated the ethics of the situation for at least a few seconds, and then we started to analyze the information. We noticed that some numbers were being chosen by lucky people and avoided by unlucky people. We slowly identified the "most likely" winning numbers: 1, 7, 17, 29, 37, and 44. For the first and only time in my life, I bought a lottery ticket. The UK National Lottery draw takes place every Saturday night and is broadcast live on prime-time television. As usual, the forty-nine balls were placed in a rotating drum; six balls and a special "bonus" ball were randomly selected. The winning numbers were 2, 13, 19, 21, 45, 32. We hadn't managed to match any of the numbers. But had the lucky and unlucky people in our experiment fared any better? Actually, there was no difference. Lucky people did no better than unlucky people, and those using any kind of superstitious ritual were just as unsuccessful as those choosing their numbers randomly. There were also no differences between decisions based on birth dates, children's ages, or pets' behavior. In short: Rationality 1; Superstition 0.

Other researchers have taken more unusual approaches to the issue. One of my favorite experiments was conducted by an American high school student named Mark Levin.[18] Levin and his friends set out to test the popular belief that if a black cat crosses your path, bad luck will result. First they asked people to measure their fortune by playing a simple computerized coin-tossing game in which they had to guess whether a coin would land heads or tails. Next, highly skilled cat wranglers ensured that a black cat walked across these people's paths as they ambled along a corridor. Finally, all the participants played the coin-tossing game a second time in order to reassess the state of their fortune. After much coin tossing and cat crossing, the results revealed that the black cat had absolutely no effect on good or bad fortune. To make certain that they had left no stone unturned, the researchers repeated the experiment with a white cat, and again obtained null results. Levin ended his article by noting that critics of his experiment might argue that the bad fortune associated with a black cat manifests itself only in real-life situations, not in an experiment involving a coin-tossing game, but he refuted the idea: "I own a black cat, and although she has crossed my path hundreds of times, I see no degradation in my school work or social life."

Similar work has been carried out in those most apparently rational of places: hospitals. Doctors are a surprisingly superstitious lot, as shown by work on alleged behavioral effects associated with a full moon. When a team of American researchers examined almost 1,500 records of trauma victims admitted to a hospital during a twelve-month period, they found no relationship between there being a full moon and number of admissions, mortality rate, type of injury, or length of stay.[19] Despite this, a survey conducted in 1987, and reported in a paper titled "Lunacy," revealed that 64 percent of emergency physicians were convinced that the full moon affected patient behavior.[20] Of these, 92 percent of nurses reported that working during a full moon was more stressful, although there is reason for skepticism about this latter finding given that the same people also argued that such stress justified "lunar pay differentials."

It doesn't stop there. In the same way that well-wishing is considered unlucky in the theater (causing actors to tell their fellow thespians to "break a leg"), so doctors working in emergency rooms consider that comments such as "looks as though it will be a quiet night" can bring on a flood of new patients. This superstition was put to the test by Andrew Ahn and his colleagues from Massachusetts General Hospital, and described in the pages of the *American Journal of Medicine*.[21] Thirty doctors were randomly assigned to one of two groups. A "jinxed" group received this message: "You will have a great on-call day." Those in the control group received a blank piece of paper.

The jinxed group did not receive any more admissions, or any less sleep, than a control condition (if anything, those receiving the message seemed to have fewer patients and more sleep than those receiving the blank piece of paper).

As with all important findings in science, this work has now been replicated in different parts of the world. In one test, two British medics, Patrick Davis and Adam Fox, randomly assigned each of their days on an emergency ward to one of two conditions: a control day or a *Q* day.[22] During the control days, the team discussed the weather; during a *Q* day they spoke about how they all thought it would be a quiet night. In line with the results obtained by their counterparts in the United States, the British physicians found no significant differences between the numbers of admissions between the two conditions.

What is probably the most systematic and thorough test of superstition dates back to the turn of the last century. In the 1880s, an American Civil War veteran, Captain William Fowler, decided to tempt fate by creating a Thirteen Club in New York.[23] The idea was simple. He would invite twelve guests to join him for dinner on the thirteenth day of each month and then break various widely held superstitions such as spilling salt on the table, crossing forks, and opening umbrellas indoors. The scheme was an instant success and the Thirteen Club quickly became one of New York's most popular social clubs. As the club's membership grew, Fowler had to hire ever-larger rooms capable of holding several tables each containing thirteen guests. Over the next forty years or so, the club's membership ran into the thousands, and its list of honorary members included no less than five successive American presidents. The members' strength of feeling against the superstitious mind-set should not be underestimated. In a speech to the club on December 13, 1886, the politician, agnostic, and orator Robert Green Ingersoll noted:

> The most important thing in this world is the destruction of superstition. Superstition interferes with the happiness of mankind. Superstition is a terrible serpent, reaching in frightful coils from heaven to earth and thrusting its poisoned fangs into the hearts of men. While I live, I am going to do what little I can for the destruction of this monster.[24]

Ingersoll went on to explain that if he discovered there was an afterlife when he died, he would spend his time there continuing to argue with those who believed in the supernatural. Despite consistently engaging in behavior that allegedly attracted little but ill-fortune, death, and disease, the members of the Thirteen Club proved remarkably healthy and happy. At the club's thirteenth dinner in 1895, Fowler reported that the death rate of members was slightly *below* that of the general population. The positive effects of breaking superstitious taboos were underlined by the comments made by one-time club leader, J. Arthur Lehman, in 1936: "My advice to anyone that wants real luck and happiness and health is to break every possible known superstition today. . . . All of the members of the Club that I can remember had good luck . . . I'm seventy-eight now and I defy you to find anyone happier or healthier than I am."

So if superstitions have no validity, why have they survived the test of time and been passed down from generation to generation? Part of the answer takes us from the islanders off the coast of New Guinea to Israelis trying to cope with SCUD attacks during the first Gulf War.

Melanesians and Missiles

Bronislaw Malinowski was one of the world's greatest anthropologists. He grew up in Poland, where he studied mathematics and the physical sciences. However, a chance encounter changed Malinowski's life. While preparing for a foreign-language exam, he came across a copy of *The Golden Bough* by the renowned anthropologist Sir James Frazer. Frazer's book was a detailed study of magic and religion in diverse cultures across the world. The book persuaded Malinowski to travel to Britain and pursue a career in anthropology. In

1914, partly to escape possible internment at the outbreak of World War I, Malinowski traveled to Melanesia, a small island off the coast of New Guinea, to immerse himself in the culture of an isolated community known as the Trobriand Islanders. His book describing his subsequent work there, *Argonauts of the Western Pacific,* is now universally regarded as a masterpiece.[25]

Malinowski studied many aspects of the Trobrianders' daily lives, and he was especially interested in one aspect: their superstitious behavior. He noticed that the Trobrianders used standard fishing techniques when they worked in the relatively calm waters of a lagoon, and engaged in elaborate magical and superstitious rituals only when they ventured onto the much more dangerous open seas. Malinowski speculated that superstitious behavior had its roots in the unpredictability of the islanders' lives. When fishing in the lagoons, the Trobrianders faced little uncertainty. However, the situation was completely different on the open seas: Here they knew that life was far more unpredictable, and so they attempted a variety of magical rituals in a vain attempt to gain control of the situation and decrease the danger.

It might be nice to believe that irrationality was confined to a group of isolated islanders in the 1920s, but exactly the same pressures that forced the Trobrianders to carry out elaborate rituals in the open seas around Melanesia also cause us to touch wood, cross our fingers, and reach for the lucky rabbits' feet.

By the middle of the 1920s, inflation in Germany was so high that paper money was carried in shopping bags. People were eager to spend their money the moment they had it for fear that it would be severely devalued the following day. By 1932, almost half the population was unemployed. In 1982, Vernon Padgett from Marshall University and Dale Jorgenson from the California State University published a paper comparing the number of articles on astrology, mysticism, and cults that appeared in major German magazines and newspapers between the two world wars and the degree of economic threat during those years.[26] Articles on gardening and cooking were also counted as controls. An index of economic threat was calculated on the basis of wages, percentage of unemployed trade union members, and industrial production. When people were suffering an economic downturn, the number of articles on superstition increased. When things were going better, they decreased. The strong relationship between the two factors caused the authors to conclude that "just as the Trobriand islanders surrounded their more dangerous deep sea fishing with superstitions, Germans in the 1920s and 1930s became more superstitious during times of economic threat."

The authors linked their findings to much broader social issues, noting that in times of increased uncertainty people look for a sense of certainty, a need that can cause them to support strong leadership regimes and to believe in such irrational determinants of their fate as superstition and mysticism.

A study carried out in Israel by psychologists at the University of Tel Aviv during the 1991 Gulf War graphically illustrated the same idea.[27] Soon after the war began it became clear that some cities, such as Tel Aviv and Ramat Gan, were in danger of attack from SCUD missiles; others, such as Jerusalem and Tiberias, were relatively safe. The researchers wondered whether the increased stress associated with living in the more dangerous areas would encourage people to become more superstitious. To test this idea, they put together a questionnaire about superstition. Some of the items asked about well-known examples of magical thinking, such as whether it was a good idea to shake hands with a lucky person, or to carry a lucky charm. Others concerned newly formed types of superstitious behavior that had emerged since the onset of the attacks. For example, since the mid-1980s, buildings in Israel had been constructed with a room capable of being sealed with plastic in order to protect its occupants from a gas attack. The questionnaire asked people whether they thought it best always to step into the sealed room right foot first and whether the chances of being hit during an attack were greater if a person whose house had already been hit was present in the sealed room. Next, the researchers went door to door in both high- and low-risk areas asking about two hundred people whether they carried out these behaviors. The researchers' speculations were confirmed: People living in areas subjected to severe missile attacks had developed far more superstitious beliefs and behaviors than those living in less dangerous parts of the country.

The research from New Guinea, Germany, and Israel all suggests that many people become superstitious to help them cope with uncertainty. However, other work shows that these beliefs can also develop for quite different reasons and have far more negative consequences.

Contagious Thinking

Sir James Frazer, in his classic text on magic and religion, describes several types of magical thinking. One of the most fundamental is the "law of contagion." According to the theory, once an object has been in contact with a person, the object somehow possesses the "essence" of that person. In certain magical rituals, a person trying to cast a spell may try to obtain the hair or fingernail clippings of an intended victim and use this to exert some kind of (usually negative) influence over them.

Paul Rozin, a psychologist at the University of Pennsylvania, wondered whether this way of thinking was alive and well in modern-day Western society, and whether it might even underlie certain types of prejudice and irrationality. To find out, Rozin and his colleagues conducted a series of unusual, but insightful, experiments. One of the tasks the researchers gave their subjects concerned clothing: "Rate how you would feel about wearing a nice, soft, blue sweater, big and bulky, unisex in style. It was laundered a couple of days ago, but it's new, has never been owned or worn by anyone."[28]

Not surprisingly, people said that they had no problem wearing the sweater. The experimenters also asked them to imagine that the sweater had been worn by someone who had contracted AIDS through a blood transfusion. The experimenters said that the sweater had been laundered a couple of days ago, and that the person with AIDS had only worn it for thirty minutes. Suddenly people didn't want to wear the sweater. Even though they knew there was no health or hygiene issue, the superstitious theory of contagion kicked in, and they could not bring themselves to wear it. When Rozin and his colleagues varied the imaginary sweater owners, they discovered that the idea of the sweater's having once belonged to someone who personified evil (such as a mass murderer or a fanatical leader) elicited the strongest reaction. In fact, Rozin's results revealed that people would rather wear a sweater that had been dropped in dog feces and not washed (raising genuine health concerns) than a laundered sweater that had once belonged to a mass murderer.

It's a Small, Small World, and Year on Year Shrinkage

People often develop magical beliefs about the world because they have experienced something seemingly weird. With the concept of coincidences, events appear to coincide in ways that seem meaningful and to defy the odds. Some of the best-known coincidences surround the deaths of Presidents John Kennedy and Abraham Lincoln. Lincoln was killed in the Ford Theater; Kennedy was assassinated while travelling in a Lincoln car, built by Ford. Lincoln was elected to Congress in 1846, Kennedy in 1946. Lincoln was elected president in 1860, Kennedy in 1960. The surnames of both men contain seven letters, and both killings took place on a Friday. After their deaths, both presidents were succeeded by men named Johnson. Andrew Johnson was born in 1809, Lyndon B. Johnson in 1909.

These sorts of amazing moments do not restrict themselves to American presidents but pop up from time to time in most people's lives. In the 1920s, three strangers were traveling through Peru by train. Sitting in the same car, they introduced themselves to one another, only to find that the first man's surname was Bingham, the second man's was Powell, and the third man's was Bingham-Powell. Another remarkable coincidence took place at London's Savoy Hotel, home of Kaspar the lucky black cat, in 1953. A television reporter named Irv Kupcinet was staying at the hotel to cover Queen Elizabeth II's coronation. Opening one of the drawers in his room, he found some items belonging to his friend Harry Hannin, manager of the well-known basketball team the Harlem Globetrotters. Just two days later, Kupcinet received a letter from Hannin in which he explained that he had been staying at the Hotel Meurice in Paris and had found one of Kupcinet's ties in a drawer in his room. Faced with such curious incidents, many people would simply say, "What are the chances of that?" and leave it there. But some scholars, such as the Stanford mathematician Persi Diaconis, have delved deeper.

Diaconis has been invited by Las Vegas casinos to determine whether their card shuffling machines really do randomize the order of decks (they don't); he has used high-speed cameras taking 10,000 frames per second to analyze human coin tossing (revealing that coins show a tiny bias toward landing the same way that they started), and persuaded a team of Harvard technicians to create a machine capable of producing a perfectly random coin toss. Diaconis has also written one of the seminal papers on the mathematics and psychology of coincidences, arguing that certain little-known statistical laws make some seemingly impossible events surprisingly likely. The law of large numbers is one example.

Almost every week in Britain, a truly amazing coincidence takes place, an event that we know is extremely unlikely to happen by chance alone. In fact, the odds of this event's happening are 15 million to one: Someone wins the lottery jackpot. Why does this unlikely event routinely happen week after week? Because a huge number of people buy lottery tickets. It is exactly the same with other coincidences. There are millions of people in the world living complex lives, and so it is not surprising that once in a while someone wins the coincidence jackpot and experiences a genuinely unlikely event. Although it is tempting to see these events as a sign from the gods or evidence of a mysterious sense of connection between people, in reality it may all come down to chance. Arthur Conan Doyle put it beautifully in "The Adventure of the Blue Carbuncle": "Amid the action and reaction of so dense a swarm of humanity, every possible combination of events may be expected to take place, and many a little problem will be presented which may be striking and bizarre."

The same idea also applies to amazing anagrams that seem to contain hidden messages or wonderfully succinct descriptions of people or events. The words "U.S. President Ronald Reagan" are a precise anagram of "repulsed and ignorant arse"; "President Clinton of the U.S.A." can be scrambled to make "to copulate he finds interns."

My favorite anagram was discovered by the puzzle creator Cory Calhoun, and it involves the famous phrase from Shakespeare's *Hamlet:* "To be or not to be: that is the question, whether 'tis nobler in the mind to suffer the slings and arrows of outrageous fortune." This phrase is an exact anagram of a statement that provides a perfect summary of the entire play: "In one of the bard's best-thought-of tragedies, our insistent hero, Hamlet, queries on two fronts about how life turns rotten." Although these examples may look amazing, nothing magical is taking place. It is simply the law of large numbers at work. Given the large number of combinations of letters in the words, and the huge amount of text in plays and books, it is not surprising that once in a while amazing anagrams emerge. What *is* perhaps more surprising is that some people are prepared to invest significant amounts of their time looking for them.

Although the law of large numbers accounts for many coincidences, sometimes there is a deeper psychology at work. A 1993 survey showed that one of the most frequently experienced coincidences is that of the "small-world phenomenon," in which two strangers meet at a party only to discover that they have a mutual acquaintance.[29] Almost 70 percent of people claimed to have had this experience, and about 20 percent experienced it frequently. In the 1960s, the phenomenon intrigued the well-known psychologist Stanley Milgram.

Milgram was a remarkable man who was responsible for conducting some of the world's most famous psychology experiments. Starting in late 1960, Milgram carried out a series of studies examining whether ordinary people would be prepared to inflict pain and suffering on others simply because they were told to do so by an experimenter.[30] In the study, an experimenter asked participants to deliver increasingly dangerous electric shocks to another participant (actually an actor who was simply pretending to receive the shocks). If the participants expressed any concern about what they were doing, the experimenter encouraged them to persevere with the procedure, using phrases such as "Please continue" and "The experiment requires you to go on." Milgram's results revealed that about 60 percent of participants were prepared to deliver what they thought was a potentially lethal shock to the hapless victim because they were told to do so by a man wearing a white coat.

Milgram's electric shock study is very well known. It can be found in almost every introductory psychology textbook and is one of the very few behavioral studies to have exerted a significant effect on the broader culture. In 1974, Milgram described it in a popular book called *Obedience to Authority.* In the mid-1970s, CBS broadcast a dramatization of the electric shock experiments with William Shatner playing the role of Milgram; and in 1986, the musician Peter Gabriel wrote a song titled "We Do What We're Told (Milgram's 37)," referring to one of Milgram's experiments in which thirty-seven out of forty participants were fully obedient. What is not so well known is that his work inspired several equally striking follow-up studies. Professors Charles Sheridan and Richard

King, concerned that participants might have correctly realized that the participant receiving the shocks was an actor, repeated the study in the 1970s; this time, real shocks were administered to puppies.[31] The resulting paper, titled "Obedience to Authority with an Authentic Victim," describes how just over 50 percent of men delivered the maximum shock to the puppies, versus 100 percent of women.

Milgram continued to devise and carry out unusual and thought-provoking experiments throughout his academic career. In fact, he had developed such a reputation for the work that when he burst into a colleague's lecture hall on November 22, 1963, and announced the assassination of Kennedy, many of the students assumed that it was all part of yet another Milgram experiment.[32]

In the mid-1960s, building on theoretical work being undertaken at the Massachusetts Institute of Technology, Milgram decided to take a hands-on approach to understanding the small-world phenomenon.[33] One hundred and ninety-eight people living in Nebraska were sent a letter in which they were asked to help ensure that it made its way to a "target person"—a particular stockbroker who worked in Boston and lived in Sharon, Massachusetts. There was, however, a catch. Participants could not mail the letter directly to the stockbroker; they had to send it to people they knew on first-name terms and who they thought might know the stockbroker. Each recipient was asked to do the same; and again, the recipients had to send the letter to people they knew on first-name terms.

How many people were needed to link complete strangers? Given the tens of millions of people in America, many were surprised to discover that there tended to be just six people linking the initial volunteer and the target person—giving rise to the popular notion that we are all connected by just six degrees of separation. The results suggest that society is much more closely knit than might first be imagined, and helps explain why jokes, gossip, and fads can rapidly spread simply by word of mouth. In addition, by examining the relationship between the people in each of the completed chains, Milgram was able to gain some insights into the social structure of 1960s America. People were far more likely to pass the letter onto someone of their own, rather than the opposite, sex, and most links involved friends and acquaintances rather than relatives. The implications of Milgram's findings are not limited to social systems; they also explain a diverse range of other networks, including the operation of power grids, the spread of disease, the way in which information is passed around the Internet, and the neural circuitry underpinning brain function.[34]

Writing about Milgram's work in 1995, the mathematician John Allen Paulos noted: "It's not clear how one would carry out studies to confirm this, but I suspect that the average number of links connecting an arbitrary pair of people has shrunk over the last fifty years. Furthermore, this number will continue to shrink because of advances in communication and despite an increasing population."[35]

Given the importance of Milgram's giant game of pass the parcel, and Paulos's speculations about a shrinking world, it's surprising that hardly any researchers have attempted to repeat the experiment. So in 2003, my colleague Emma Greening and I teamed up with Roger Highfield, science editor of the *Daily Telegraph,* and the Cheltenham Science Festival to address this issue.[36] We wanted to carry out the first British replication of Milgram's classic piece of quirkological research and test two ideas. First, would we obtain the same number of links, or even as Paulos suggested, fewer, than Milgram? Second, was it possible to use the phenomenon to explain another mystery that had emerged during my work studying lucky and unlucky people? Lucky people claim to have lots of chance encounters, and these seem to have remarkably beneficial effects on their lives. They bump into someone at a party, discover that they know people in common, and from these connections they end up getting married or doing business. Or when they need something, they always seem to know someone who knows someone who can solve their problem. In contrast, unlucky people rarely report such experiences. We wondered whether lucky people report lots of small-world experiences because they know lots of people and so are, without realizing it, making their own good fortune by constructing, and inhabiting, an especially small world.

I published a short article in the *Telegraph* inviting readers who wished to participate in a "small-world" experiment to contact me. One hundred volunteers were then sent a package containing some instructions along with a set of postcards and envelopes. The instructions explained that the purpose of the experiment was to ensure that the parcel made its way to a certain "target person."

Rather than using a stockbroker in Boston, our target person was Katie Smith, a twenty-seven-year-old event planner working in Cheltenham. As with Milgram's original study, all initial volunteers and subsequent recipients were asked to send the parcel only to those they knew on first-name terms. The original participants, and all their subsequent recipients, were also asked to return one of the postcards to us so that we could track the packages as they moved around the country.

There tended to be just four people linking our initial volunteers to Katie—two fewer than obtained in Milgram's experiment. Some of the chains in our study provide striking illustrations of just how well-connected apparent strangers actually are. For example, one of our initial volunteers was a textile agent called Barry. Barry lives in Stockport and, perhaps not surprisingly, doesn't know Katie Smith. Barry passed the package onto his friend Pat because she lived close to Cheltenham Racecourse. Pat also doesn't know Katie. However, Pat sent the package to her friend David, who happened to be the head of the Cheltenham Science Festival. Bingo! David knew Katie and so was able to complete the chain and pass the package directly to her.

Our study was the first British replication of Milgram's famous experiment. The decrease in the average number of links taken to reach our target person may be due to Britain's being better connected than America. Or the results could be seen as supporting the intriguing possibility that the world has become substantially smaller over the last forty years. Perhaps, as a result of vast increases in electronic communication, telephone networks, and travel, we are all connected to one another as never before. Maybe, on a social level, science and technology have genuinely shrunk the world.

Possible evidence of global shrinkage is all well and good, but did we find evidence to suggest that lucky people are especially well connected, and therefore live in a smaller world than most? To find out, we asked the initial volunteers involved in the study to rate their general levels of luckiness prior to taking part. Thirty-eight volunteers did not send their parcels to anyone, therefore guaranteeing that their packages would never reach Katie. Interestingly, the vast majority of these people had previously rated themselves as unlucky. We wanted to discover what lay behind this curious behavior. These volunteers had gone to considerable lengths to ensure that they participated in the study, but they had effectively dropped out at the first stage. We wrote asking why they had failed to participate. Their replies were telling—the majority said that they couldn't think of anyone they knew on first-name terms who could help deliver the parcel. As a result, from the outset it appears that the lucky participants knew far more potential recipients for the parcels than unlucky people and were far more successful when it came to forwarding them. These results provide substantial support for the notion that lucky people are living in a much smaller world than unlucky people and that this, in turn, helps maximize their potential for "lucky" small-world encounters in life.

Walking on Hot Coals and Things That Go Bump in the Night

Some people appear to be able to walk on fire, crossing unharmed across a long bed of burning coals with a surface temperature of approximately 1,000 degrees Fahrenheit. The scientific explanation for this amazing feat is that the thermal conductivity of coal is low and, providing the bed of embers is relatively short, little heat will be transferred to the walkers' feet. However, many firewalkers earn a good living expounding a more extraordinary explanation. According to them, they use the power of the mind to create a magical "energetic" force field that protects them from harm, and they claim they can teach this skill to others. Whereas science would predict that people can walk across approximately fifteen feet of embers without being burned, the paranormalists boast that they can walk any distance safely.

In 2000, I worked with the BBC science show *Tomorrow's World* to stage a dramatic test of this claim.[37] The program spent a large sum of money burning fifty tons of wood to create a sixty-foot-long bed of red-hot embers. Live on television, the alleged miracle mongers put their paranormal theory to the test: Each jumped off the bed at around the twenty-five-foot mark, and they all suffered second-degree burns on their feet. I interviewed the firewalkers afterward and discovered that they had a different explanation for their failure. One spoke about how the bright television lights had prevented him from going into the deep trance needed for a successful demonstration. Another explained that her guardian angel had unexpectedly left her a few moments before the start of the walk. It was a remarkable demonstration of how belief in the impossible can be bad for your health. Even second-degree burns hadn't caused them to question their paranormal abilities.

Fortunately, most people do not think they possess superhuman abilities. Many, however, believe that they have experienced equally strange phenomena. About a third of people believe in ghosts, and around one in ten claims to have actually encountered one. I have no idea whether ghosts exist, but I am fairly sure that people are quite capable of fooling themselves into believing that this is the case. For many years my colleagues and I have carried out unusual experiments into the psychology of ghostly experiences.[38] Britain has more than its fair share of haunted homes, and much of the work has taken place at some of the best-known "haunted" locations in the country. We were the first researchers to be invited to investigate the alleged ghostly goings-on at an official Royal Palace, spending ten days at the splendid Hampton Court on the outskirts of London. In other work, we staged a study in a series of apparently haunted vaults deep under the historic streets of Edinburgh, Scotland.

People always seem to be a little disappointed to discover that our experiments are quite different from the sorts of studies portrayed in *Ghostbusters.* We tend not to wander around in jumpsuits with vacuum cleaners strapped to our backs, and, for the record, we have never caught a spirit form in a ghost trap. However, we don't set out to prove or disprove the existence of ghosts. Instead, our work is all about trying to understand why people consistently report odd experiences in certain parts of these allegedly haunted locations.

Most of the studies have involved asking members of the public to walk carefully through the locations in a systematic way and to describe any strange and unusual phenomena that they experience. Then, by examining the types of people who report these experiences, and the places in which they tend to report them, one can slowly start to piece together the psychology of the haunting.

We have discovered that some people are far more sensitive to the presence of alleged ghosts than others. Many volunteers will wander through a "haunted" location and experience absolutely nothing; a few moments later, another person will walk through exactly the same spot, instantly feel uneasy, and report a weird sense of presence. Those who experience strange phenomena tend to have very good imaginations. They are the types of people who make excellent hypnotic subjects; often they cannot remember whether, for instance, they turned off the iron before leaving the house or simply imagined doing so. It seems that they are able to convince themselves that a spirit may really be standing right behind them or hiding in a dark alcove. As a result, they genuinely feel scared and cause their bodies and brains to produce the signals associated with fear, such as the hairs on the back of their neck standing up and a sudden sense of cold.

The work also suggests that context plays a vitally important role in the proceedings. This was brilliantly illustrated in an experiment published in 1997 by Jim Houran, a psychologist and a collaborator of mine.[39] Jim took over a disused movie theater that had no reputation for being haunted and had two groups of people walk around it and rate the number of unusual phenomena they experienced. Members of one group were told that the place was associated with lots of ghostly phenomena and so they were on the lookout for spirit activity. The others were told that the theater was currently undergoing renovation and that they were there to rate how each room made them feel. The two groups visited exactly the same locations in the theater, but they perceived them through completely different mind-sets: The "ghost-busters" reported significantly more unusual experiences than members of the other group.

So does that mean that all ghostly experiences are the result of an overactive imagination combined with the correct context? Not necessarily. Other work, carried out by the late Vic Tandy, suggested that some ghostly experiences might really have been the result of something strange in the air.[40] Vic, an electrical engineer by training, spent much of his time looking into phenomena that pricked his curiosity, including conjuring and ghosts. In 1998, he was working at a company that designed and manufactured life-support equipment for hospitals. The firm ran a small laboratory that Vic shared with a couple of other scientists. This laboratory also had a reputation for being haunted, and the cleaning staff sometimes reported feeling odd in the building. Vic had always put this down to suggestion, or perhaps the result of the small furry animals that inhabited parts of the building. That was until he himself had a strange experience. Working alone late at night, he started to feel increasingly uncomfortable and cold. Next, he had the distinct impression that he was being watched, and looked up to see an indistinct gray figure slowly emerge in the left side of his peripheral vision. The hair on the back of his neck stood up and, he later recalled, "It would not be unreasonable to suggest that I was terrified." Vic eventually built up the courage to turn and look at the figure. As he did, it faded away and disappeared.

Being the good scientist that he was, Vic thought that maybe some of the bottles that held anesthetic agents might have leaked, causing him to hallucinate. A quick check revealed that this wasn't so. Stumped and stunned, he went home.

The following day, he planned to enter a fencing competition and so brought his foil into the lab for last-minute repairs. As he clamped the foil into a vise, it started to vibrate frantically. Although some may have been tempted to attribute the movement to poltergeist activity, Vic again searched for a rational explanation. This time, he found one. By carefully sliding the vise along the floor, he was able to observe that the movement was at its maximum in the center of the laboratory and petered out toward each end of the room. Vic figured out that the room contained a low-frequency sound wave that fell below the human hearing threshold. Further investigation confirmed his suspicions. He traced the source of the wave back to a newly fitted fan in the air-conditioning system. When the fan was switched on, the fencing foil vibrated. When the fan was turned off, the foil remained stationary. But could Vic's discovery explain the seemingly ghostly phenomena of the night before?

Vic knew that although these waves, usually referred to as "infrasound," can't be heard, they carry a relatively large amount of energy, and so are capable of producing weird effects. In the 1960s, NASA was eager to discover how the infrasound produced by rocket engines might affect astronauts during launching. Their tests showed that it did possess the potential to vibrate the chest, affect respiration, and produce gagging, headaches, and coughing. Additional research suggested that certain frequencies can also cause vibration of the eyeballs and therefore the distortion of vision. The waves can also move small objects and surfaces and even cause the strange flickering of a candle flame. Writing about his experiences in the pages of the *Journal of the Society for Psychical Research,* Vic speculated that some buildings contain infrasound (perhaps caused by strong winds blowing across an open window, or the rumble of nearby traffic), and that the strange effects of such low-frequency waves might cause some people to believe that the place is haunted.

The idea is plausible, because infrasound is deeply strange. It can be produced naturally from ocean waves, earthquakes, tornadoes, and volcanoes. The 1883 Krakatoa eruption produced infrasound that circled the globe several times and was recorded on instruments worldwide. These low-frequency sound waves are also a by-product of nuclear explosions, thus explaining the network of infrasonic listening posts that constantly monitor the environment for possible evidence of nuclear bomb tests.

Several animals are sensitive to frequencies undetectable by the human ear, including ultrasound (high frequency) and infrasound (low frequency). Research into the detection and use of these extreme vibrations within the animal kingdom has a long history. In the early 1880s, the pioneering scientist Francis Galton placed an ultrasonic whistle in the end of his hollow walking stick and wandered around Regents Park Zoo noting down which animals responded to the high-frequency sounds produced whenever he pressed a rubber bulb at the top of the stick: "Some curiosity is inevitably aroused by the unusual uproar my perambulations provoke in the canine community," Galton reported after using this forerunner of the modern-day dog whistle.

More recent, but conceptually similar, research has shown that whales, elephants, squid, guinea fowl, and rhinoceros are all sensitive to low-frequency sounds, using these signals to migrate and communicate over vast distances. This, combined with the fact that infrasound is a natural by-product of some earthquakes and tornadoes, led some researchers to suggest that they might also be able to detect the infrasound emitted from such natural disasters and use it as a kind of early-warning system. Some have suggested that this accounted for the alleged fleeing of animals before the 2004 tsunami in Asia.

Low-frequency sound has also been investigated by the military as a possible basis for acoustic weaponry, and is informally referred to as the dreaded "brown note" because it can allegedly vibrate people's bowels, causing them to defecate. Although sound engineers have known about this possibility for years, in 2000 the concept entered the public domain when an episode of the cartoon *South Park* depicted one of its child characters inadvertently broadcasting the note on the radio, causing the entire nation simultaneously to empty their bowels. Because of the resulting coverage, the science show *Myth Busters* tested the concept by subjecting people to high levels of infrasound. Although the presenters reported feeling nauseous, the study failed to produce the much-rumored effect.

There was, however, one problem. Most of the military and industrial investigations had used very high levels of infrasound, whereas Vic was speculating that much lower levels might be enough to induce a weird ghostly experience or two. It was time for an experiment.

A Small Draft, or a Cost-Effective Way of Finding God

Sarah Angliss, a long-time friend of mine, studies acoustics and produces sound installations for museums and other public spaces. One evening we were chatting about ghosts and Vic's low-frequency sound hypothesis. Sarah was also interested in infrasound and suggested that we team up and conduct an experiment. We needed an event that would attract large numbers of people, and one in which they could rate how they felt while infrasound was either present or absent. Sarah had the idea of piping infrasound into certain pieces being played at a live concert to discover whether the secret sound wave affected the way in which the audience felt about the music. Could it, for example, induce the types of strange experiences often associated with the presence of a ghost, such as a sense of being watched, sudden feelings of cold, and a tingling on the back of the neck?

Sarah led the crack squad of engineers and physicists who built a high-tech infrasound wave generator that allowed us to produce infrasound at will. In reality, this was a seven-meter-long sewage pipe equipped with a low-frequency speaker in the middle. Sarah was present when the system was first turned on: "The pipe began to resonate strip lights, furniture and other objects. As the pipe made very little audible noise, this was an odd experience. Seeing objects vibrate for no apparent reason, it is easy to imagine how infrasonic energy could be mistaken for a ghostly sighting."[41]

Teaming up with my PhD student at the time, Ciarán O'Keeffe, and two National Physical Laboratory acousticians, Richard Lord and Dan Simmon, we hired one of the main concert rooms on London's South Bank and staged two unusual concerts. Each concert would consist of various pieces of contemporary piano music, performed by the acclaimed Russian pianist GéNIA. At four points during the concert, the audience would be asked to complete a questionnaire that measured emotional responses to the music and to note any unusual experiences, such as tingling sensations or suddenly feeling cold. Just before two of these points, the auditorium would be flooded with infrasound.

The two concerts would be identical, except for the timing of the infrasound. If the generator was turned on in one piece in the first show, it would be turned off in that piece in the second show. This counterbalancing procedure would enable us to minimize other sources of emotional effects, such as differences between the pieces of music. We would also be careful to produce a level of infrasound that was on the cusp of perception and this, coupled with the fact that it was masked by GéNIA's music, would help ensure that members of the audience were never consciously aware of its presence.

Staging the concert was far from easy. The South Bank concert rooms were not far from the London Zoo, and there was an initial concern that some of the animals might be affected by the infrasound, thus re-creating the "unusual uproar" initiated by Galton's sound studies over a century before. A few "back of the envelope" calculations revealed that our four-legged friends at the zoo had nothing to worry about. However, the same calculations also showed that if we were not careful, the humans in the hall did. High levels of infrasound can cause unpleasant effects on people's bodies; naturally, we wanted to expose the audience only to levels that were safe. The potential problem was that as the infrasound bounced around the hall, there would possibly be areas of the auditorium where the waves added together to create an unusually loud, and potentially dangerous, effect. To prevent this happening, it was important to turn on the pipe before the concert, and then to have Richard and Dan carefully sweep through the auditorium checking the infrasound levels.

The team assembled on the morning of the concerts, the pipe was installed at the back of the hall and turned on to maximum power, and the sweep began. Thankfully, the results revealed that no parts of the hall were exposed to dangerously high levels of infrasound. Relieved, we continued with our preparations.

My role was to be master of ceremonies. To welcome people, explain the purpose of the experiment, and ensure that the questionnaires were properly completed. Ciarán had decided which pieces of music would include the infrasound and so sat with Richard and Dan as they controlled the pipe. Sarah was team leader, and also presented a talk after the concert explaining the science underpinning the event. GéNIA played each of the pieces during the concert.

Conducting these types of live events is always nerve-wracking. There can usually be only one chance to get everything right and, if anything does go wrong, there is a high potential for public humiliation. Good publicity had ensured that the event was a sell-out, and GéNIA and I waited nervously backstage as two hundred members of the public filed into the hall for the first concert. The lights in the auditorium slowly dimmed, and I walked onto the stage and welcomed people to the unique event. GéNIA played each of the pieces perfectly, the pipe was turned on and off on cue, and the audience had a thoroughly enjoyable time. Everyone completed the questionnaires at the end of the four experimental pieces of music and handed them to us as they left the hall. I needn't have been nervous. The whole concert ran like clockwork. About an hour later, we repeated the entire process for the two hundred people attending the second concert, and then we retired to the nearest bar.

The following week, my research assistant entered the questionnaire data into a computer and analyzed the results. Had all of Sarah's careful planning and preparation paid off? Had the infrasound really produced any spooky effects in our concert going guinea pigs? If so, this would be the first experimental evidence to suggest that Vic was right to think that some alleged ghostly experiences may be due to low-frequency sound waves. The good news was that no member of the audience had experienced the dreaded "brown note" phenomenon. The very good news was that, as predicted, they had reported significantly more strange experiences during the pieces that incorporated infrasound. The effect was far from trivial, with people reporting, on average, about 22 percent more unusual experiences with infrasound present. People's description of their unusual experiences made for fascinating reading. When the infrasound was flooding into the concert room during one piece, one audience member reported a "shivering on my wrist, odd feeling in stomach"; another said that he had an "increased heart rate, ears fluttering, anxiety." At another point in the concert, one man said he "felt like being in a jet before it takes off," and a woman reported a "pre-orgasmic tension in body and arms, but not in legs."

These findings were reported by the world's media. As a result, the team was contacted by theme parks asking whether they could use infrasound to make their scariest rides even more terrifying. But this was not the most curious spin-off from the project. We had shown that some "ghostly" experiences may be caused by infrasound. And some academics have taken the idea one step further, suggesting that the same low-frequency waves might also play a key role in creating allegedly sacred experiences. Aeron Watson and David Keating from Reading University have constructed a computer model of a Scottish Neolithic passage grave.[42] Using this model, the researchers have argued that the site has an infrasonic resonant frequency such that a person beating a 30-centimeter drum could produce powerful low-frequency sounds.[43] Others have suggested that some large organ pipes found in certain churches and cathedrals are also capable of producing similar effects.

As part of the preparation for the concert, the team visited several churches and cathedrals that contained especially large organ pipes and discovered that some were indeed creating significant levels of infrasound. This suggests that people who experience a sense of spirituality in church may be reacting to the extreme bass sound produced by the pipes. Further support for the idea came from one pipe manufacturer who informally told the team that the sounds from these pipes are inaudible, and that they can be viewed either as a very expensive way of creating a small draft or as a cost-effective way of helping the congregation find God.

4 Making Your Mind Up

The Strange Science of Decision Making

Imagine that you decide to buy a nice new calculator. You go to your local electronics store and the salesperson shows you a range of devices. After careful consideration, you choose a model that costs $20. At this point, the clerk looks slightly anxious and explains that the following day the store is going to have a sale. If you come back then, the calculator will cost $5. Do you buy the calculator then and there, or return the following day?

Now let's imagine a slightly different scenario. This time you decide to buy a new computer. You're shown a range of machines. After careful consideration, you choose a computer costing $1,999. Once again, the assistant looks anxious, and then explains that the following day there will be a sale. If you come back then, the computer will be reduced to $1,984. Do you buy the computer, or return the following day?

Researchers examining the psychology of decision making have presented these two scenarios to lots of people. In both instances, there is the opportunity to save identical amounts of money, and so it would be rational to treat each choice the same way. People should either buy the calculator and computer right away or, if they want to save $15, return the following day. However, most people treat the two scenarios very differently. About 70 percent of people say that they would put off buying the calculator until the following day, but purchase the computer right then and there.

Even without a calculator, it is clear that the figures don't add up. Why do so many people act in such an irrational way? It seems that they view their potential saving not in absolute terms but rather as a percentage of the amount of money they are spending. In absolute terms, each time they stand to save $15. However, this represents 75 percent of the price of the calculator, but just 1.5 percent of the price of the computer. Seen in relative terms, the former seems to be a much better deal than the latter, and so well worth waiting for.

This is just one example from the large amount of research investigating how people make up their minds. The work has examined how people make many different types of decisions, including whom they should marry, which political party they should support, the type of career they wish to pursue, the sort of house they should live in, the size of car they should have, and whether they should give it all up and move to the countryside.

Here are just a few of the questions this unusual research has explored: whether subliminal messages can increase sales of Coke, popcorn, and bacon; whether something as simple as the height of political candidates can cause voters to switch allegiance from one party to another; whether your surname influences where you live and the career you pursue; whether Hollywood movies influence the verdicts returned in courtrooms around the world; and why certain online chat rooms and personal ads are more effective than others.

We start by delving deep into the strange world of subliminal perception.

Drinking Coke, Eating Popcorn, and Buying Bacon

In September 1957, a market researcher named James Vicary announced the results of a remarkable experiment proving that subliminal stimuli exerted a powerful influence over people's buying behavior.[1] According to Vicary, moviegoers in New Jersey had been secretly exposed to the subliminal messages "Drink Coke" and "Eat Popcorn" while watching their favorite films. The messages had been flashed onto the screen from a high-speed projector designed by Vicary, with each exposure lasting just one three-thousandth of a second. Although the audience had been unaware of the messages, sales of Coke and popcorn had increased by 18 percent and 58 percent, respectively. Vicary's announcement generated a considerable furor among the public and the politicians. Could people's thoughts and behavior really be manipulated by subliminal messages? Could they be persuaded to buy products they didn't want, to vote for politicians they didn't support? Could these messages even be broadcast on national television and influence an entire nation?

Word about the possible power of subliminal stimuli spread like wildfire, with a survey conducted just nine months after Vicary's press conference revealing that more than 40 percent of respondents had heard about the story. The resulting hullabaloo caught the attention of Melvin DeFleur, an expert in communication studies from Indiana University. DeFleur had gained his doctorate for CIA-funded research examining how information about food and shelter could be communicated effectively to the public in the event of a nuclear war.[2] DeFleur had been especially interested in the effectiveness of two low-tech methods of dissemination—word of mouth and the bombarding of towns with thousands of leaflets.

To avoid widespread panic, DeFleur and his colleagues often disguised the real reason for their work. In one part of the project, researchers visited a fifth of homes in an isolated town in Washington State posing as marketers for the Gold Shield Coffee Company. They told people that the company had developed a new slogan ("Gold Shield Coffee—Good as Gold"), and that three days later they would interview all the inhabitants in the town and give a pound of coffee to everyone who could name the slogan. In addition to this face-to-face attempt to create a caffeine-related buzz, the U.S. Air Force was also ordered to bombard the town with 30,000 leaflets describing the scheme. When the investigators arrived three days later, they discovered that 84 percent of inhabitants were able to tell them accurately that Gold Shield Coffee was as good as gold. In their resulting report, the researchers noted that this figure may represent an unrealistically high level of dissemination because the price of coffee had risen dramatically just before the study began, and the public might have been highly motivated to discover the slogan.

DeFleur was curious about James Vicary's claims concerning subliminal perception, and he teamed up with his colleague Robert Petranoff to investigate.[3] The two decided to conduct a realistic test by presenting hidden messages on national television. They knew that they had to be quick. The National Association of Broadcasters had already recommended that subliminal stimuli were not to be used on the media, and it seemed likely that a full ban was on its way. DeFleur and Petranoff carried out two experiments on the television station WTTV Channel 4, in Indianapolis.

The first part of the study was designed to determine whether hidden messages could affect the public's viewing habits. As part of its normal nightly programming, WTTV Channel 4 broadcast a two-hour feature film, followed by a news program hosted by a well-known presenter named Frank Edwards. The experimenters obtained permission to superimpose the subliminal message "Watch Frank Edwards" throughout the entire two-hour film in the hope that it would persuade more people to tune into the Edwards show.

A second aspect of the experiment examined the possibility that subliminal stimuli might alter people's buying behavior. John Fig, Inc., a wholesale bacon distributor in Indiana, allowed the experimenters to flash the subliminal message "Buy Bacon" during its television commercials, and then track the resulting effect on sales across the region.

Throughout July 1958, people watching WTTV Channel 4 were bombarded with hidden messages that told them to watch Frank Edwards and to buy bacon. Before the experiment, an average of 4.6 percent of the public had been tuning into Frank Edwards. After being exposed to two hours of continual subliminal messages, that figure fell to just 3 percent. The effect of the subliminal messages on buying behavior was just as unimpressive. Before the experiment, John Fig, Inc., sold an average of 6,143 units of bacon per week to the good folk of Indiana. By the end of the study, the figure had shown a modest increase to 6,204 units per week. In short, the subliminal stimulation had had almost no effect on bacon sales and, if anything, had persuaded a considerable number of people to avoid Frank Edwards. The effects of the subliminal onslaught had been less than remarkable.

DeFleur and Petranoff concluded that the public could sleep easily at night, safe in the knowledge that they were not having their thoughts and behavior secretly manipulated by subliminal stimuli. Their conclusions were bolstered by another study carried out just a few months before theirs. In February 1958, the Canadian Broadcasting Company briefly presented the phrase "Phone Now" more than 350 times during a popular Sunday night program called *Close-Up,* and they asked viewers to write in if they noticed any strange changes in their behavior. CBC saw no noticeable increase in telephone usage during, or after, the program. The station did, however, receive hundreds of letters from viewers describing how they had experienced an unaccountable urge to drink beer, visit the bathroom, or take the dog for a walk. Despite the impressive lack of evidence suggesting that televised subliminal stimuli had any effect on viewers, in June 1958 the National Association of Broadcasters responded to public and political pressure by banning the use of these messages on American networks.

So why the discrepancy between the increase in sales of popcorn and Coke claimed by James Vicary, and the lack of bacon buying reported by DeFleur and Petranoff? The mystery was finally resolved in 1962, when Vicary was interviewed in the magazine *Advertising Age.* He explained how his story about subliminal stimuli and buying behavior had been leaked to the media far too early. In fact, he had collected only the minimum amount of data needed to file a patent, and he admitted that his investigations were much too small to be meaningful. The entire public and political debate had been based on fiction, not on fact. Toward the end of his interview, Vicary added: "All I accomplished, I guess, was to put a new word into common usage. . . . I try not to think about it anymore." Vicary did far more than simply encourage people to use the word "subliminal." His fictitious study has become the stuff of urban legend, and is still referred to by those who believe that buying behavior can be influenced by subliminal messages.

The lack of evidence to support a link between televised subliminal messages and behavior has not stopped present-day politicians from worrying about the possible effect of subtle signals on voters. During the 2000 U.S. presidential elections, the Republicans produced a television advertisement criticizing the Democrats' policy toward prescription drugs for the elderly. As part of the advertisement, various words slowly moved from the foreground to the background. As the word "bureaucrats" came into view, one frame of the ad contained just the last four letters of the word, spelling "rats." The Democrats perceived this as an attempt to sway the electorate via subliminal perception and asked the Federal Communications Commission to investigate the matter. The Republicans dismissed the appearance of the "rats" word as coincidence, and argued that the advertisement was about health care and not rodents.

James Vicary is not the only person to claim that subliminal stimuli can exert a powerful effect on behavior. Others have written best-selling books claiming that advertisers regularly implant sexually arousing images in photographs to help boost sales. Alleged examples include women with bare breasts embedded in ice cubes, a man with an erection pictured on cigarette packs, and the word "sex" embedded several times on each side of one of the world's best-selling biscuits. In addition, several companies have marketed subliminal audiotapes containing hidden messages that claim to produce all sorts of desirable effects, including increased self-esteem, sexual prowess, and intelligence. This is not small business. In 1990, it was estimated that sales of subliminal audiotapes exceeded $50 million annually in the United States alone.[4] Most of these claims have not been subjected to any form of scientific testing, and the few studies that have been carried out on the topic have failed to support the efficacy of such hidden messages.[5] In one study, overweight people listened to subliminal audiotapes designed to help them drop a size. They lost no more weight than a control group not listening to any tapes.[6] In another experiment, police officers spent more than twenty weeks listening to tapes designed to improve their marksmanship.[7] The results revealed that the group ended up with the same shooting abilities as their non-subliminally stimulated colleagues.

So, does this mean that our thinking and behavior isn't influenced by small, subtle signals? In fact, a large amount of research suggests that many aspects of our everyday behavior are affected by factors outside our awareness. These factors are not to be found being briefly flashed up on movie and television screens; instead, they are right in front of our noses and can exert a considerable influence on the way we think and behave. Like something as simple as your name.

Mr. Bun the Baker

In 1971, two psychologists, Barbara Buchanan and James Bruning, asked a group of people to rate how much they liked a thousand or so first names.[8] Strong stereotypes emerged, the vast majority of people giving the thumbs-up to the likes of *Michael, James,* and *Wendy,* but showing an equally strong dislike for *Alfreda, Percival,* and *Isidore.* It would be nice to think that these emotional reactions don't have a significant effect on people's lives. Nice, but wrong.

In the late 1960s, the American researchers Arthur Hartman, Robert Nicolay, and Jesse Hurley examined whether people with unusual names were more psychologically disturbed than their normally named peers.[9] They examined more than 10,000 psychiatric court records, and identified eighty-eight people whose first names were highly unusual, such as Oder, Lethal, and Vere. They then looked through the same set of records and put together a control group of eighty-eight normally named people who were matched on gender, age, and place of birth. Those with unusual names were significantly more likely than the control group to be diagnosed as psychotic. As the researchers note in their paper, "A child's name . . . is generally a settled affair when his first breath is drawn, and his future personality must then grow within its shadow."

Other studies have also documented the downside of having a name that stands out from the crowd. Research has shown that teachers award higher essay grades to children with likeable names,[10] that college students with undesirable names experience high levels of social isolation, and that people whose surnames happen to have negative connotations (such as "Short," "Little," or "Bent") are especially likely to suffer feelings of inferiority.[11] The psychiatrist William Murphy has examined several case histories illustrating this final point. In one instance, a patient admitted to wearing an athletic supporter to bed when he was a boy to prevent his penis becoming erect. The supporter failed to have the desired effect, and instead caused the boy's penis to bend downward. Unfortunately, the patient's last name was Bent, and this, coupled with the fact that his nickname was "Dinkey," constantly reminded him of the sexual problems that he had experienced as a boy. This, in turn, made him feel anxious about sex, resulting in psychosexual impotence and reinforcing his feelings of inadequacy.

Nicholas Christenfeld, David Phillips, and Laura Glynn from the University of California, San Diego, uncovered evidence in 1999 suggesting that even a person's initials may become an issue of life or death.[12] The team used an electronic dictionary to generate every three-letter word in the English language. They then worked their way through the list, identifying words that were especially positive (such as "ace," "hug," and "joy") and those that had very negative connotations ("pig," "bum," and "die"). Using a computerized database of California death certificates, they examined the ages at which people with "positive" and "negative" sets of initials passed away. Controlling for factors such as race, year of death, and socioeconomic status, the researchers discovered that men with positive initials lived around four and a half years longer than average, whereas those with negative initials died about three years earlier than average. Women with positive initials lived an extra three years, although there was no detrimental effect for those with negative initials. When discussing the possible mechanisms behind the effect, the authors noted that people with negative initials "may not think well of themselves, and may have to endure teasing and other negative reactions from those around them." This idea was supported by the fact that those with negative initials were especially likely to die from causes with psychological underpinnings, such as suicides and accidents.

But it is not all doom and gloom for the unusually named and negatively initialed. Another team of researchers have questioned the findings of the Christenfeld study. In a paper titled "Monogrammic Determinism?" Stilian Morrison and Gary Smith from Pomona

College in California criticized the statistical methods used in the original experiment and failed to replicate the findings using what they consider to be more sophisticated analyses.[13]

Richard Zweigenhaft, a psychologist from Guilford College in North Carolina, has argued that there are several potential benefits associated with having an unusual name.[14] He notes that one of the most frequently voiced complaints by those with common names is that there are too many other people with the same name. The same point was well made by Samuel Goldwyn who, upon hearing that a friend had named his son John, quipped, "Why did you name him John? Every Tom, Dick, and Harry is named John." Zweigenhaft also notes that unusual names are more memorable and cites several instances in which the fame enjoyed by well-known sports people may have been due, at least in part, to their unusual names. As one *New York Post* sportswriter noted when discussing the Oakland Athletics' pitcher Vida Blue, "America knew it instantly. Vida Blue! Vida Blue tripped off the tongue like Babe Ruth and Ty Cobb and Lefty Grove."

Taking a more empirical look at the potential positive effects of unusual naming, Zweigenhaft randomly selected 2,000 people from *The Social Register* (described as the "best guide to the membership of the national upper classes"), and identified those who were mentioned only once; this process generated a list of 218 people. Zweigenhaft then generated a control group by randomly selecting 218 people who did not have unusual names in the original sample of 2,000. Next, he consulted *Who's Who* (described as a book listing "the best known men and women in all lines of useful and reputable achievement") to discover whether people with usual or unusual names tended to obtain eminence. Of the total of 436 possibilities (2 x 218), 30 were listed. Of these,

23 from the unusual names group were listed in *Who's Who,* versus just 7 of those with more usual names. In short, evidence that under certain circumstances, an unusual name can be good for your career.

Work examining the effects that people's names have on their lives is not just concerned with whether a name is unusual or usual. The remarkable research of Brett Pelham and his colleagues at the State University of New York at Buffalo suggests that people's names may influence the towns in which we choose to live, the career paths we follow, whom we marry, and even the political parties we support.[15]

By looking at a huge number of U.S. census records, Pelham has uncovered an overrepresentation of people called Florence living in Florida, George in Georgia, Kenneth in Kentucky, and Virgil in Virginia. In another study, the team examined the Social Security death records of 66 million American people who had died in cities starting with the term "Saint" (for example, St. Anne, St. Louis, etc.). Once again, they found proportionately more people called Helen in St. Helen, more Charleses in St. Charles, more Thomases in St Thomas, and so on. Further analyses suggested that these effects do not occur because parents name their offspring after the children's places of birth but because people drift toward cities and towns containing their own names.

Could the same effects even influence people's choice of marriage partner? Are people more likely to marry someone whose surname starts with the same letter as their own? Pelham and his colleagues looked at more than 15,000 marriage records between 1823 and 1965.[16] An intriguing pattern emerged: Significantly more couples had family names with the same initial than predicted by chance. Worried that the effect might be due to ethnic matching (that is, members of certain ethnic groups being likely to marry one another and have surnames starting with certain letters), the team repeated the study, but this time focussed on the five most common American surnames: Smith, Johnson, Williams, Jones, and Brown. Once again the effect emerged; for instance, people named Smith were more likely to marry another Smith than someone called Jones or Williams, and people called Jones were more likely to say "I do" to another Jones than a Brown or even a Johnson.

Pelham's work is not restricted to examining the relationship between people's names, where they choose to live and die, and the people they marry. He has also examined how surnames may influence choice of occupation. Searching the online records of the American Dental Association and American Bar Association, the researchers found that there were more dentists whose first names began with "Den" than with "Law." Likewise, a greater preponderance of lawyers had first names beginning with "Law" than with "Den." Then there is the data from hardware and roofing companies. Using the *Yahoo Internet Yellow Pages,* the team searched for all the hardware stores and roofing companies in the twenty largest U.S. cities; then they examined whether the owners' first names or surnames began with the letter *H* or *R.* The results revealed that the names of owners of hardware companies tended to start with the letter *H* (such as Harris Hardware), and the names of those in charge of roofing companies tended to start with *R* (such as Rashid's Roofing). According to Pelham, the same effect even extends into politics. During the 2000 presidential campaign, people whose surnames began with the letter *B* were especially likely to make contributions to the Bush campaign, whereas those whose surnames began with the letter *G* were more likely to contribute to the Gore campaign. Writing about his results in paper titled "Why

Susie Sells Seashells by the Seashore: Implicit Egotism and Major Life Decisions," Pelham concludes that perhaps we should not be surprised by these effects, noting that they "merely consist of being attracted to that which reminds us of the one person most of us love most dearly."

In addition to being interesting in its own right, Pelham's work may at last provide an explanation for an effect that has fascinated psychologists for decades: Why does a surname so often match the bearer's chosen occupation?

In 1975, Lawrence Casler from the State University of New York at Geneseo compiled a list of more than two hundred academics working in fields associated with their last names.[17] Casler's list includes an underwater archaeologist called Bass, a relationship counselor called Breedlove, a taxation expert named Due, a gynecologist named Hyman, and an educational psychologist studying parental pressure called Mumpower. In the later 1990s, *New Scientist* magazine asked readers to send in similar examples from their own lives. The resulting list included music teachers Miss Beat and Miss Sharp, members of the British Meteorological Office called Flood, Frost, Thundercliffe, and Weatherall, a sex therapist named Lust, Peter Atchoo the pneumonia specialist, a firm of lawyers named Lawless and Lynch, private detectives Wyre and Tapping, and the head of a psychiatric hospital, Dr. McNutt. My own favorites are the authors of the book *A Student's Guide to the Seashore:* John and Susan Fish.

Pelham's work suggests that examples such as these may not happen entirely by chance; rather, some people may be unconsciously drawn to occupations related to their names. As a professor of psychology called Wiseman, I am in no position to be skeptical about the theory.

Hidden Persuaders

Our names are assigned to us the moment we are born and, for most people, remain throughout their lives. However, some of the other factors that influence our thoughts and behavior are far more subtle. Sometimes, it can just be a single sentence, a short piece of music, or a newspaper headline.

It really doesn't take much to change the way in which a person thinks, feels, and behaves. The concept is beautifully illustrated in two studies recently published in one of the world's most prestigious academic publications, the *Journal of Personality and Social Psychology.*

In the first of these, conducted by John Bargh and his colleagues at New York University, participants were asked to rearrange a series of scrambled words to form a coherent sentence.[18] Half the participants were shown mixed up sentences that contained words relating to the elderly, such as "man's was skin the wrinkled." The remaining participants were shown the same mixed-up sentences, but the one word relating to the elderly was replaced with a word not associated with old age, such as "man's was skin the smooth." Once participants had carefully worked their way through the sentences, the experimenter thanked them for taking part and gave them directions to the nearest set of elevators. The participants thought the experiment was over. In reality, the important part was just about to begin. A second experimenter was sitting in the hallway armed with a stopwatch. When participants emerged from the laboratory, this second experimenter secretly recorded the time taken for them to walk down the hallway to the elevators. Those who had just spent time unscrambling the sentences that contained words relating to old age took significantly longer than those who had spent time with the nonelderly sentences. Just spending a few minutes thinking about words such as "wrinkled," "gray," "bingo," and "Florida" had completely changed the way people behaved. Without realizing it, those few words had "added" years to their lives and they were walking like elderly people.

A similar study, conducted by Ap Dijksterhuis and Ad van Knippenberg from the University of Nijmegen in Holland, asked participants to spend five minutes jotting down a few sentences about the behavior, lifestyle, and appearance of a typical football hooligan, while others did exactly the same for a typical professor.[19] Everyone was then asked about forty Trivial Pursuit questions, such as "What is the capital of Bangladesh?" or "Which country hosted the 1990 Soccer World Cup?" Those who had spent just five minutes thinking about a typical football hooligan managed to answer 46 percent of the questions correctly, whereas those who had generated sentences related to a typical professor were right 60 percent of the time. Although people were unaware of it, their ability to answer questions correctly was dramatically altered by simply thinking about a stereotypical football hooligan or a professor.

This is all well and good within the relatively artificial confines of a laboratory, but how do the same effects influence people's behavior in the real world?

Americans leave about $26 billion in restaurant tips every year. You would think the size of the tip would depend on the quality of food, drink, or service provided, but secret studies conducted in bars and restaurants around the globe have revealed the hidden factors that really determine our tipping behavior. Mood plays a large part in the process. Happy eaters are bigger tippers. In one study, French bar staff were asked to give their customers a small card with the bill.[20] Half the cards contained an advertisement for a local nightclub; the other half contained the following joke:

> An Eskimo had been waiting for his girlfriend in front of a movie theater for a long time, and it was getting colder and colder. After a while, shivering with cold and rather infuriated, he opened his coat and drew out a thermometer. He then said loudly, "If she is not here by fifteen degrees, I'm going!"

Those receiving the joke showed a higher level of laughing and, more important, tipping. Researchers have replicated the relationship between happiness and tipping time and again. Waiters receive bigger tips when they draw happy faces, write "Thank you" at the bottom of a bill, or give a big smile to customers.[21] People tip more when the sun is shining, and even when waiters tell them that the sun is shining.[22] Other studies have shown that tipping is dramatically increased when waiters introduced themselves by their first name, or refer to customers by name.[23]

Then there is the power of touch. Describing their work in a paper titled "The Midas Touch: The Effects of Interpersonal Touch on Restaurant Tipping," April Crusco and her collegue explain how they trained two waitresses to touch diners' palms or shoulders for exactly one and a half seconds as they gave them the bill.[24] Both kinds of touching produced more tipping than the hands-off approach adopted in the control condition, with palm touching doing slightly better than a tap on the shoulder.

Leaving relatively small amounts of money to waiters and bar staff is one thing, but do these subtle effects persuade people to part with much larger sums of cash? In the 1990s, researchers Charles Areni and David Kim from Texas Tech University investigated exactly this issue by systematically varying the music being played in a downtown wine shop.[25] Half the customers were subjected to classical tunes, including Mozart, Mendelssohn, and Chopin; the other half heard pop songs, including Fleetwood Mac, Robert Plant, and Rush. By disguising themselves as shop assistants making an inventory of stock, the experimenters were able to observe customers' behavior, including the number of bottles they picked up from the shelves, whether they read the labels, and, most important of all, the amount of wine they bought.

The results were impressive. The music did not affect how long people stayed in the cellar, how many bottles they examined, or even the number of items they bought. Instead, it had a dramatic effect on just one aspect of their behavior—the cost of the wine they bought. When the classical music was playing, people bought bottles of wine that were, on average, more than three times more expensive than those they bought when the pop music was playing. The researchers believe that hearing the classical music unconsciously made shoppers feel more sophisticated, and this in turn caused them to buy significantly more expensive wine.

There is even some evidence to suggest that the same sort of subtle stimuli influence matters of life and death. Jimmie Rogers (not Kenny), a professor of sociology, analyzed more than 1,400 country songs and discovered that the lyrics often refer to topics associated with negative life experiences, including unrequited love, alcohol abuse, financial problems, hopelessness, fatalism, bitterness, and poverty.[26] In the mid-1990s, Steven Stack from Wayne State University and Jim Gundlach from Auburn University wondered whether continual exposure to downbeat topics might make people more likely to commit suicide.[27] To find out, the researchers looked at the suicide rate and the amount of country music played on national radio in forty-nine areas across the United States. After controlling for several other factors, such as poverty, divorce, and gun ownership, the researchers did find that the more country music played on the radio, the higher the suicide rate.

The results may sound far-fetched, and they have been challenged by several other researchers.[28] However, the basic premise is supported by a wealth of other work suggesting that the mass media plays an important role in determining whether people decide to end their lives, of which the work exploring the "Werther Effect" is an excellent example.

In Goethe's novel *The Sorrows of Young Werther*, a young man named Werther falls in love with a woman who is already promised to another. Rather than face a life without her, Werther decides to end his life by shooting himself. The book was a remarkable success. In fact, in many ways it was a little too successful, inspiring a series of copycat suicides that eventually resulted in its being banned in several European countries.

In 1974, David Phillips, a sociologist from the University of California, San Diego, decided to examine whether media reports of suicides may create a modern-day Werther Effect.[29] In an initial study examining the suicide statistics in the United States between 1947 and 1968, he discovered that a front-page suicide story was associated, on average, with an excess of almost sixty suicides. Moreover, the types of suicides reflected the methods of death described in the media, and the level of publicity received by the suicides was directly related to the number of subsequent deaths. On average, the number of suicides increased by roughly 30 percent within two weeks of media reports, and the effect was especially pronounced after a celebrity death. Phillips calculated, for example, that the death of Marilyn Monroe in August 1962 increased the national suicide rate by about 12 percent. Since Phillips's groundbreaking work, more than forty scientific papers have been written on the topic, prompting several countries to produce media guidelines for reporting suicides, urging journalists not to sensationalize them or to describe the methods used.[30]

Another part of Phillips's work has investigated the relationship between televised boxing matches and murder rates. He carefully analyzed daily murder rates in the United States, and showed that they tended to increase in the week following the television broadcast of a high-profile heavyweight boxing match. There was a direct relationship not only between the amounts of publicity the fight received and the number of murders, but also between the racial backgrounds of the boxers and the murder victims. If a white boxer lost the fight, Phillips found an increase in the number of white, but not black, people murdered. Likewise, if a black boxer lost, there was an increase in the number of black, but not white, people killed.

All this adds up to one simple fact: The ways in which we think and feel are frequently influenced by factors outside our awareness. Our names influence our self-esteem and choice of career. Just reading a sentence influences how old we feel and our recall of general knowledge. A simple smile or a subtle touch influences how much we tip in restaurants and bars. The music played in shops creeps into our unconscious and influences the amount of money we spend. But do the same sorts of strange persuaders also influence the way in which we see others? Could they even dictate the politicians that we vote for, and the way in which we decide on the guilt or innocence of our fellow citizens?

Inching Forward in the Polls

Thousands of years ago there were evolutionary advantages to hanging around with taller people because their physical size afforded all sorts of benefits when it came to gathering food and defeating foes. Although height no longer offers a physical advantage, our primate brains hold on to their evolutionary past: We still associate tall people with success, a faulty but persuasive perception that plays out in interesting ways.

The psychologists Leslie Martel and Henry Biller asked university students to rate men of varying heights on many different psychological and physical attributes.[31] Reporting the results in their book *Stature and Stigma,* they describe how men and women rated men shorter than five feet five as less positive, secure, masculine, successful, and capable. Even our language reflects the value of height. Those held in high esteem are "big men" that we "look up" to. Run out of money, and you are "short" of cash.

Even in the world of romance and mating, size matters. Robin Dunbar, an evolutionary psychologist from Liverpool University, and his colleagues analyzed data from more than 4,000 healthy Polish men who had undergone compulsory medical examinations between 1983 and 1989.[32] They found that childless men were about three centimeters shorter than men who had fathered at least one child. The only exceptions to the pattern were men born in the 1930s. Dunbar believes that this was because they emerged into the marriage market just after World War II, a time when single men were relatively scarce and so women had few choices.

This association between mating success and height appears to be universal. In the 1960s, Thomas Gregor, an anthropologist from Vanderbilt University, lived among a tropical-forest people of central

Brazil known as the Mehinaku.[33] Even here, height matters. Among the Mehinaku, tall men are seen as attractive and are respectfully referred to as "wekepei." Those short in stature are referred to by the derisive term "peritsi," which rhymes with "itsi," the word for penis. Wekepei were far more likely than peritsi to be associated with wealth, power, participation in rituals, and reproductive opportunities. Gregor discovered that the taller the man, the more female mates he had access to, with the three tallest men having had as many affairs as the seven shortest men.

Does height also matter when it comes to careers? It seems so. In the 1940s, psychologists found that tall salesmen were more successful than their shorter colleagues, and a 1980 survey found that more than half the CEOs of America's Fortune 500 companies are at least six feet tall. More recent research from the *Journal of Applied Psychology* shows that when it comes to height in the workplace, every inch counts.[34] Timothy Judge, a business professor from the University of Florida in Gainesville, and his colleague Daniel Cable analyzed the data from four large studies that had followed people through their lives, carefully monitoring personality, height, intelligence, and income. Focusing on the relationship between height and earnings, Judge discovered that each inch above average corresponds to an additional $789 in pay each year. Someone who is six feet tall therefore earns an extra $4,734 more each year than an equally able five-feet-five colleague. Compounded over a thirty-year career, a tall person enjoys an earning advantage of hundreds of thousands of dollars over shorter colleagues.

Politics has also been scrutinized. Of the forty-three American presidents, only five have been below average height, and it has been more than a hundred years since voters elected someone who was shorter than average (President William McKinley, who was five feet seven, took office in 1896 and was referred to by the press as a "little boy"). Most presidents have been several inches above the norm. Ronald Reagan was six feet one, and George Bush Sr. and Bill Clinton both stand tall at six feet two. There is also some evidence to suggest that some candidates realize the influence of height on voters and take steps to make the most of an advantage. In the 1988 presidential debate, George Bush Senior greeted Michael Dukakis with an exaggeratedly long handshake—a move apparently orchestrated by Bush's campaign manager to have them stand together as long as possible and thus make the most of the fact that Bush was taller.

The psychological relationship between status and height works in both directions. Not only do we think that tall people are more competent, but we also believe that competent people are tall. This explains why we are so often surprised to discover that some Hollywood stars are below average height. Dustin Hoffman, for example, is just five feet five, and Madonna is five feet four. The Web site www.celebheights.com (by-line: "In the Land of Hollywood Pygmies, the Elevator-Shoed Dwarf Is King") is dedicated to discovering the true heights of celebrities, often sending people of a known height to have their photographs taken next to celebrities so that their heights can be accurately determined. The author Ralph Keyes speculated about the fact that so many actors are short in his book *The Height of Your Life.* Keyes thought that some smaller people have a need to show that they are strong and overcome their height disadvantage by developing assertive personalities.

This relationship leads to an interesting phenomenon—that the perceived height of a person can change with that person's apparent status. The first scientifically controlled experiment into this curious phenomenon was conducted by Paul Wilson, a psychologist from the University of Queensland.[35] Wilson introduced a fellow academic to different groups of students and asked them to assess his height. Unbeknownst to the students, Wilson changed the way in which he introduced the academic each time. On one occasion, he told the class that the man was a fellow student; the next time he said that he was a lecturer; then the man was introduced as a senior lecturer; and finally as a full professor. The students' perception of the man's height varied with his perceived status. When he was just a fellow student he was seen as being about seventy inches tall. However, simply saying that he was a lecturer added about one inch to his height. Promoting him to senior lecturer meant that he gained another inch in the eyes of the students, and his rapid promotion to professor added an extra inch, bringing him up to about seventy-three inches.

In 1960, Harold Kassarjian from the University of California asked 3,000 voters whether they would be supporting Kennedy or Nixon in the forthcoming election, and which they believed to be the taller of the two candidates.[36] In reality, Kennedy was an inch taller than Nixon. However, this was not how his voters saw it. Forty-two percent of Nixon supporters said that Nixon was the taller candidate, compared to just 23 percent of Kennedy supporters. Other research, conducted in the early 1990s by Philip Higham and William Carment from McMaster University in Canada, took matters a stage further.[37] Higham and Carment asked voters to estimate the heights of the leaders of the three main political parties (Brian Mulroney, John Turner, and Ed Broadbent) in Canada before, and after, a general election. Mulroney won the election, resulting in a half-inch gain in the height polls. After losing the election, Tuner and Broadbent were seen to have shrunk by about a half an inch and one and a half inches, respectively.

I wondered whether it might be possible to use this effect to measure the perceived status of politicians before an election. In 2001, I worked with Roger Highfield, the science editor at the *Daily Telegraph,* to carry out an unusual political opinion poll.[38] We asked a representative sample of 1,000 respondents to estimate the height of the leaders of the UK's two main political parties. According to their party headquarters, the Labour and Conservative leaders at that time, Tony Blair and William Hague, were both six feet tall. But this is not how the electorate saw things.

In line with Harold Kassarjian's findings from the 1960s, we found differences when people estimated the heights of the leader they supported and the leader they opposed. Significantly more Labour than Conservative voters thought that Blair was five feet nine or taller. Likewise, more Conservatives than Labour supporters thought that Hague was five feet nine or taller. In short, voters saw their own candidates as taller than the opposition. However, what did our stature poll predict about the results of the forthcoming election? Whereas only 35 percent of voters thought that Blair was less than the average male height of five feet nine inches, 64 percent of voters thought this of William Hague. So voters perceived Blair as relatively tall and Hague as a real shorty.

And the results of the 2001 election?

A massive landslide victory for Tony Blair's Labour Party.

If the Face Fits

We all used to be a lot hairier than we are now. As apes, we were covered in facial and body hair but, over the course of tens of thousands of years, we have shed our fur. There is considerable debate about why this happened. Some researchers believe that it was a result of our needing less hair to keep warm as we ventured away from the shady forests and out into the hot savannas. Others have suggested that a lack of body and facial hair was associated with a lower incidence of disease-carrying ticks and parasites. Either way, some men choose to turn back the hands of evolutionary time and sport various types of facial hair. In doing so, they are unconsciously altering the way in which they are perceived by the people around them.

In 1973, the psychologist Robert Pellegrini studied the effects of facial hair on perceived personality.[39] He managed to find eight full-bearded young men who were happy to have their facial hair removed in the name of science. Pellegrini took a photograph of each of the men before the experimental barber got at them. Next, each man was photographed when he had a goatee and a moustache, then just a moustache, and finally when he was clean-shaven. Groups of randomly selected people were asked to rate the personality of the people in the photographs. There was a positive relationship between the amount of beard and traits such as masculinity, maturity, dominance, self-confidence, and courage. "It may well be that inside every clean-shaven man there is a beard screaming to be let out," Pellegrini noted. "If so, the results of the present study provide a strong rationale for indulging that demand."

Pellegrini's work, although insightful, failed to ask about one important trait: honesty. Had he done so, his conclusions about beards may not have been so positive. Recent surveys show that more than 50 percent of the Western public believe clean-shaven men to be more honest than those with facial hair. Apparently, beards conjure up images of diabolical intent, concealment, and poor hygiene. Although there is no relationship between honesty and facial hair, the stereotype is powerful enough to affect the world—perhaps explaining why everyone on the Forbes 100 list of the world's richest men is clean-shaven, and why no successful candidate for the American presidency has sported a beard or a moustache since 1910.

The beard studies are just one tiny aspect of a large amount of research conducted by psychologists into the effects of facial appearance on perceived personality and abilities. According to research recently published by Alexander Todorov and his colleagues at Princeton University, facial appearance is vitally important in politics.[40] Todorov presented students with pairs of black-and-white photographs containing head shots of the winners and runners-up for the U.S. Senate in 2000, 2002, and 2004. For each pair of photographs, Todorov asked the students to choose which of the pair looked more competent. Even though the students saw the pairs of photographs for just one second, choosing which of the two looked more competent predicted the election results about 70 percent of the time. Not only that, but the degree of disagreement among the students also predicted the margin of victory. When the students all agreed on which of the two candidates appeared the most competent, that candidate emerged the clear winner at the polls. When there was less agreement among the students, the election results were not so clear-cut.

Todorov's work suggests that when it comes to winning seats in the Senate, it is important to have a face that fits. But does a person's facial features also influence the most important political process of them all—the race for the White House? To find out, I recently teamed up with an expert in facial perception—Rob

Jenkins, a psychologist from the University of Glasgow—and carried out an unusual experiment involving twelve of the most powerful men in history.

Most people are quick to associate certain personality traits with certain types of faces. They see a baby-faced individual with large eyes and a round head and instantly assume that the person is honest and kind. Or they meet someone with close-set eyes and a crooked nose and suddenly question whether that person is to be trusted. Like it or not, such stereotypes influence many aspects of our everyday lives, and so it wouldn't be especially surprising if presidents tend to have the types of faces that are perceived as especially trustworthy and competent.

However, Rob and I were curious about whether facial appearance affects voters in a far more subtle and interesting way. Not surprisingly, research suggests that Democrats and Republicans value different personality traits in their leaders, Democrats being attracted to those who are more liberally oriented and Republicans going for more authoritarian types. Assuming that people unconsciously associate such traits with different facial features, are Democrats and Republicans drawn to very different-looking leaders? Such an effect might influence the way in which party members choose candidates to run for the presidency, or how voters decide which one to put into the White House. Either way, if there is something to the idea, then Democratic and Republican presidents should have very different facial features because different selection pressures are in operation. Rob and I set out to discover whether this was the case.

The work involved a sophisticated computer program that accurately blends several different faces into a single average, or "composite," image. The principle behind the technique is simple. Imagine having photographic portraits of two people. Both have bushy eyebrows and deep-set eyes, but one has a small nose and the other a much larger nose. To create a composite of their two faces, researchers first scan both photographs into the computer, control for differences in lighting, and then manipulate the images to ensure that key facial attributes—such as the corners of the mouth and eyes—are in roughly the same position. Next, one image is laid on top of the other, and an average of the two faces calculated. If both faces have bushy eyebrows and deep-set eyes, the resulting composite would also have these features. If one face has a small nose and the other a large one, the final image would have a medium-sized nose. The process is totally automated and can be used to merge any number of faces.

Rob tracked down photographic portraits of the last six Democratic (Roosevelt, Truman, Kennedy, Johnson, Carter, and Clinton) and Republican (Eisenhower, Nixon, Ford, Reagan, Bush Sr., and Bush Jr.) U.S. presidents, ensuring that the portraits in each group showed the presidents with the same facial expression and looking in the same direction. He then digitally removed Harry Truman's glasses, fed all the images into a computer, and created a composite for each group of presidents. The results were astonishing. As predicted, the blend of the six Democratic presidents looked very different from the six Republican presidents: The Democratic composite looked remarkably Clinton-like and the Republican composite bore a striking similarity to George Bush Jr. (see fig. 5).

We wondered whether these results came about because the composites contained images of Bill Clinton and George Bush Jr., and so we excluded both of these faces, and re-ran the analysis.

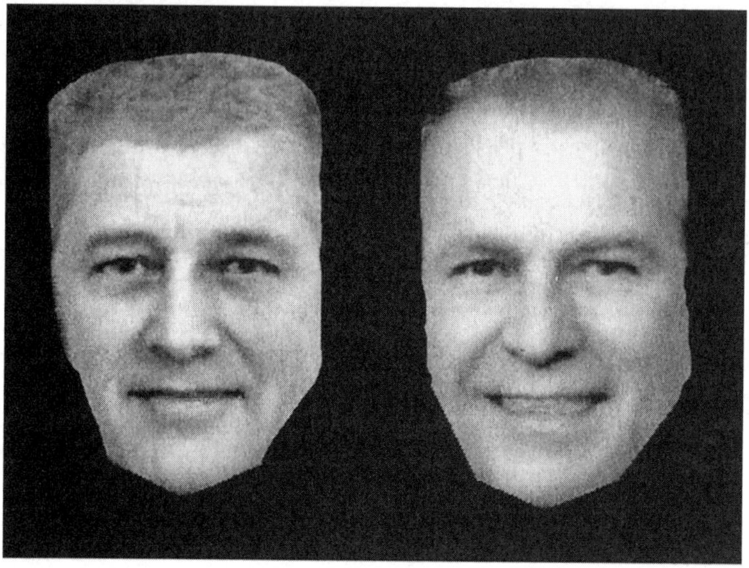

Fig. 5 Composites of the last six Democratic (left) and Republican (right) presidents.

Even without Clinton and Bush, the results were almost exactly the same. The Democratic composite still looked far more Clinton than Bush, and the Republican composite was clearly more Bush than Clinton (see fig. 6). In short, evidence that Democratic and Republican voters are drawn to leaders that conform to very different facial "types."

Were these differences really driven by Democrats' attraction to faces that appear more liberally orientated and Republicans' preferences for more authoritarian types? To find out, we asked a group of people to rate the faces shown in figure 6. For each face, they were presented with various adjectives, such as "caring," and "authoritarian," and asked to indicate whether they believed that the person shown in the photograph possessed that trait. They had no

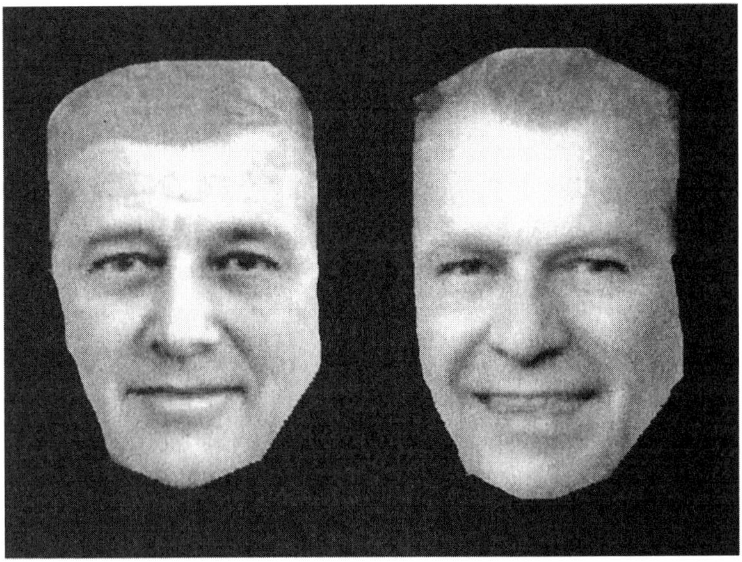

Fig. 6 Composites of the last six Democratic (left) and Republican (right) presidents, excluding Bill Clinton and George Bush Jr.

idea that the faces were based on presidents, or that the experiment was even related to the psychology of voting. Even so, large differences emerged. The Republican composite was rated as significantly more authoritarian than the Democratic composite, and the Democratic composite was seen as far more caring and open-minded than the Republican one.

Even when it comes to one of the most important and powerful political positions in the world, voters do indeed appear to ask themselves a key question: Does the face fit?

If facial stereotypes can influence winning or losing at the ballot box, are there other situations where looks matter? Could these same types of stereotypes even influence whether people determine the guilt of defendants in a courtroom?

And So I Ask the Jury . . . Is That the Face of a Mass Murderer?

In chapter 2, I described how my first mass-media psychology experiment with the help of Sir Robin Day had explored the psychology of lying. Three years later, I went back to the same studio to conduct a second study. This time the experiment was bigger and far more complicated than before. This time we wanted to discover whether justice really is blind.

The idea for the study had occurred to me when I had come across a Gary Larson *Far Side* cartoon. The cartoon was set in a courtroom, and the lawyer was talking to the jury. Pointing at his client, the lawyer said, "And so I ask the jury . . . is that the face of a mass murderer?" Sitting in the dock is a man wearing a suit and tie, but instead of a normal head, he has the classic "smiley" face consisting of just two black dots for eyes and a large semicircle grin. Like all good comedy, Larson's cartoon made me laugh, but then it made me think.

The decisions made by juries have serious implications, and so it is important that they are as rational as possible. I thought it would be interesting to put this alleged rationality to the test. During a live edition of the BBC's leading science program, *Tomorrow's World,* the members of the public were asked to play the roles of jury members. They were shown a film of a mock trial, had to decide whether the defendant was guilty or innocent, and then record their decisions by telephoning one of two numbers.

Unbeknownst to them, we would cut the country into two huge groups. We discovered that the BBC broadcasts to the nation via thirteen separate transmitters. Usually they all carry an identical signal, so the whole of the country watches the same program.

However, for this experiment, we obtained special permission to send out different signals from the transmitters, allowing me to split Britain in two and to broadcast different programs to each half of the country.

Everyone saw exactly the same evidence about a crime in which the defendant had allegedly broken into a house and stolen a computer. However, half the public saw a defendant whose face showed characteristics of the stereotype of a criminal—he had a broken nose and close-set eyes. The other half saw a defendant whose face matched a stereotypical innocent person—he was baby-faced and had clear blue eyes. To ensure that the experiment was as well controlled as possible, both defendants were dressed in identical suits, stood in exactly the same position in the dock, and had the same neutral expression on their faces.

We carefully scripted a judge's summing-up, describing how the defendant had been accused of a burglary. The evidence presented did not allow for a clear guilty or not guilty decision. For example, the defendant's wife said that he was in a bar at the time of the crime, but another witness saw him leave about thirty minutes before the burglary. A footprint at the scene of the crime matched the defendant's shoes, but these were a fairly common brand of shoe owned by many people.

After transmission, we stood anxiously by the telephones and waited to see how many calls we would receive. The experiment had obviously struck a chord with the public. For the lying experiment we had received about 30,000 calls. This time, more than twice as many people telephoned. A fair and rational public would have focused solely on the evidence when deciding guilt or innocence. However, the unconscious tendency to succumb to the lure of looks proved too much. About 40 percent returned a guilty verdict on the man who just happened to fit the stereotype of a criminal. Only 29 percent found the blue-eyed, baby-faced man guilty. People had ignored the complexity of the evidence and made up their minds on the basis of the defendants' looks.

It would be nice to think that this result is confined to the relatively artificial setting of a television studio. That is not, however, the case. John Stewart, a psychologist from Mercyhurst College in Arizona, spent hours sitting in courts rating the attractiveness of real defendants.[41] He discovered that good-looking men were given significantly lighter sentences than their equally guilty, but less attractive, counterparts.

In his book *Influence,* the psychologist Robert Cialdini, from Arizona State University,[42] makes a fascinating link between this work and a highly unusual experiment exploring the use of plastic surgery in prisons. In the late 1960s, a group of prisoners in a New York City jail were given plastic surgery to correct various facial disfigurements. Researchers discovered that these prisoners were significantly less likely to return to prison than a control group of prisoners with uncorrected facial disfigurements. The degree of rehabilitation, such as education and training, did not seem to matter. Instead, looks appeared to be everything. This result caused some social policymakers to argue that societal stereotyping was causing some people to turn to a life of crime, and that changing the way they looked had provided an effective way of preventing them from offending again. This may have been the case. However, Cialdini used the data obtained by John Stewart to argue for another interpretation of the results. It was possible that the corrective surgery had little effect on whether they re-offended, but simply meant that they were less likely to be sent to prison.

THE HIDDEN INFLUENCE OF HOLLYWOOD

Research shows that we link looks with likeability. Whenever we see an attractive face, we unconsciously associate it with traits such as "kindness," "honesty," and "intelligence." Good-looking people are more likely to be offered jobs than their ugly competitors, and to be given higher salaries than their equally competent colleagues.

But where do these sorts of irrational effects come from and why do they persist? Some researchers place the blame firmly at the door of Hollywood. Stephen Smith, from North Georgia College, and his colleagues decided to discover whether this was true. In the first of two highly revealing experiments, the researchers collected twenty of the top-grossing films for each decade between 1940 and 1989.[43] They then asked a group of people to watch the films, rating all the characters identified by name on various scales, including how attractive they were, how moral, how intelligent, how friendly, and whether they lived happily ever afterward. After sitting through everything from *It's a Wonderful Life* to *Around the World in 80 Days* (the 1956 version), and *Last Tango in Paris* to *Beetlejuice,* the raters evaluated 833 characters. The researchers discovered that physically attractive characters were depicted as more romantically active, morally good, intelligent, and far more likely than others to live happily every after.

Although interesting, this doesn't prove that such depictions cause stereotypical thinking. To investigate this, the experimenters conducted a second study. They chose a few films that either did or didn't portray attractive people in a stereotypical way. For example, *Pride of the Yankees* relates the true-life story of the famous baseball player Lou Gehrig. A good-looking Gary Cooper played Gehrig, showing his success on the field, and how in the prime of his life Gehrig begins having serious health problems but deals with the illness with incredible dignity. At the opposite end of the spectrum came films such as *Up the Down Staircase,* in which a young and spirited teacher tries to make a difference in a troubled inner-city school. Sandy Dennis, who played the lead in the film, was a highly acclaimed actress. However, unlike other stars, such as Gary Cooper, she did not look like a classic Hollywood idol and tended to stammer her way through lines.

Groups of people were asked to watch one of the films and rate certain aspects of it. Then they were asked to help out with a second study. They were told that a nearby university wanted people to rate the qualifications of various graduate students. Each member of the group was presented with a folder containing a resume and a photograph of a student. In reality, all the resumes were identical, but were accompanied by one of two pictures—one showing an attractive person and the other showing an unattractive one. Those who had just seen *Pride of the Yankees,* or a film like it, assigned especially high ratings to the attractive candidate, and especially low ratings to the unattractive candidate. The effect disappeared when the researchers examined the corresponding data from participants who had seen *Up the Down Staircase* or similar films. Just on the showing of one film, people's perception had changed significantly. Although they weren't aware of it, the stereotypes depicted in the film had seeped into their brains and affected the way they saw others. The experiment involved just one film. It is not difficult to imagine the effects of a lifetime of watching thousands of similarly biased television shows, advertisements, and movies.

IF YOU WERE A PIZZA TOPPING, WHAT WOULD YOU BE?

Knowing how your thoughts, feelings, and behavior are influenced by subtle factors allows you to use information to your own advantage. For example, right now, millions of single people all over the world are desperate to find the perfect partner (or, for many, any partner at all). The good news is that help is at hand. For several years, researchers have been exploring how an understanding of the psychology of attraction can help budding Casanovas impress others. Like so much of the strange science described here, the work has not been carried out in laboratories but in the real world: during speed-dating events, in personal ads, and, as with our starting point, high above a river in British Columbia.

In 1974, two psychology professors, Donald Dutton and Arthur Aron, conducted an unusual study on two bridges above the Capilano River in British Columbia.[44] One was a swaying footbridge suspended about two hundred feet above the rocks; the other was much lower, and more solidly built. Young men walking across each of the bridges were stopped by a female experimenter posing as a market researcher. The woman asked the men to complete a simple questionnaire, and then offered them her telephone number in case they would like to find out more about her work. As predicted by the experimenters, the offer of the telephone number was not only accepted by significantly more men on the high bridge, but a greater proportion of men on the high bridge subsequently telephoned the female experimenter. Why should someone's position above the Capilano River have anything to do with that person's accepting the telephone number of a woman and then calling her for a chat?

Prior to the bridge study, researchers had confirmed what poets had suspected for hundreds of years. When a person finds someone attractive, the heart beats faster as the body prepares itself for potential action. Dutton and Aron wondered whether the opposite was true—that people whose hearts were already beating faster would be more likely to find someone attractive. Hence the experiment on the two bridges. The precarious nature of the high, swaying bridge meant that people using this way of crossing the river had higher heart rates than those on the lower bridge. When the men on the high bridge were approached by the female market researcher, they unconsciously attributed their increased heart rates to her rather than to the bridge. As a result, their bodies fooled their brains into thinking that they found her attractive, and so were more likely to accept her telephone number and subsequently give her a call. In addition to showing how the body can deceive the brain, the results have an important implication for our lives. This is why, when you want someone to fall in love with you, some scholars believe that you and your date should stay away from calming New Age music, country walks, and wind chimes. Instead, your chances of success are increased by attending a rock concert, riding on a roller coaster, or watching a frightening film.

The work conducted by Dutton and Aron is just one of several unusual experiments exploring the psychology of love and attraction. Other work has tackled the rather thorny issue of pick-up lines.

If you really want to impress a potential date, what is the best opening gambit? Searching the Internet certainly won't help, with the most frequently cited lines likely to depress rather than impress ("Is it hot in here or is it just you?" "If I could rearrange the alphabet, I'd put U and I together," and "I lost my phone number. Can I have yours?"). To help discover the pick-up lines most likely to attract a potential partner, researchers from the University of Edinburgh had people rate various types of classic openings.[45]

The results showed that straight appeals for sex ("Well, hey there, I may not be Fred Flintstone, but I bet I can make your Bed Rock!") and compliments ("So there you are! I've been looking all over for *you,* the girl of my dreams") did not play big. In fact, they were so unsuccessful that the researchers wondered why they should have evolved at all. After much head scratching, they concluded that these lines might be "used by men to identify sociosexually unrestricted women" (think "tart"). Instead, lines suggesting a potential for spontaneous wit, a pleasant personality, wealth, and an appreciation of culture were much more effective. The study was all well and good, but, as the authors themselves admit, it is one thing to check the "yes, that is a good pick-up line" box on an anonymous questionnaire and quite another to make the decision in real life.

I recently teamed up with the Edinburgh International Science Festival with my academic colleagues James Houran and Caroline Watt to examine the best pick-up lines and conversational topics when searching for the love of your life. The project revolved around a large-scale, experimental, speed-dating event.

A few months before the event, we issued a media appeal for single people who wished to participate in a study exploring the science of seduction. We had about five hundred replies, and invited a hundred randomly selected participants (fifty men and fifty women) to our love laboratory.

The event took place in a large beautiful ballroom at one of Edinburgh's oldest and most palatial hotels. At the beginning of the evening, our one hundred participants arrived and were randomly seated at one of five long tables. At each table, men were seated on one side, women on the other. The people at four of the tables were asked to talk about a specified topic throughout all their speed dates. We chose four of the most frequently used topics: hobbies, film, travel, and books. Our fifth table acted as a "control," and we allowed the people there to chat about whatever they liked. As we started to play the romantic strains of Carole King, each person was asked to chat to the person opposite them. Three minutes later, participants were asked to rate their potential beaus. Did they find them physically attractive? What was the level of "chemistry" between them? How quickly had they made up their minds? And, perhaps most important, would they like to meet each other again? A few moments later, everyone was paired up with a different person, and the entire procedure repeated again. Two hours and ten speed dates later, the experiment was over. It proved to be a huge success, and lots of people were hanging around in the bar afterward. Some shared their telephone numbers with one another.

The following day, we entered more than 1,500 pages of data into a giant spreadsheet. Whenever two people had indicated that they would be happy to meet up again, we sent them each others' telephone numbers. Around 60 percent of those attending walked away with the contact details of at least one other person. Some people did really well, with about 20 percent getting the details of four others. Women proved to be about twice as picky as men, but the top-rated man and woman of the evening had a 100 percent success rate: All their dates wanted to meet them again.

The conversation topics had produced different success rates. When talking about movies, less than 9 percent of the pairs wanted to meet up again, compared to 18 percent when participants spoke about the top topic—travel. A clue to why would-be lovers might want to avoid chatting about movies comes from additional data from the study. At the beginning of the evening, we asked everyone to indicate their favorite types of films. The results revealed that men and women have very different tastes. For instance, 49 percent of men liked action films compared to just 18 percent of women, and 29 percent of women liked musicals, compared to only 4 percent of men. Whenever I walked past the table where participants were talking about films, all I heard was arguing. In contrast, the conversations about travel tended to revolve around great holidays and dream destinations, and that makes people feel good and so appear more attractive to one another.

The data also revealed other surprises. Although men are traditionally seen as shallow people who judge women very quickly, our findings suggested that women were making up their minds much sooner than men, with 45 percent of women's decisions being made in less than thirty seconds, compared to just 22 percent of men's decisions. Since a man has only a few seconds to impress a woman, his opening comments are important.

To uncover the best type of pick-up lines, we compared the conversations of participants rated as very desirable by their dates with those seen as especially undesirable. Failed Casanovas either tended to employ old chestnuts ("Do you come here often?") or else struggled to impress with comments such as "I have a PhD in computing" and "My friend is a helicopter pilot." Those more skilled in seduction encouraged their dates to talk about themselves in an unusual, fun, quirky way. The most memorable lines from the top-rated man and woman in the study illustrate the point. The top-rated male's best line was: "If you were on *Stars in Their Eyes*, who would you be?"; the top-rated female asked: "If you were a pizza topping, what would you be?"

Why should these latter types of lines be so successful? The answer was revealed by an unusual experiment involving drinking straws and funny voices.

In 2004, Arthur Aron (of the 1974 bridge study) and Barbara Fraley, a psychologist from the State University of New York at Stony Brook, randomly paired strangers and had them carry out one of two sets of slightly strange behaviors.[46] In one condition, one stranger was blindfolded and the other was asked to hold a drinking straw between his or her teeth (which made that person's voice sound funny). The two then carried out a series of tasks designed to make them laugh. The blindfolded person had to learn a series of dance steps by listening to instructions read by the straw-holding colleague. In another example of laboratory-based hilarity, they were asked to act their favorite television commercial using a made-up language.

The other, more straight-faced condition did not involve drinking straws. Here, the dance steps were learned without the blindfold and the silly voice, and the commercials were acted in English. Participants were then asked to complete a questionnaire about how much fun they had had. The results confirmed that the blindfold, drinking straw, and silly language had resulted in significantly more hilarity. Then came the crunch question: All the participants were asked to draw two overlapping circles to indicate the degree of closeness they had felt with their partners. The results revealed that those who had participated in the shared humor experience felt significantly closer to their partners, and also found them more attractive.

The successful pick-up lines in our study were the speed-dating equivalent of putting a straw in your mouth to make your voice sound silly: They elicited a shared funny experience that promoted a sense of closeness and attraction.

"Minimalist Seeks Woman": The Psychology of Personal Ads

Imagine that you are going to write a personal ad. What choice of words do you think would prove most successful and attract the largest number of replies? This was exactly the question tackled in another aspect of our journey into the science of seduction.

We asked everyone involved in the speed-dating experiment to write a short personal ad containing about twenty words. We then showed these to more than a hundred men and women and asked them to indicate which ads they would be most likely to answer. The results provided important clues into a hitherto unexplored aspect of ads.

Previous work into personals had examined the type of person most frequently sought by men and women.[47] The results haven't yielded many big surprises. Men tend to look for women who are physically attractive, understanding, and athletic. In contrast, women are searching for someone who is understanding, humorous, and emotionally healthy. I decided to take a different tack.

I looked through the ads we had received and noticed something odd. There was a large variation in the number of words that people used to describe themselves compared to the number of words used to describe the person they were looking for. Which type of ad would attract the greater number of replies—the one that describes you in greater detail or the one that describes the person you are looking for?

To find out, I counted the number of words the advertisers used for themselves and for those they sought. I then used these two numbers to derive a "self versus other" percentage. At one extreme were the "it's all about you" people, who obtained a near 0 percent score by saying very little about themselves and instead focused almost entirely on their wish lists:

> Brunette, 27, looking for someone kind, romantic, spontaneous, caring, and who is willing to take a risk. We can always tell them we met in the supermarket!

In the middle of the range were the "it's about the two of us" people who split the wording more evenly, describing themselves and their potential partners, and who obtained a 50 percent score:

> Laid-back guy, good sense of humor, into sport, travel, lethal coffee, eating out, seeks creative, funny, sunny, happy, charismatic girl to while away long summer nights.

Then, at the other end of the spectrum were the "it's all about me" people who obtained a 100 percent score by focusing almost entirely on themselves:

> Bright, fun, gym-loving, nonsmoker, singer-songwriter, into detective novels, funny films, American comedy shows, and long walks on sunny beaches.

I then looked at the relationship between the score assigned to each ad and the number of people indicating that they would reply to that ad. The results were revealing. Only a small number of people indicated that they would reply to "it's all about you" ads. The "it's all about me" ads fared a little better, but still didn't attract many replies. A balance between the two extremes turned out to be the winning formula. The results showed that a 70 percent "this is me" versus 30 percent "this is what I am looking for" balance attracted the greatest number of replies. It seems that if you devote more than 70 percent of the ad to describing yourself, you look self-centered. Less than 70 percent and you look suspicious.

Our two top ads fitted the pattern, and contained the rough 70:30 split. Around 45 percent of men said that they would reply to the winning female ad:

> Genuine, attractive, outgoing, professional female, good sense of humor. Enjoys keeping fit, socializing, music, and travel. Would like to meet like-minded, good-natured guy to share quality times.

Similarly, almost 60 percent of women indicated that they would be attracted to the top male ad:

> Male, good sense of humor, adventurous, athletic, enjoys cooking, comedy, culture, film, seeks sporty, fun female for chats and possible romantic relationship.

Our study also provided another top tip for those wishing to write winning ads. We asked our group of one hundred people to indicate which ads they thought members of the opposite sex would be likely to answer. The results showed a remarkable difference between the sexes.

First, let's have a look at the ads written by men. We compared the percentage of women who said that they would reply to each ad with the percentage of men who *thought* that women would reply. So, one of the ads read:

> Tall, slim, athletic, fashionable male with a good sense of humor looking for slim to average girl with good sense of humor interested in cars, music, clothes, and cuddles.

About 11 percent of women said that they would reply to the ad. Interestingly, men said that they thought 15 percent of women would reply—a remarkably accurate prediction. Another ad noted:

> Tall, energetic male with his head in the clouds and feet on the ground. Would like to meet a woman who is fun, positive, and isn't afraid of a challenge.

This time, 39 percent of women checked the "yes" box. Again, men's predictions were remarkably accurate, predicting that 32 percent of women would answer this ad. And so it went on. For ad after ad, men were able to predict accurately which ads women would find attractive and which they would avoid. Overall, men's predictions were, on average, 90 percent correct.

A very different story emerged when women predicted men's behavior. Look at the following ad, written by a female:

> Cute and quirky professional with a passion for good food, wine, and company looking for the proverbial tall, dark, and handsome with cracking wit and fit body.

Only 5 percent of the men said that they would reply to the ad. Women were convinced that this would act as a man-magnet, predicting that about 44 percent of them would reply. How about:

> Relaxed, upbeat, friendly woman who enjoys relaxing, laughing, exploring the world, and wants to dance the night away!

Once again, women thought that this would attract the majority of men, but they were wrong. Only about 22 percent of men indicated that they would respond.

The pattern repeated itself across the ads. Women simply had very little idea about what actually attracted men. So why are women so inaccurate? Perhaps the unsolicited "questionnaire graffiti" that women thought men were interested only in the physical attributes of women is a clue. Time and again, we came across comments such as "They are just interested in one thing," and "They are only interested by two things." Our research suggests that perhaps men are not quite so shallow. Regardless, the implication for women using personals is simple: If you want to attract lots of beaus, get a guy to write your ad.

LOVE AT FIRST SIGHT?

Take a quick look at the two images shown in figure 7. Do you prefer the image on the left or the one on the right? Your decision may feel like little more than guesswork, but in reality there is a considerable amount of psychology at work, and I recently used this task to understand more about that most curious of human experiences: love at first sight.

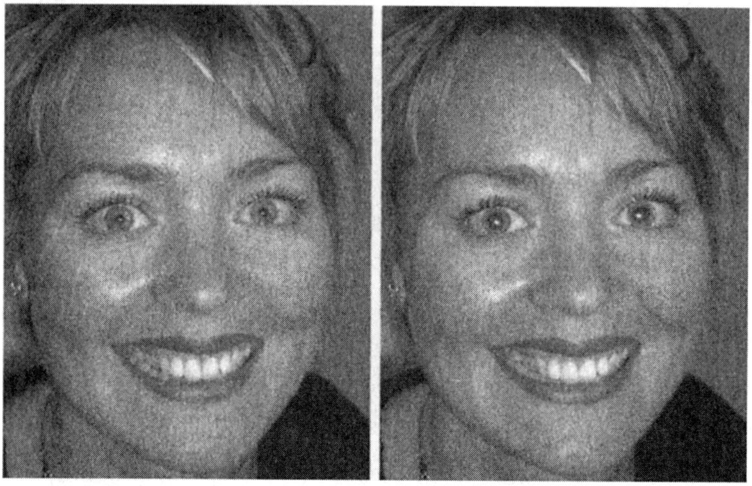

Fig. 7 Which image do you find more attractive?

The study was initiated by an e-mail from a middle-aged woman called Jenny. Jenny had been one of the participants in the speed-dating study, and she was writing to let me know that she had since met the man of her dreams under somewhat unusual circumstances. Her e-mail described how, a few months before, she had arrived at a friend's party and immediately noticed a man standing on the other side of the room. Their eyes met for a split second and Jenny had the sudden, and surreal, experience of instantly "knowing" that this was the man she was going to marry. The man smiled, walked over, and the two of them started to chat. A few hours later, he admitted to having felt the same instant attraction toward Jenny, and the two of them arranged to meet again. Jenny ended her e-mail by explaining that they had been together for six months now, and were planning to marry.

Jenny's e-mail made me curious about the idea of love at first sight. A search through psychology journals and books revealed that there had been no academic work into the topic, and so the area seemed ripe for some quirky research. A month later, I launched a two-part online experiment to take an initial look at the phenomenon.

The first part of the study tackled several questions. What percentage of people have experienced love at first sight? Do more women than men report the phenomenon? Did the experience lead to a romantic relationship and, if so, how long had those relationships lasted? More than six hundred members of the public agreed to take part, and the results were fascinating.

Almost 70 percent of respondents said that they had indeed experienced love at first sight, with roughly equal numbers of men and women reporting the sensation. These are not once-in-a-lifetime experiences. Forty percent of respondents said that they had experienced the phenomenon more than once, one in ten people having experienced it several times. The results also suggested that there is far more to these experiences than just wishful thinking. In 40 percent of instances, people reported that the objects of their desire had experienced exactly the same feelings, 60 percent of the experiences had led to romantic relationships, and one in four of these relationships had lasted longer than ten years.

The second part of the study presented participants with the task described at the beginning of this section. Take another look at the two images shown in figure 7. There is only one very small difference between the images—the pupils in the image on the right have been digitally enhanced and so are larger than the pupils in the image on the left. People's pupils tend to become larger when they see something, or somebody, that appeals to them. Moreover, because we tend to like people who like us, people with enlarged pupils are often seen as especially attractive. The signal is subtle, but the effect is powerful. It has also been known about for a long while. During the seventeenth century, Venetian women would place an extract of the plant belladonna, which contains a toxin that dilates the pupil, into their eyes to appear more attractive. This unusual practice explains the origin of the plant's name: *bella donna* means "beautiful lady" in Italian. The toxin would also have had the side effect of making the Venetian women's vision somewhat blurry, perhaps also giving rise to the expression "Love is blind."

What has all of this to do with love at first sight? My theory was that people who experienced this phenomenon may, without realizing it, be especially sensitive to nonverbal signals of attraction. If this was correct, then in the experiment such people would be especially likely to be drawn to the images containing enlarged pupils. During the experiment, people were shown several pairs of photographs and were asked to indicate which image in each pair they found most attractive. The data was fascinating. First, women were far more sensitive to pupil size than men. Time and again they would choose the image with the larger pupils, but the men tended to check the "uncertain" box. Second, when I focused on those people who had experienced love at first sight, this effect was much more striking. Women who had experienced love at first sight were super-sensitive to signals of attraction, whereas men who had experienced this strange phenomenon were relatively insensitive to the same cues. This provides tentative evidence that the love-at-first-sight experience, at least in women, may be driven by an enhanced ability to detect subtle signals of attraction.

The study revealed that love at first sight is surprisingly frequent, often leads to long-lasting relationships, and might be driven (at least in women) by a sensitivity to certain types of subtle nonverbal cues. In short, that there is far more to this curious phenomenon than first meets the eye.

5 THE SCIENTIFIC SEARCH FOR THE WORLD'S FUNNIEST JOKE

Explorations into the Psychology of Humor

In the 1970s, the cult comedy show *Monty Python's Flying Circus* created a sketch based entirely around the idea of finding the world's funniest joke. In the 1940s, a man named Ernest Scribbler thinks of the joke, writes it down, and promptly dies laughing. The joke turns out to be so funny that it kills anyone who reads it. Eventually, the British military realize that it could be used as a lethal weapon, and so they arrange to have a team of people translate the joke into German. Each person translates just one word at a time in order not to be affected by the joke. The joke is then read out to German forces, and it is so funny that they are unable to fight because they are laughing so much. The sketch ends with footage from a special session of the Geneva Convention in which delegates vote to ban the use of joke warfare.

In a strange example of life imitating art, in 2001 I headed a team carrying out a year-long, scientific search for the world's funniest joke. Instead of exploring the potential military applications of jokes, we wanted to take a scientific look at laughter.

In addition to finding the joke that had maximum mass appeal, my Pythonesque project resulted in a string of surreal experiences involving the internationally syndicated humorist Dave Barry, a giant chicken suit, the Hollywood actor Robin Williams, and more than five hundred jokes ending with the punch line "There's a weasel chomping on my privates."

More important, the project also provided considerable insights into many of the questions facing modern-day humor researchers. Do men and women laugh at different types of jokes? Do people from different countries find the same things funny? Does our sense of humor change over time? And if you are going to tell a joke involving an animal, are you better off making the main protagonist a duck, a horse, a cow, or a weasel?

Why Did the Chicken Cross the Road?

In June 2001, I was contacted by the same august scientific body that had commissioned my study into financial astrology, the British Association for the Advancement of Science (BAAS). The BAAS were eager to create a project that would act as a centerpiece for a year-long national celebration of science, and they wanted a large-scale experiment that would attract public attention. Would I be interested in creating it and, if so, what would I choose to investigate?

After a few "close, but no cigar" moments, I happened to see a rerun of the *Monty Python* sketch involving Ernest Scribbler, and I started to think about the possibility of *really* searching for the world's funniest joke. I knew that there would be a firm scientific underpinning for the project because some of the world's greatest thinkers, including Sigmund Freud, Plato, and Aristotle, had written extensively about humor. In fact, the Austrian philosopher Ludwig Wittgenstein was so taken with the topic that he once stated that a serious work in philosophy could be written entirely of jokes. I then discovered that whenever I mentioned my idea to people, it provoked a serious discussion. Some queried whether there really was such a thing as the world's funniest joke. Others thought that it was impossible to analyze humor scientifically. Almost everyone was kind enough to share a favorite joke with me. The rare mix of good science and popular appeal meant that the idea felt right.

I presented the BAAS with my plans for an international, Internet-based project called LaughLab. I would set up a Web site that had two sections. In one part, people could input their favorite jokes and submit them to an archive. In the second section, participants could answer a few simple questions about themselves (such as sex, age, and nationality), and then rate how funny they found various jokes randomly selected from the archive. During the year, we would slowly build a huge collection of jokes and ratings from around the globe; from this we would be able to discover scientifically what makes different groups of people laugh and which joke made the whole world smile. Everyone at the BAAS nodded, and LaughLab got the green light.

The success of the project hinged on being able to persuade thousands of people worldwide to come online and participate. To help spread the word, the BAAS and I launched LaughLab by staging an eye-catching photograph based around perhaps the most famous (and, as we would go on to prove scientifically, least funny) joke in the world: "Why did the chicken cross the road? To get to the other side." Toward the end of 2001, I found myself standing in the middle of a road dressed in a white laboratory coat and holding a clipboard (see fig. 8). Next to me was a student dressed in a giant chicken suit. Several national newspaper photographers were lined up in front of us, snapping away, and I can still vividly remember one of them looking up and shouting: "Can the guy playing the scientist move to the left?" I shouted back "I *am* a scientist," and then looked sheepishly at the giant chicken standing next to me. It was the type of surreal experience that was to occur all too frequently throughout the next twelve months.

The launch was successful, and LaughLab made its way into newspapers and magazines all over the world. Within a few hours of opening the Web site for business, we received more than five hundred jokes and 10,000 ratings. Then we hit a major problem: Many of the jokes were a tad crude. Actually, I am understating the issue. They were absolutely filthy. One especially memorable submission involved two nuns, a large bunch of bananas, an elephant, and Yoko Ono. We couldn't allow these submissions into the archive because we had no control over who would visit the site to rate the jokes. With a backlog of more than three hundred jokes from the first day alone, we needed someone to work full time to vet them. My research assistant, Emma Greening, came to the rescue. Every day for the next few months, Emma carefully looked at every joke and excluded those that were not suitable for family viewing. She was often frustrated by seeing the same jokes again and again (the joke "What is brown and sticky?" "A stick" was submitted more than three hundred times); but on the upside,

Fig. 8 A giant chicken crosses the road to help promote LaughLab.

Emma now owns one of the largest collections of dirty jokes in the world.

Participants were asked to rate each joke on a 5-point scale ranging from "not very funny" to "very funny." To simplify our analyses, we combined the 4 and 5 ratings to make a general "yes, that is quite a funny joke" category. We could then order the jokes on the basis of the percentage of responses that fell into this category. If the joke really wasn't very good, then it might have only 1 or 2 percent of people assigning it a rating of 4 or 5. In contrast, the real rib-ticklers would have a much higher percentage of top ratings. At the end of the first week, we reviewed some of the leading submissions. Most of the material was pretty poor and so tended to obtain low percentages. Even the top jokes fell well short of the 50 percent mark. Around 25 to 35 percent of participants found the following jokes funny, and so they came toward the top of the list:

A teacher decided to take her bad mood out on her class of children and so said, "Can everyone who thinks they're stupid, stand up!" After a few seconds, just one child slowly stood up. The teacher turned to the child and said, "Do you think you're stupid?"

"No," replied the child, "but I hate to see you standing there all by yourself."

Did you hear about the man who was proud when he completed a jigsaw within thirty minutes, because it said "5–6 years" on the box?

Texan: "Where are you from?"

Harvard graduate: "I come from a place where we do not end our sentences with prepositions."

Texan: "Okay—where are you from, Jackass?"

An idiot was walking alongside a river when she spied another idiot on the other side of the river. The first idiot yelled to the second idiot: "How do I get to the other side?" The second idiot responded immediately: "You're already *on* the other side!"

The top jokes have one thing in common—they create a sense of superiority in the reader. The feeling arises because the person in the joke appears stupid (the man with the jigsaw), misunderstands an obvious situation (the idiots on the riverbank), pricks the pomposity of another (the Texan answering the Harvard graduate), or makes someone in a position of power look foolish (the teacher and the child).

These findings provided some empirical support for the adage about the difference between comedy and tragedy: "If *you* fall down an open manhole, that's comedy. But if *I* fall down the same hole . . . "

The observation that people laugh when they feel superior to others dates back to around 400 BC, and was described by Plato in his famous text *The Republic.* Proponents of this "superiority" theory believe that the origin of laughter lies in the baring of teeth, akin to "the roar of triumph in an ancient jungle duel." Because of these animalistic and primitive associations, Plato was not a fan of laughter. He thought that it was wrong to laugh at the misfortune of others and that hearty laughter involved a loss of control that made people appear to be less than fully human. In fact, the father of modern-day philosophy was so concerned about the potential moral damage that could be created by laughter that he advised citizens to limit their attendance at comedies and never to appear in this lowest form of the dramatic arts.

Plato's view was echoed by the later writings of his fellow Greek thinker, Aristotle. Unfortunately, we have only indirect references to Aristotle's thoughts on the subject because the original treatise is lost (and is the manuscript that lies at the heart of Umberto Eco's mystery *The Name of the Rose*). Aristotle apparently argued that many successful clowns and comedians make us laugh by eliciting a sense of superiority. It is easy to find support for the theory. In the Middle Ages, dwarves and hunchbacks caused much merriment. In Victorian times, people laughed at the mentally ill in psychiatric institutions and at those with physical abnormalities in freak shows. There is also the 1976 study showing that when the public were asked to list adjectives describing comedians, they tended to produce the words "fat," "deformed," and "stupid."[1]

The superiority theory is also used to poke fun at entire groups of people. The English traditionally tell jokes about the Irish, the Americans like to laugh at the Polish, the Canadians pick on the Newfies, the French on the Belgians, and the Germans on the Ostfriedlanders.[2] All are about one group of people trying to make themselves feel good at the expense of another.

In 1934, Harold Wolff and his colleagues from Harvard University published the first experimental study of the superiority theory.[3] The researchers asked groups of Jews and Gentiles to rate how funny they found various jokes. To ensure that the presentation of jokes was as controlled as possible, the researchers printed them on strips of cloth 140 feet long and four inches wide; they passed the strips behind an aperture in the laboratory wall at a constant speed, ensuring that participants saw each joke one word at a time. When participants saw the symbol of a star that had been printed at the end of each strip, they were asked to shout out how funny they had found the joke on a scale between minus 2 (very annoying) and plus 4 (very humorous).

As predicted by Aristotle and Plato, the Gentiles tended to laugh more at jokes disparaging Jews, and the Jews preferred the jokes that put down the Gentiles. Another part of the experiment explored whether a "control" group—the Scots—would prove equally amusing to both Jews and Gentiles. The researchers presented participants with a series of anti-Scottish jokes, such as the classic "Why are Scotsmen so good at golf? The fewer times they hit the ball, the less it will wear out," and were surprised to find that the Gentiles found them significantly funnier than the Jews. The experimenters initially wondered whether this might have been because Gentiles have a better sense of humor than Jews, but then realized that the anti-Scots jokes were a bad choice of control. Both the Jews and Scots are often portrayed as "stingy" in jokes, and this had caused the Jews to sympathize with the Scots and find the anti-Scottish jokes unfunny.

Taking part in this groundbreaking study apparently wasn't easy on people. Some participants complained that they had heard many of the jokes before, and one man noted that he would rather be subjected to electric shocks than additional one-liners. Modern researchers have worked hard to overcome these problems, and their findings have helped expand and refine the superiority theory.

We now know that the more superior a joke makes people feel, the harder they laugh. Most of us do not find a disabled person slipping on a banana skin funny, but replace the disabled person with a traffic warden and suddenly people are slapping their thighs. This simple idea explains why so many jokes attack those in power, such as politicians (thus David Letterman's famous quip: "The traffic was so bad I had to squeeze through spaces that were narrower than President Clinton's definition of sex"), and judges and lawyers ("What do you call a lawyer with an IQ of 10? A lawyer. What do you call a lawyer with an IQ of 15? Your honor"). People in positions of power often do not see the funny side of these and so treat them as a real threat to their authority. Hitler was sufficiently concerned about this potential use of humor that he set up special "Third Reich joke courts" that punished people for many acts of inappropriate humor, including naming their dogs "Adolf."[4]

Some research suggests that such jokes can have surprisingly serious consequences. In 1997, Gregory Maio, a psychologist from Cardiff University of Wales, and his colleagues, looked at the effect that reading superiority jokes had on people's perception of those who were the butt of the jokes.[5] The study was carried out in Canada, and so centered around the group who were frequently portrayed as stupid by Canadians, namely, Newfoundlanders ("Newfies"). Before the experiment, participants were randomly assigned to one of two groups. The people in each group were asked to read one of two sets of jokes into a tape recorder, supposedly to help determine the qualities that make a voice sound funny or unfunny. Those in one group read jokes that did not involve laughing at Newfies (such as Seinfeld material); the other group read classic Newfie put-down humor (such as the classic thigh slapper: "A Newfie friend of mine heard that every minute a woman gives birth to a baby. He thinks she should be stopped"). Afterward, participants were asked to indicate their thoughts about the personality traits of Newfoundlanders. Those who had just read out the Newfie jokes rated Newfoundlanders as significantly more inept, foolish, dim-witted, and slow than those who had delivered the Seinfeld material.

Just as worrying, other work has revealed that superiority jokes have a surprisingly dramatic effect on how people see themselves.[6] Jens Förster, a professor from the International University Bremen in Germany, recently tested the intelligence of eighty women of varying hair color. Half were asked to read jokes in which blondes appeared stupid. Then all participants took an intelligence test. The blond women who had read the jokes obtained significantly lower scores than their blond counterparts in the control condition, suggesting that jokes have the power to affect people's confidence and behavior and so actually create a world in which the stereotypes depicted in the jokes become a reality.

Very early in LaughLab, we saw the superiority theory appear by virtue of the age-old battle of the sexes. The following joke was rated as being funny by 25 percent of women, but just 10 percent of men:

> A husband stepped on one of those penny scales that tell you your fortune and weight and dropped in a coin. "Listen to this," he said to his wife, showing her a small white card. "It says I'm energetic, bright, resourceful, and a great person." "Yeah," his wife nodded, "and it has your weight wrong, too."

One obvious possibility for the difference in ratings between the sexes is that the butt of the joke is a man, and so appeals more to women. However, that is not the only possible interpretation of the result. It could, for example, be that women generally find jokes funnier than men. A year-long study of 1,200 examples of laughing in everyday conversation revealed that 71 percent of women laugh when a man tells a joke, but only 39 percent of men laugh when a woman tells a joke.[7]

To help try to tease apart these competing interpretations, we studied the LaughLab archive to find jokes that put down women, such as:

> A man driving on a highway is pulled over by a police officer. The officer asks: "Did you know your wife and children fell out of your car a mile back?" A smile creeps onto the man's face and he exclaims: "Thank God! I thought I was going deaf!"

On average, 15 percent of women rated jokes putting down women as funny, compared to 50 percent of men. The points awarded to these jokes revealed that the superiority theory did explain the differences between what makes men and women laugh. But this is not to say that there are no differences between the sexes when it comes to humor and jokes. Research suggests that men tell a lot more jokes than women. In one study, two hundred college students were asked to record all of the jokes that they heard during a one-week period and make a note of the joke-teller's sex. The group reported 604 jokes, with 60 percent of them coming from men rather than women.[8] This difference has been observed in many countries, and is present even when children first start to tell jokes to other another.[9]

Some scholars believe that these differences occur because women avoid jokes that are of a sexual nature or involve acts of aggression ("What do you call a monkey in a minefield? A BABOOM!"). Others think that the difference has its roots in the link between laughter, jokes, and status. People with high social status tend to tell more jokes than those lower down in the pecking order. Traditionally, women have had a lower social status than men, and thus may have learned to laugh at jokes rather than to tell them. Interestingly, the only exception to this status/joke-telling relationship concerns self-disparaging humor, by which people who have low social status tell more self-disparaging jokes than those with high status. In line with this idea, researchers examining the amount of self-disparaging humor produced by male and female professional comedians found that 12 percent of male scripts contained self-disparaging humor, compared to 63 percent of female scripts.[10]

We took our first in-depth look at our data three months into the project. The project's technical guru, Jed Everitt, downloaded the

10,000 jokes and ratings from the 100,000 people who had agreed to tell us how funny they found each of the rib-ticklers. The top joke at that early stage had been rated as funny by 46 percent of participants. It had been submitted by Geoff Anandappa, from Blackpool in the northwest of England, and involved the famous fictional detective Sherlock Holmes and his long-suffering sidekick, Dr. Watson:

> Sherlock Holmes and Dr. Watson were going camping. They pitched their tent under the stars and went to sleep. Sometime in the middle of the night Holmes woke Watson up and said: "Watson, look up at the stars, and tell me what you see."
>
> Watson replied: "I see millions and millions of stars."
>
> Holmes said: "And what do you deduce from that?"
>
> Watson replied: "Well, if there are millions of stars, and if even a few of those have planets, it's quite likely there are some planets like Earth out there. And if there are a few planets like Earth out there, there might also be life."
>
> And Holmes said: "Watson, you idiot, it means that somebody stole our tent."

It is a classic example of two-tiered superiority theory. We laugh at Watson for missing the absence of the tent and also at the pompous way in which Holmes delivered the news to Watson.

Two thousand years ago, Plato speculated that the sense of superiority plays a key role in the creation of humor. Our findings suggested not only that he was right but also that the animalistic release of a victorious roar at other people's misfortune is still alive and well in the twenty-first century.

"A Cigar May Just Be a Cigar, but a Joke Is Never *Just* a Joke"

Although the initial stages of the experiment had been a huge success, we still wanted more people to visit our virtual laboratory. Because of this, we announced our initial findings to the media. After the success of our "Why did the chicken cross the road?" photograph, we staged a second striking photograph involving an actor dressed as a clown lying on the actual couch used by Sigmund Freud. Why Freud? Well, he was fascinated by humor, and in 1905 he produced his classic treatise on the topic, *Jokes and Their Relation to the Unconscious.*

Freud's basic model of the mind revolved around the notion that we all have sexual and aggressive thoughts, but that society does not allow us to express these ideas openly. As a result, they are repressed deep into the unconscious and emerge only in the odd slip of the tongue (the "Freudian slip"), in dreams, and in certain forms of psychoanalysis.

According to Freud, jokes act as a kind of psychological release valve that help prevent the repressed pressure from becoming too great—in other words, a way of dealing with whatever it is that causes us to feel anxious. The simple act of telling a joke, or of laughing at someone else's joke, reveals a great deal about the unconscious, and caused Freud to once quip: "A cigar is sometimes just a cigar, but a joke is never *just* a joke." Given that in Freudian terms a cigar is often seen as symbolizing a penis, I have always found Freud's choice of image for his famous line interesting.

There is a great deal of debate about Freud's contribution to the psychology of humor, with one group of academics noting that "it would be exceedingly difficult to find a person of at least average intelligence who knows less about humor than did Freud."[11] This from a group of researchers who described the superiority theory of humor using the following paragraph:

> Let S believe J is a joke in which A seems to S victorious and/or B appears the butt. Then the more positive S's attitude towards A and/or towards the "behaviour" of A, and/or the more negative S's attitude towards B and/or towards the "behaviour" of B, the greater the magnitude of amusement S experiences with respect to J.

The Freud Museum is based in the North London house where the great mind doctor worked during the final part of his life. The building contains a wonderful collection of books and artifacts and, of course, Freud's famous couch. This five-foot-long chaise longue was apparently given to him by a grateful patient in the 1890s. During a typical therapy session, a patient would recline on the couch, and Freud would sit in a large armchair. He devised various techniques to reach the activities of the unconscious. Sometimes he would ask patients to talk about their dreams; at other times, he would say a certain word and have patients respond with the first word they thought of. Since the couch has come to symbolize Freud's approach to understanding the human mind, it provided the perfect backdrop for the second LaughLab photograph. The BAAS contacted the museum and were delighted when the director granted us special permission to have a clown recline on this most famous of couches.

On a cold December morning in 2001, the LaughLab team (plus clown) arrived at the museum and were shown into Freud's office.

It is an impressive room. One wall is lined with bookshelves containing Freud's extensive collection of books and manuscripts. Egyptian, Greek, and Roman antiquities are scattered around the room. The couch sits in one corner of the room next to Freud's large leather armchair.

The photographers arrived and we took up our positions. Our clown carefully reclined on the couch, and I picked up a clipboard and took my place in the armchair. Sitting in the chair that had once been occupied by the world's most famous psychiatrist, and being greeted from his couch by a man wearing a huge bright blue wig, a greasepaint grimace, and massive red shoes, proved to be another surreal LaughLab moment. The photographers liked the setup and merrily snapped away. To help induce a sense of realism into the pictures, one of them asked me to conduct an informal therapy session with the clown. Although not a Freudian psychologist, I was happy to try. I asked my "patient" what the problem was, and the quick-thinking clown said that he was upset because no one took him seriously.

Although Freud claimed to be a scientist, many of his ideas are completely untesticle. Even so, many of the jokes submitted into LaughLab certainly supported Freud's ideas. Time and again, we would get jokes about the stresses and strains of loveless marriage, inadequate sexual performance, and, of course, death:

> I've been in love with the same woman for forty years. If my wife finds out, she'll kill me.

> A patient says to his psychiatrist: "Last night I made a Freudian slip; I was having dinner with my mother-in-law and wanted to say: 'Could you please pass the butter.' But

instead I said: 'You silly cow, you have completely ruined my life.'"

A guy goes to the hospital for a check-up. After weeks of tests, a doctor comes to see him and says that he has some good news and some bad news.

"What's the bad news?" asks the man.

"I am afraid we think you have a very rare and incurable disease," says the doctor.

"Oh, my God, that's terrible," says the man. "What's the good news?"

"Well," replies the doctor, "we are going to name it after you."

Some of the submissions allowed us to explore Freud's theories. Given that older people tend to be especially anxious about the effects of aging, would they find gags about memory loss and the like funnier than younger people would? Freud would have argued that this should be the case, but would our data support this? We carefully sifted through the joke archive and selected several jokes that centered on the difficulties associated with getting old, such as the following:

An elderly couple had dinner at another couple's house, and after eating, the wives left the table and went into the kitchen.

The two elderly gentlemen were talking, and one said: "Last night, we went out to a new restaurant, and it was really great. I would recommend it very highly."

The other man said: "What was the name of the restaurant?"

> The first man thought and thought and finally said: "What is the name of that flower you give to someone you love? You know . . . the one that is red and has thorns."
>
> "Do you mean a rose?"
>
> "Yes," the man said. He then turned toward the kitchen and yelled:
>
> "Rose, what's the name of that restaurant we went to last night?"

and:

> A man in his late sixties suspects that his wife is going deaf, so he decides to test her hearing. He stands on the opposite side of the living room from her and asks: "Can you hear me?" No answer. He moves halfway across the room toward her and asks: "Can you hear me now?" No answer. He moves and stands right beside her and says: "Can you hear me now?" She replies: "For the third time, yes!"

The results were as Freud would have predicted. Younger people didn't like these types of jokes. On average, about 20 percent of people under the age of thirty found each joke funny, versus 50 percent of people in the "sixty or over" age category. The message is clear—we laugh at the aspects of life that cause us the greatest sense of anxiety.

We also inadvertently conducted a second experiment testing this idea. Emma Greening, our joke-vetting expert, had done a grand job keeping the crude material away from the Web site. However, she did allow one joke through by mistake:

> A guy goes to his priest and says, "I feel terrible. I am a doctor and I have slept with some of my patients." The priest looks concerned, and then tries to make the man feel better by saying, "You aren't the first doctor to sleep with their patients and you won't be the last. Perhaps you shouldn't feel so guilty."
>
> "You don't understand" says the man, "I'm a vet."

It is a classic Freudian joke, and it revolves around one of the most basic forms of societal taboos—sex with animals. Interestingly, it obtained a very high score, about 55 percent of people finding it funny. Draw your own conclusions from the fact that men found it funnier than women, and people from Denmark found it funniest of all.

THE HUMOR OF THE HEMISPHERES

Scientists are not known for their sense of humor. However, since we were conducting an experiment, we thought it appropriate to approach some of Britain's best-known scientists and science writers and ask them to submit their favorite jokes to LaughLab. They all proved obliging, and we ended up receiving material from some of the UK's top thinkers, including: Baroness Susan Greenfield, the director of the Royal Institution; Colin Pillinger, the planetary scientist and principal investigator of the ill-fated Beagle 2 Mars lander project; Steve Jones, the evolutionary biologist; and Simon Singh, the best-selling science author.

The joke that went on to win the "best joke submitted by a well-known scientist or science writer" category was submitted by Sir Harry Kroto, the Nobel laureate. Kroto, a professor of chemistry, is best known for being part of the team that discovered a new form of carbon known as C60 Buckminsterfullerene, and not quite so well known for describing himself as adhering to four "religions": humanism, atheism, amnesty-internationalism, and humorism. It may have been this last interest that gave him the edge over his fellow scientists, his winning joke being that old chestnut involving two men and a dog:

> A man walking down the street sees another man with a very big dog.
>
> The man says: "Does your dog bite?"
>
> The other man replies: "No, my dog doesn't bite."
>
> The first man then pats the dog, has his hand bitten off, and shouts, "I thought you said your dog didn't bite."
>
> The other man replies: "That's not my dog."

Overall, the jokes submitted by scientists did not fare especially well. In fact, they came in the bottom third of all jokes submitted, and even Sir Harry Kroto's winning entry beat only 45 percent of other jokes.[12]

We also examined another source of humor: computers. LaughLab attracted lots of jokes about this topic ("The software said it needed Windows 98 or better, so I bought a Mac"). However, it also contained a few jokes actually written by a computer.

A few years ago, Graham Ritchie and Kim Binsted of the University of Edinburgh created a computer program that could produce jokes.[13] We were keen to discover whether computers were funnier than humans, and so we entered several of the computer's best jokes into LaughLab. The majority of them received some of the lowest ratings in the archive. However, one example of computer comedy was surprisingly successful, and it beat about 250 human jokes: "What kind of murderer has fiber? A cereal killer."

It's an example of the most basic form of joke—the simple pun. The most popular theory about why we find these sorts of jokes funny revolves around the concept of "incongruity." The idea is that we laugh at things that surprise us because they seem out of place. It's funny when clowns wear outrageously large shoes (especially when they are not performing), when people have especially big noses, or when politicians tell the truth. In the same way, many jokes are funny because they involve ideas that run against our expectations. A bear walks into a bar. Animals and plants talk. But there is more to this theory than simple forms of incongruity. In many jokes, there is an incongruity between the setup and the punch line. For example:

> Two fish in a tank. One turns to the other and says: "Do you know how to drive this?"

The set-up line leads us to think about two fish in a fish tank. But the punch line surprises us—why should the fish be able to drive a fish tank? Then, a split second later, we suddenly realize that the word "tank" has two meanings, and that the fish are actually in an army tank. Scientists refer to this as the "incongruity-resolution" theory. We resolve the incongruity caused by the punch line, and the accompanying feeling of sudden surprise makes us laugh.

The LaughLab team decided to find out what was happening in people's brains when they laughed at these types of jokes. To help, I contacted Adrian Owen, a neuroscientist at the MRC Cognition and Brain Sciences Unit in Cambridge, England. I chose Adrian for two reasons. First, he is one of the leading brain imagers in the world. Second, the two of us studied psychology at college together, devised and performed in the *Captain Fearless* magic show during our summer breaks, and, despite it all, remain good friends. Adrian teamed up with his colleague Steve Williams, a professor from the Institute of Psychiatry, and used a technique known as functional magnetic resonance imaging (or fMRI) to examine what was happening inside people's brains when they laughed at some of the best puns from the project.

Brain scanning is used to study all sorts of psychological phenomena. One of my favorite experiments was conducted by Gert Holstege, a professor at the University of Groningen, and examined how women fake orgasms.[14] In the study, women's heads were scanned while their partners stimulated them manually to achieve a real orgasm. The women were also asked to fake an orgasm. Comparing the two scans revealed that faking was associated with certain parts of the brain, providing a very expensive way of knowing whether an orgasm was genuine. Curiously, the researchers also discovered that many couples were put off because their feet were cold. When they gave the couples socks to wear, about 80 percent of the couples were able to achieve orgasm compared with 50 percent in the "no sock" condition.

Our scans were far more straightforward to obtain, but no less surreal. The work involved carefully placing people's heads inside a million-dollar scanner and asking them to read some of the top-rated puns. The results revealed that the left side of the brain plays a key role in setting up the initial context for the joke ("There are two fish in a tank . . . "), and that a small area in the right hemisphere provides the creative skills necessary to realize that the situation can be seen in a completely different, and often surreal, way ("One fish turns to the other and says: 'Do you know how to drive this?'"). One of the resulting brain scans is shown in figure 9. This scan shows two areas in the left hemisphere being activated after being shown some of the set-up lines from LaughLab jokes.

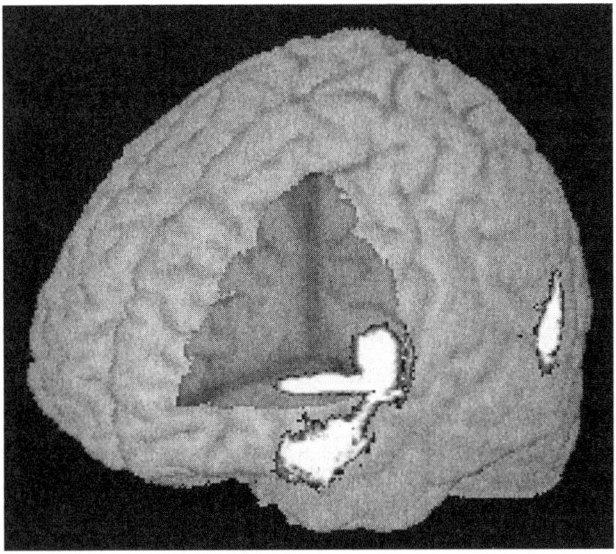

Fig. 9 A 3D scan showing the parts of the brain involved in finding jokes funny.

This work supported other research showing that people who have experienced damage to the right hemisphere are less able to understand jokes, and so they don't see the funny side of life.[15] Take a look at the following setup line and then the three possible punch lines, and see whether you can choose the correct one:

> A man went up to a lady in a crowded square. "Excuse me," he said, "Do you happen to have seen a policeman anywhere around here?"
>
> "I'm sorry," the woman answered, "but I haven't seen one for ages."

Potential punch lines:

- A "Oh, OK, can you give me your watch and necklace then."
- B "Oh, OK, it's just that I've been looking for one for half an hour."
- C "Baseball is my favorite sport."

The first punch line is obviously correct. The second one makes sense, but isn't funny. And the third does not make sense, *and* isn't funny. People with damage to the right side of the brain tended to choose the third punch line far more often than people who did not have any brain damage. It seems that these people know that the end of the joke should be surprising, but they have no way of knowing that one of the punch lines could be reinterpreted to make sense. Interestingly, these people still find films of slapstick comedians funny—although they haven't lost their sense of humor, they have lost the ability to work out why certain incongruities are funny and others aren't. Some of the researchers conducting this work summed up the situation this way: "While the left hemisphere might appreciate some of Groucho's puns, and the right hemisphere might be entertained by the antics of Harpo, only the two hemispheres united can appreciate a whole Marx Brothers routine." As the journalist Tad Friend dryly noted in his *New Yorker* article on LaughLab, neither hemisphere seems to find Chico funny.[16]

WEASELS, AND THE COMEDY *K*

In January 2002, Emma Greening walked into my office and said, "I just don't get it, we are receiving a joke every minute, and they all end with the same punch line: 'There's a weasel chomping on my privates.'" We were five months into the project and, unbeknown to us, Dave Barry had just devoted an entire column to our work in the *International Herald Tribune*.[17] In a previous column, Barry claimed that any sentence can be made much funnier by the insertion of the word "weasel."[18] In his column about LaughLab, Barry repeated his theory and urged his readers to submit jokes to our experiment that ended with the punch line "There's a weasel chomping on my privates." In addition, he asked people to assign any weasel joke a maximum 5 points whenever it was chosen from the archive. Within just a few days, we had received more than 1,500 "weasel chomping" jokes.

Barry is not the only humorist to develop a theory about which words, and sounds, make people laugh. The results from one of the mini-experiments that we conducted during LaughLab supported the most widely cited of these theories: the mysterious comedy potential of the letter *k*.

Early in the experiment, we received the following submission:

> There were two cows in a field. One said: "Moo." The other one said: "I was going to say that!"

We decided to use the joke as a basis for a little experiment. We reentered the joke into our archive several times, using a different animal and noise. We had two tigers going "Gruurrr," two birds going "Cheep," two mice going "Eeek," two dogs going "Woof," and so on. At the end of the study, we examined what effect the different animals had had on how funny people found the joke. In third place came the original cow joke, second were two cats going "Meow," but the winning animal noise joke was:

> Two ducks were sitting in a pond. One of the ducks said: "Quack." The other duck said: "I was going to say that!"

Interestingly, the *k* sound (as in the "hard *c*") is associated with both "quack" and "duck" and has long been seen by comedians and comedy writers as being especially funny. The idea of the comedy *k* has certainly made it into popular culture. In the *Star Trek: The Next Generation* episode "The Outrageous Okona," a comedian refers to the idea when attempting to explain humor to the android Data. There was also an episode of *The Simpsons* in which Krusty the Clown (note the *k*'s) visits a faith healer because he has paralyzed his vocal chords trying to cram too many "comedy *k*'s" into his routines. After being healed, Krusty exclaims that he is overjoyed to get his comedy *k*'s back, celebrates by shouting out "King Kong," "cold-cock," and "Kato Kaelin," and then kisses the faith healer as a sign of gratitude.

Why should the *k* sound produce such pleasure? It may be due to an odd psychological phenomenon known as "facial feedback." People smile when they feel happy. However, evidence suggests that the mechanism also works in reverse; that is, people feel happy simply because they have smiled. In 1988, Fritz Strack and his colleagues from the University of Mannheim, Germany, had people judge how funny they found Gary Larson's *Far Side* cartoons under one of two conditions.[19] The participants in one group were asked to hold a pencil between their teeth, but to ensure that it did not touch their lips. This forced the lower part of their faces into a smile. Those in the other group were asked to support the end of the pencil with just their lips, and not their teeth. This forced their faces into a frown. The results revealed that people actually experience the emotion associated with their expressions. Those who had their faces forced into a smile felt happier; they found the *Far Side* cartoons much funnier than those who were forced to frown did.

Interestingly, many words featuring the *k* sound force the face into a smile (think "duck" and "quack"), and they may account for why we associate the sound with happiness. Regardless of whether this explains the "comedy *k*" effect, the explanation certainly plays a key role in another aspect of humor—the contagious nature of laughter.

In 1991, Verlin Hinsz and Judith Tomhave, psychologists from North Dakota State University, visited various shopping centers to examine smiling.[20] One member of the team smiled at a random selection of people while another experimenter, secreted inside a fake food stand, carefully observed whether the person reciprocated with a smile. After hours of smiling and observing, they discovered that half of people responded to the experimenter's smile with another smile. Their results caused them to suggest that the old saying "Smile, and the whole world smiles with you" should be altered to the more scientifically accurate "Smile, and *half* the world smiles with you."

The ability automatically, and unconsciously, to mimic the facial expressions of those around us plays a vitally important role in group survival, cohesion, and bonding. By copying the expressions of others, we quickly feel how they feel, and so find it much easier to empathize with their situations and to communicate with them. One person in the group smiles, and others automatically copy the smile and cheer up. Another feels sad or afraid or panicked and, again, the emotion can spread from person to person. This, combined with the results from the pencil experiment, explains why laughter is contagious. When people see or hear another person laugh, they are far more likely to copy the behavior, start laughing themselves, and therefore actually find the situation funny. This is the reason why so many television comedy programs carry laughter tracks, and why nineteenth-century theater producers would hire a "professional" audience member (known as the *rieur*) whose especially infectious laugh encouraged the entire audience to giggle and guffaw.

Although this contagion usually has limited effects, sometimes it can get out of hand, and an otherwise inexplicable epidemic of laughter can sweep through thousands of people. In January 1962, three teenaged girls attending a missionary-run boarding school in Tanzania started laughing.[21] Their hilarity quickly spread to 95 of the 159 pupils at the school, and by March the school was forced to close. It is reported that the attacks of laughing lasted from minutes to hours, and although debilitating, did not result in any fatalities. The school reopened in May but was again forced to close within weeks when another 60 pupils were struck down with the "laughter plague." The closure created its own problems: Several of the girls returned to their hometown of Nshamba, promptly causing more than two hundred of the 10,000 residents of the town to descend into uncontrollable giggling. It is not known whether the girls' teacher had a *k* in his or her name.

COMEDIANS ON THE COUCH

After a few months we had received more than 25,000 jokes, about a million ratings, and a large amount of international publicity. It was around this time that I was contacted by John Zaritsky, an Oscar-winning Canadian documentary maker, asking whether I should like to help make a film based on LaughLab that would examine humor around the world. I quickly agreed, and together we traveled the world looking at what makes different parts of the globe guffaw, titter, and groan.

As part of the film, John invited me to Los Angeles to road test some of the material that was obtaining high ratings. I carefully searched through the database and identified two types of jokes—those that the British found especially funny and those that appealed to Americans. In June 2002, I found myself standing in the wings of the Ice House, a comedy club in Pasadena, California. The MC, a sassy young woman named Debi Gutierrez, was standing on the stage explaining what was about to happen. She described the LaughLab project and said that I would deliver some of the jokes that had proved most popular with the British and that she would deliver the gags that had received high ratings from the Americans. A few moments later and I was onstage. It was another of those surreal moments. Debi opened with a classic:

> Woman to a male pharmacist: "Do you have that Viagra drug?"
>
> Pharmacist "Yes."
>
> Woman: "Can you get it over the counter?"
>
> Pharmacist: "Only if I take two of them."

Debi managed to mess up the punch line, and the joke fell flat. Not even a titter. Then it was my turn. I decided to open with a "Doctor, Doctor" joke that proved very popular with the British people visiting our virtual laboratory:

> A guy goes to the doctor and has a checkup. At the end of the examination, he turns to the doctor and asks how long he has to live. The doctor replies, "Ten." The guy looks confused, and says, "Ten what? Years? Months? Weeks?" The doctor replies, "Nine, eight, seven . . . "

Again, it was a tumbleweed moment. You could have heard a pin drop. Or a duck drop, if it's funnier. After a few more jokes obtained exactly the same negative response, Debi finally produced the only laugh of the session with the improvised opening of a nonexistent joke: "Two faggots and a midget walk into a bar . . . "

According to our data, about a third of the audience should have found the jokes funny. In reality, that figure was embarrassingly close to zero. So what went wrong? It was horses for courses. The people voting in our experiment represented a wide cross section of the public, whereas the people at the comedy club were into a certain type of comedy—bold, brash, offensive, and aggressive. When it comes to comedy, there is no magic bullet, no single joke that everyone will find really funny. It is a question of matching the joke to the person, and we had missed by a mile. It was a point that was to come up repeatedly when we announced our winning joke at the end of the experiment.

Although being on stage at the Ice House was no fun, waiting backstage with the other performers proved to be more interesting. Professional comedians are, if you will excuse the pun, a funny group of people. They have chosen to make a living in a difficult and highly stressful way. They have to stand onstage, night after night, and make a group of complete strangers laugh out loud. No matter how they feel, or what is happening in their own lives, they have to be funny. In view of this, a small number of psychologists have been interested in analyzing their minds.

Woody Allen once remarked: "Most of the time I don't have much fun, the rest of the time I don't have fun at all." But how much truth is there in the popular stereotype of the sad clown? It is easy to think of high-profile examples, including the British comedian Spike Milligan (who suffered from manic-depression throughout his life) and the American performers Lenny Bruce and John Belushi (both of whom are believed to have committed suicide).

In 1975, the psychiatrist Samuel Janus published a groundbreaking paper on the psychology of comedians. Keen to investigate the truth behind the popular notion of the sad clown, Janus interviewed fifty-five well-known professional comedians about their lives.[22] Janus gathered together some of the top names in comedy, working only with those who were earning at least a six-figure salary and were known nationally. The results revealed that the vast majority of the group possessed above average intelligence (with few achieving the classification of "genius"), 80 percent had sought psychotherapy at some point in their lives, and nearly all were extremely anxious about losing their star status. This last finding caused Janus to conclude that "several were able to enjoy life and reap the benefits of their fame and fortune, but they were in a very small minority." His report also shows the problems of working with highly successful, but angst-ridden, professional comedians. Although almost all performed well on the tests of intelligence, Janus noted that "the problem was not one of getting them to respond, it was one of continuously allaying their anxiety and reassuring them that they were indeed doing well." Also, when asked about their experiences with psychotherapy, Janus describes how several of his participants said that the therapist had asked them to "lie down on the couch and tell me everything you know," shortly followed by the comment: "And now he's doing my act in Philadelphia."

PRETEND THE WORLD IS FUNNY AND FOREVER

Janus's image of "comedian as sad clown" was not supported by work published in 1981 by Seymour and Rhoda Fisher, psychoanalysts from the State University of New York at Syracuse.[23] The Fishers conducted an extensive investigation into more than forty well-known comedians and clowns, including Sid Caesar, Jackie Mason, and Blinko the Clown, and published their findings in a wonderful book titled *Pretend the World Is Funny and Forever.*

As part of the work, they administered the classic test known as the Rorschach Inkblot Test, in which participants were asked to look at an ambiguous inkblot and say what the inkblot resembles. The test has been used extensively in research and even features in a well-known Freudian joke:

> A man goes to a psychoanalyst. The analyst gets out a stack of cards containing ink blots, shows them to the man one at a time, and asks him to say what the ink-blots remind him of. The man looks at the first ink blot and says, "Sex." Then he looks at the second ink blot and says,

> "Sex," again. In fact, he goes through the whole stack of images, saying the word "sex" in response to every one. The psychiatrist looks concerned and says, "I don't wish to worry you, but you seem to have sex on the mind." The man looks surprised, and answers, "I can't believe you just said that—you are the one with all the dirty pictures."

Since most of the tests took place in restaurants and circus dressing rooms, the Fishers often found them difficult to administer because of constant interruptions by members of the public and fellow performers.

Contrary to the popular conception of the "sad clown" and to Janus's previous results, the Fishers found little evidence of psychopathology. They were surprised to discover that their interviewees appeared remarkably resilient and well adjusted despite the stressful nature of working as professional comedians.

Another aspect of the Fishers' work examined the childhood experiences of the comedians and clowns. They noted that the majority of their interviewees started young, and were often considered the "class clown." In line with the "superiority" theory, many related instances in which they would use humor to get one up on their teachers. One performer recalled how the teacher had asked him to go to the blackboard and spell "petroleum." He promptly walked up to the front of the class, picked up a piece of chalk, and wrote the word "oil." Professional comedians tend to come from relatively low-income families and to have been unhappy as children, and thus their performances may represent an attempt to compensate for these difficult early experiences by gaining the affection of an audience. There is considerable anecdotal evidence to support the idea. Woody Allen once said that the need to be accepted was one of his primary motivations for being funny; Jack Benny didn't enjoy a holiday in Cuba because no one recognized him; and W. C. Fields once explained why he liked making people laugh: "At least for a short moment, they love me."

The second element of the Fishers' research examined the psychological qualities associated with being funny. Several performers admitted that they were intensely curious about people and behavior, reporting how they would endlessly watch others go about their lives until they found some small idiosyncrasy that could form the basis for a new joke or routine. The Fishers noted that there were many parallels between comedians and social scientists. They argued that both groups are constantly on the prowl for novel perspectives on human behavior, the only major difference being that in the first case such insights make people laugh and in the others, they form the basis for academic papers. Having spent my career reading such publications, I would venture that this alleged distinction fails to clearly separate the two groups.

The Fishers also set out to examine the relationship between comedy and anxiety. When presented with inkblots, people often report that after seeing one image they realize that the blot can be seen in a different way. After carefully analyzing the types of images that the comedians reported seeing in the random inkblots, the Fishers concluded that their participants often produced a unique class of "nice monster" imagery, wherein threatening figures would be transformed into something far more pleasant. A "dragon with flames shooting out of his mouth" would become a noble and misunderstood figure, and a "dirty hyena" would change into a lovely cuddly pet. The Fishers interpreted this as evidence that comedians and clowns are unconsciously motivated to use humor as a way of coping with distressing events.

James Rotton, a psychologist from Florida International University, also questioned the notion that comedy is inevitably associated with sadness and psychopathology. He examined a copy of Hoffman's *Entertainment Personalities of the Past* for the years of birth and death of well-known comedians and compared it to a control group of noncomedic entertainers born in the same years. (Rotton restricted his list to male comedians after discovering that the ages of many female comedians were unreliable because they didn't match other bibliographic sources, suggesting a possible chronopsychology of comedy).[24]

Rotton described his findings in a paper titled "Trait Humor and Longevity: Do Comics Have the Last Laugh?" and argued that comedians were no more likely to die younger than other entertainers. A subsequent analysis of the cause of death of comedians (gleaned by examining the obituaries of performers published in *Time* and *Newsweek* between 1980 and 1989) revealed no evidence of an excess of heart attacks, cancers, pneumonia, accidents, or suicides. In short, there is no evidence to suggest that the obvious stresses and strains associated with having to be funny night after night leads to an early demise.

Rotton's findings are in line with other work suggesting that being able to laugh at life reduces anxiety and that, if anything, comedy may actually be good for your health. In the thirteenth century, the surgeon Henri de Mondeville speculated that laughter may promote recovery from illness: "The surgeon must forbid anger, hatred, and sadness in the patient, and remind him that the body grows fat from joy and thin from sadness." A few hundred years later, William Shakespeare echoed the same sentiment: "Frame your mind to mirth and merriment, which bars a thousand harms and lengthens life."

Recent research has supported a link between laughter, coping with stress, and psychological and physical well-being. According to this work, people who spontaneously use humor to cope with stress have especially healthy immune systems, are 40 percent less likely to suffer a heart attack or stroke, experience less pain during dental surgery, and live 4.5 years longer than most.[25]

In 1990, researchers discovered that watching a video of Bill Cosby performing his stand-up routine results in enhanced production of salivary immunoglobulin A—a chemical that plays a key role in preventing upper respiratory tract infection (apparently these beneficial effects were significantly reduced when participants listened to Mel Brooks and Carl Reiner's classic "2,000-Year-Old-Man" routine).[26] In 2005, Michael Miller and his colleagues from the University of Maryland studied the relationship between finding the world funny and the inner lining of blood vessels. When such vessels expand, they increase blood flow around the body and promote cardiovascular well-being. Participants were shown scenes from films that were likely either to make them feel anxious (such as the opening thirty minutes of *Saving Private Ryan*) or to make them laugh (such as the "orgasm" scene from *When Harry Met Sally*). Overall, participants' blood flow dropped by around 35 percent after watching the stress-inducing films, but rose by 22 percent after seeing the more humorous material. On the basis of the results, the researchers recommend that people laugh for at least fifteen minutes each day.

In a similar vein, James Rotton examined the effects that watching different kinds of videos had on hospital patients recovering from orthopedic surgery.[27] Patients in one group were asked to select funny films from a list that included *Bananas, Naked Gun,* and *The Producers;* those in another group were denied access to any material that might induce a smile, and they were instead asked to select movies from a "serious" list, including titles such as *Die Hard II, Casablanca,* and *The Hunt for Red October.* The experimenters secretly monitored the quantity of major pain relievers that the patients consumed via a self-controlled pump. Those watching funny films used about 60 percent fewer pain-relieving drugs than those looking at the serious movies. In an interesting twist to the experiment, the researchers also included another group of patients who were not allowed to select which comedy films to watch but instead were given the movies selected by others. This group administered significantly more drugs than either of the other groups, scientifically proving that there is nothing more painful than watching a comedy that doesn't make you laugh.

Finally, a team of researchers asked participants to reflect on their mortality by constructing mock wills, completing their own death certificates (including an estimate of their dates and causes of death), and writing the eulogies for their own funerals.[28] Researchers discovered that those who had exhibited a prior tendency to laugh at the absurdities of life did not find the tasks as stressful as the more gloomy participants had found them. Exactly the same effect has emerged in more realistic settings. Bereavement counselors interviewing people six months after they had lost their spouses found that those who could laugh about the loss were more able than others to come to terms with the situation and to move on with their lives.[29] However, as one of the jokes submitted to LaughLab illustrates, it is possible to take this idea too far:

A man dies and his wife telephones her local newspaper, and says, "I would like to print the following obituary: Bernie is dead."

The man at the newspaper pauses, and says, "Actually, for the same price you could print six words."

The woman replies, "Oh, okay, can I go with: Bernie is dead. Toyota for sale."

HEARD THE ONE ABOUT THE RELIGIOUS FUNDAMENTALISTS?

Given the physical and psychological benefits of laughter, it isn't surprising that some scientists have investigated the characteristics of people who do, and do not, see the funny side of life. Some of the most intriguing work in the area has been carried out by Vassilis Saroglou, a psychologist from the Université Catholique de Louvain in Belgium, who looked at the relationship between laughter and religious fundamentalism.

Saroglou argues that there is a natural incompatibility between religious fundamentalism and humor.[30] The creation and appreciation of humor requires a sense of playfulness, an enjoyment of incongruity ("Two fish in a tank . . . "), and a high tolerance for uncertainty. Humor also frequently involves mixing elements that don't go together, that threaten authority, and that contain sexually explicit material. In addition, the act of laughter involves a loss of self-control and self-discipline. All these elements, argues Saroglou, are the antithesis of religious fundamentalism, and research shows that those who subscribe to it tend to value serious activities over playfulness, certainty over uncertainty, sense over nonsense, self-mastery over impulsiveness, authority over chaos, and mental rigidity over flexibility. Saroglou supports his argument by noting that many scholars have written about the deep mistrust that exists between humor and religion, citing evidence from various religious texts. When discussing examples of biblical humor, Saroglou notes: "One might wonder, for instance, why Christ didn't simply say 'blessed are you that weep now, for you shall laugh' (Lk 6:21), but went on to add 'woe to you that laugh now, for you shall mourn and weep' (Lk 6:25)."

Additional evidence comes from a monastic rule regarding priests playing with children: "If a brother willingly laughs and plays with children . . . he will be warned three times; if he does not stop, he will be corrected with the most severe punishment."

Eager to test his hypothesis empirically, Saroglou conducted an unusual experiment.[31] In one part of the study, participants completed a questionnaire measuring their level of religious fundamentalism and rated the degree to which they endorsed various ideas, including whether a particular set of teachings contain fundamental truths, that these truths are opposed by evil forces, and that they must be followed via a set of well-defined historical practices. In another part of the experiment, the participants were shown a set of twenty-four pictures depicting a variety of frustrating everyday situations and asked to note down how they would react. After the participants completed the picture task, the researchers rated the degree of humor in their responses. For instance, one of the cards showed someone falling to the ground in front of two friends, with one of the friends asking, "Did you hurt yourself?" A straight-faced response to this card might be something like "No, I am fine," but "I don't know, I haven't reached the ground yet" would constitute a far more humorous approach. In line with his prediction, Saroglou found a strong relationship between religious fundamentalism and humor, the fundamentalists producing far more serious-sounding answers than others.

As is almost always true with research showing a relationship between two factors, it is difficult to separate cause and effect. Perhaps having a poor sense of humor leads to a fundamentalist religious belief. Or maybe, as Saroglou hypothesized, being a fundamentalist prevents people from seeing the funny side of life. To help disentangle these two possibilities, Saroglou carried out a second study.[32] This time he split participants into three groups. One group saw funny footage from famous French comedy shows. A second group saw religiously oriented footage, including a documentary film about a pilgrimage to Lourdes, scenes from *Jesus of Montreal,* and a discussion between a journalist and a monk about spiritual values. A third group didn't see any film footage at all, and so acted as a control. Participants were then asked to complete the same humor production task as before. Overall, the people who had seen the humorous footage produced more than twice as many funny responses as the control group, and those who had seen the religious footage trailed in third place. The clever design of the experiment helped Saroglou differentiate correlation from causation, and suggests that exposure to religious material prevents people from using humor to help ease the stressful effects of everyday hassles.

The relationship between humor production and religious fundamentalism didn't stop people from submitting jokes about various deities to the LaughLab experiment. Many of them played on the incongruous idea of an omnipotent, caring God behaving out of character:

A shipwreck survivor washes up on the beach of an island and is surrounded by a group of warriors.

"I'm done for," the man cries in despair.

"No, you are not," comes a booming voice from the heavens. "Listen carefully, and do exactly as I say. Grab a spear and push it through the heart of the warrior chief."

The man does what he is told, turns to the heavens, and asks, "Now, what?"

The booming voice replies, "*Now* you are done for."

ROBIN WILLIAMS, SPIKE MILLIGAN, AND THE "WOOF WOOF" JOKE

In a 1939 edition of the *New York Times Magazine,* the Canadian humorist Stephen Leacock remarked, "Let me hear the jokes of a nation and I will tell you what the people are like, how they are getting along, and what is going to happen to them." Our Laugh-Lab data allowed us to take a scientific look at Leacock's idea by examining national differences in humor. We were not the first academics to tackle the topic.

In chapter 1, I described the groundbreaking research on astrology and personality carried out by the prolific British psychologist Hans Eysenck. During World War II, Eysenck developed an interest in the psychology of humor and did an unusual survey into British, American, and German magazine cartoons.[33] Getting hold of the material proved problematic. Large shipments of American magazines had been lost due to sinkings in the Atlantic, much of the potential British material had been destroyed in the bombings of the British Museum, and the choice of German material was restricted to magazines published before the outbreak of hostilities. Despite the problems, Eysenck soldiered on, and eventually managed to find seventy-five cartoons drawn from various magazines, including *Punch* in Britain, the *New Yorker* in the United States, and *Berliner Illustrierte* in Germany.

Eysenck then translated the German captions into English and showed all the cartoons to groups of English people. Participants were first asked to rate how funny they found the cartoons. Eysenck discovered that the cartoons from all three countries obtained roughly the same funniness ratings. Next, participants were asked to guess whether each cartoon originated in Britain, the United States, or Germany, allowing the experimenters to analyze the points awarded to the cartoons as a function of where the participants *thought* they were from. The cartoons that people thought were from Germany received much lower ratings than those believed to be from America and Britain. Further analysis revealed additional evidence of national stereotypes. When Eysenck looked closely at the cartoons that people thought were German, he found an overrepresentation of negative elements, including fat women, badly dressed girls, and old-fashioned furniture.

In the second part of his study, Eysenck had British, American, and German volunteers (actually refugees who had fled their homeland because of the war) rate the same set of jokes and limericks. His results revealed that, overall, Americans found the material funnier than people from the other two countries, but that there were few differences in the types of jokes that people from different countries found funny.

Our LaughLab data broadly supported Eysenck's findings. There were large differences in how funny the jokes were to people from different countries. Canadians laughed least at the jokes. This could be seen in one of two ways. Given that the jokes were not very good, it could be argued that Canadians have a discerning sense of humor. Alternatively, they may simply not have much of a sense of humor at all, and so would not find anything funny. Germans found the jokes funnier than people from any other country. The validity of this finding was questioned within the pages of almost every non-German newspaper and magazine reporting our findings. One British newspaper told the top-rated German joke—"Why is a television called a medium? Because it is neither rare nor well done"—to a spokesperson at the German Embassy in London. Apparently, he laughed so much he dropped the telephone and cut off the call. Few other differences emerged. On the whole, people from one country found the same jokes funny and unfunny. The comedian and musician Victor Borge once described humor as the shortest distance between two people. If he is correct, then knowing that diverse groups of people laugh at the same jokes might help bring such groups closer together.

By the end of the project we had received 40,000 jokes, and we had them rated by more than 350,000 people from seventy countries. We were awarded a Guinness World Record for conducting one of the largest experiments in history, and we made the cover story of the *New Yorker*. The top joke, as voted by Americans, was as follows:

> At the parade, the colonel noticed something unusual going on and asked the major: "Major Barry, what the devil's wrong with Sergeant Jones's platoon? They seem to be all twitching and jumping about."

> "Well sir," says Major Barry after a moment of observation. "There seems to be a weasel chomping on his privates."

Dave Barry had successfully managed to make the top American joke weasel-oriented. He had, thank goodness, less influence over the votes cast by those outside the United States. We carefully went through the huge archive and found our top joke. It had been rated as funny by 55 percent of the people who had taken part in the experiment:

> Two hunters are out in the woods when one of them collapses. He doesn't seem to be breathing and his eyes are glazed. The other guy whips out his phone and calls the emergency services. He gasps, "My friend is dead! What can I do?" The operator says, "Calm down. I can help. First, let's make sure he's dead." There is a silence, then a shot is heard. Back on the phone, the guy says, "OK, now what?"

The joke had just beaten the initial frontrunner, the one about Holmes, Watson, and the strange case of the missing tent, to first place. We contacted Geoff Anandappa, the man who had submitted the Holmes and Watson joke, and broke the bad news. Geoff was gracious in defeat, noting: "I can't believe I got knocked out in the final round! I could've been a contender . . . I want a rematch, and this time I'm going to fight dirty. Did you hear the one about the actress and the bishop?"

The database told us that the winning joke had been submitted by a psychiatrist from Manchester in Britain named Gurpal Gosall. When we contacted Gurpal, he explained how he sometimes told the joke to cheer up his patients; he noted: "It makes people feel better, because it reminds them that there is always someone out there who is doing something more stupid than themselves."

The BAAS and I announced our findings at the third, and final, press conference. For the last time, we hired a chicken suit, and had one of my lucky doctorate students dress up (see fig. 10).

Fig. 10 Another giant chicken reveals the world's funniest joke.

Our winning joke was printed on a huge banner and unveiled to the waiting press. Terry Jones, the comedian on the Python team responsible for the sketch involving the world's funniest joke, was asked by the media for his opinion.[34] He thought the joke was quite funny but perhaps rather obvious. Another journalist interviewed the Hollywood star Robin Williams about our winning entry. Like Jones, Williams thought that is was okay, but went on to explain that the world's funniest joke is probably absolutely filthy and therefore not the sort of thing you would tell in polite company.

The year-long search for the world's funniest joke concluded. Did we really manage to find it? In fact, I don't believe it exists. If our research tells us anything, it is that people find different things funny. Women laugh at jokes in which men look stupid. The elderly laugh at jokes involving memory loss and hearing difficulties. Those who are powerless laugh at those in power. There is no one joke that will make everyone guffaw. Our brains just don't work like that. In many ways, I believe that we uncovered the world's blandest joke—the gag that makes everyone smile but very few laugh out loud. But, as with so many quests, the journey was far more important than the destination. Along the way we looked at what makes us laugh, how laughter can make you live longer, how humor should unite different nations, and we also discovered the world's funniest comedy animal.

Five years after the study, I received a telephone call from my friend and brain-scanning scientist, Adrian Owen. He explained that he had just seen a documentary film about Spike Milligan, comedian and cofounder of the Goons (*The Goon Show* was a popular comedy radio program in Britain in the 1950s), and that the program contained a very early version of our winning joke. The documentary (the title of which, *I Told You I Was Ill,* was based on Spike's epitaph) contained a brief clip from a 1951 BBC program called *London Entertains* with the following early Goon sketch:

> Michael Bentine: I just came in and found him lying on the carpet there.
>
> Peter Sellers: Oh, is he dead?
>
> Michael Bentine: I think so.

> Peter Sellers: Hadn't you better make sure?
> Michael Bentine: Alright. Just a minute.
> *(Sound of two gun shots)*
> Michael Bentine: He's dead.

It is highly unusual to be able to track down the source of jokes because their origins tend to become lost in the mists of time. Spike Milligan had died in 2002, but with the help of the documentary makers, I contacted his daughter Sile, and she confirmed that it was highly likely that her father had written the material. We announced that we believed we had identified the author of the world's funniest joke, and LaughLab made headlines again.

During the ensuing interviews, several journalists asked me a question that frequently occurs whenever I speak about LaughLab: What was my favorite joke from the thousands that flooded in through the year? I always give the same reply:

> A dog goes into a telegraph office, takes a blank form, and writes: "Woof Woof. Woof Woof Woof. Woof Woof Woof Woof."
>
> The clerk examines the paper and politely tells the dog: "There are only nine words here. You could send another 'Woof' for the same price."
>
> The dog looks confused and replies, "But that would make no sense at all."

I don't really know why I like it. It just makes me laugh.

6 Sinner or Saint?

The Psychology of When We Help and When We Hinder

In the early 1930s, Richard LaPiere, a psychologist from Stanford University, spent several months driving up and down the West Coast of the United States with one of his Chinese students and the student's wife.[1] The couple had been born and raised in China and had only recently moved to the United States. To them, LaPiere appeared to be a genial professor who had kindly found the time to show them around. In reality, they were unsuspecting guinea pigs in a secret experiment that LaPiere was conducting throughout the trip.

The idea for the experiment had occurred to LaPiere when the couple had first arrived at the university, and he had taken them to the main hotel in town. A relative rarity in the United States of the 1930s, Chinese people were frequently subjected to a considerable amount of blatant prejudice. According to LaPiere, he approached the hotel with a sense of trepidation because it was "noted for its narrow and bigoted attitudes toward Orientals."

LaPiere went to the reception with his two friends and nervously asked whether they had any rooms available. To LaPiere's surprise, the clerk didn't display the prejudice for which his establishment had gained a considerable reputation, and instead quickly found them a suitable accommodation. Curious about the discrepancy between what he had heard about the hotel and his experience with the receptionist, LaPiere later telephoned the hotel and asked whether they would have a room available for "an important Chinese gentleman." He was told in no uncertain terms that the hotel would not provide accommodation.

LaPiere was struck by the difference between how people *said* that they would behave and how they *actually* acted. But he realized that his experience in the hotel could just have been atypical. To investigate the issue properly he would need to repeat the same scenario with a far larger number of hotels and restaurants, and that is when he hit upon the idea of taking his two Chinese colleagues on an experimental road trip across the United States.

The journey involved driving 10,000 miles, and visiting sixty-six hotels and 184 restaurants. At each hotel and eatery, LaPiere had his student ask about the possibility of accommodation or food. LaPiere then secretly noted whether the request was successful. The results from this initial part of the study replicated his earlier experience. His two companions received pleasant and helpful service almost everywhere they went, leading LaPiere to conclude that "the 'attitude' of the American people, as reflected in the behavior of those who are for pecuniary reasons presumably most sensitive to the antipathies of their white clientele, is anything but negative toward the Chinese."

Six months later, LaPiere conducted the second part of the study. To each of the hotels and restaurants that they had visited, he sent questionnaires asking: "Will you accept members of the Chinese race as guests in your establishment?" To help hide the exact purpose of the study, this question was one of many; the other items on the form inquired about whether each establishment welcomed Germans, French, Armenians, and Jews. The results made for disturbing reading. More than 90 percent of the respondents checked the "no, Chinese people are not welcome here" box, and almost all of the remaining 10 percent went for the "uncertain" option. LaPiere received only one "yes" response. This reply came from a hotel that LaPiere and his students had visited a few months before. The owner had added a short note to the questionnaire saying that the reason she would welcome people from China was because she had recently enjoyed a nice visit from a Chinese man and his sweet wife.

In LaPiere's study, people said that they would behave in a way that was in keeping with the societal norms of the day, but they actually behaved quite differently. In more recent studies, researchers have obtained copious evidence for the same effect, with people claiming that they are not racist (in keeping with modern societal norms), but then behaving in a prejudiced way.

It all adds up to one simple point. Asking people to rate how nice they are is unlikely to yield a genuine insight into anything other than their ability to deceive themselves and others. Because of people's reluctance, or inability, to report accurately whether they are nice or nasty, many researchers interested in these topics have done exactly what LaPiere did. They have stopped asking people to check the "saint" or "sinner" box, taken off their lab coats, put on trench coats, and carried out secret studies in the real world.

Vanishing Gloves, Attaché Cases, and Female Van Drivers

For the past twenty-five years, John Trinkaus, a professor from the City University of New York, has dedicated his academic life to the scientific observation of ordinary folk going about their everyday business. Trinkaus has investigated a huge range of topics and published his findings in almost a hundred academic papers. He has visited railway stations and noted the color of sneakers worn by men and women (79 percent of male sports-shoe wearers chose white, versus just 34 percent of female wearers);[2] compared the number of times television weather forecasters *said* that their predictions had been accurate with the number of times they were *actually* correct (only 49 percent of their allegedly accurate predictions were right);[3] traveled to inner-city neighborhoods to document the decreasing numbers of people wearing baseball caps with their peaks turned to the back (it is dropping at a rate of 10 percent per year);[4] and plotted verbal trends in providing an affirmative response by counting the number of times interviewees on television talk shows used the word "yes" when answering questions (of the 419 questions analyzed, "yes" was used 53 times, "exactly" 117 times, and "absolutely" 249 times).[5]

Trinkaus's investigations into sports shoes, weather forecasts, baseball caps, and the use of the "yes" word are all brilliantly obscure. However, some of his other research has serious implications, not least his investigations of the surprising predictability of human nature.[6] Trinkaus asked hundreds of his students to think of any odd number between 10 and 50, and found the majority chose 37. When asked to name any even number between 50 and 100, most said 68. Trinkaus then took this aspect of his research into the real world, asking a hundred people who owned attaché cases with number locks to tell him the combination.[7] He discovered that almost 75 percent of owners had not changed the factory settings on their cases, and they could be opened with the numbers 0-0-0. In his book *Surely You're Joking, Mr. Feynman,*[8] the physicist Richard Feynman describes how he used the same type of predictability to gain access to top-secret documents when he was working on the development of the atomic bomb at Los Alamos. On one occasion he opened a colleague's safe by trying various combinations he thought a physicist might use (the winning numbers were 27 18 28, after the mathematical constant e=2.71828). Feynman also discovered that no one had bothered to change the generic factory settings to one of the largest safes on the base, which could have been opened by an unskilled thief within minutes.

My favorite piece of Trinkaus research is described in a little-known paper titled "Gloves as Vanishing Personal 'Stuff': An Informal Look."[9] Here Trinkaus begins by noting how his personal belongings, including single socks, umbrellas, and one glove from each pair, often seem to disappear. He then goes on to explain that he has managed to overcome the problem with umbrellas by purchasing several inexpensive ones from a street vendor (who, according to his observations, charged 50 percent more for them on a rainy day than he did on a sunny day), but is reluctant to apply the same approach to gloves. Eager to get to the bottom of the vanishing gloves mystery, Trinkaus monitored his missing mittens during a ten-year period, carefully noting whether the vanishing glove belonged to his left or right hand. The results revealed that left-hand gloves went missing more than three times as often as right-hand gloves. This caused him to speculate that he might be removing his right glove first, pushing it down into his pocket, then removing his left glove, and pushing it on top of the glove already there. If this was true, then his left glove would be nearer the top of the pocket, and more likely to fall out.

Trinkaus's work into vanishing gloves has inspired other researchers to investigate similar topics. In 2005, Megan Lim, Margaret Hellard, and Campbell Aitken, researchers from the MacFarlane Burnet Institute for Medical Research in Melbourne, conducted an experiment to discover why teaspoons in communal kitchens disappear with annoying regularity (or, as they phrase it in their scientific paper on the topic, to answer the age-old question "Where have all the bloody teaspoons gone?").[10] The team secretly marked seventy teaspoons, placed each of them in one of eight communal kitchens at their institute, and tracked the movement of the spoons over a five-month period. Eighty percent of the teaspoons went missing during this time, half of them disappearing within the first eighty-one days. Additional questionnaire data revealed that 36 percent of people said they had stolen a teaspoon at some point in their lives, and 18 percent admitted to such a theft in the previous twelve months.

This latter result argues against the notion that the vanishing spoons are being sucked into another dimension, and instead supports a more mundane explanation: People steal them. The researchers also note that the institute's level of disappearing teaspoons, multiplied by the entire Melbourne workforce, suggests that 18 million teaspoons go missing each year in Melbourne alone, and that if these spoons were laid end to end, they would stretch around the coastline of Mozambique. Unlike the Trinkaus research into vanishing gloves, other researchers have started to replicate the "disappearing teaspoons" study across the globe. In one of the most recent pieces of follow-up work, French academics reported that 1,800 teaspoons went missing over a six-month period in a large cafeteria.[11]

The stealing of teaspoons indirectly brings us to Trinkaus's work into dishonesty and antisocial behavior. As we shall see later in this chapter, many of the other researchers interested in these types of behavior are drawn to serious acts of stealing or selfishness. Trinkaus has managed to develop his own unique approach by focusing on relatively small-scale social transgressions, such as parking in restricted areas or taking more than ten items through the supermarket express line. His findings have revealed a surprising insight into just how common these occurrences are, how they can be used to chart the moral decline of society, and the relationship between them and female van drivers.

In 1993, Trinkaus and his team of researchers visited a large supermarket in the Northeast and secretly observed customers on seventy-five separate occasions for a period of fifteen minutes each.[12] They carefully counted how many people took more than the limit of ten items through the express line. To help ensure the scientific validity of their study, they observed shoppers at various times of the day over the course of several weeks, and recorded people's behavior only when more than two other lanes were open (and they therefore had the option of taking their goods through a correct checkout). The results revealed that around 85 percent of shoppers in the express lines were breaking the rules by having more than ten items in their wagons. In 2002, Trinkaus repeated the same experiment at the same supermarket, and discovered that the percentage of deceptive shoppers had risen to 93 percent.[13] Projected forward, these figures suggest that by 2011, no one in express lines will have ten items, or fewer, in their carts.

Trinkaus also noticed a new form of dubious behavior that had developed since his 1993 study. Several shoppers in the express line placed their items on the conveyor belt in groups of ten, and then told the cashier that they would pay for each group separately. One shopper managed to get twenty-nine items through the express line by using this sneaky approach. As soon as Trinkaus spotted this new form of deceptive behavior, he realized that it could be used as a potential way of identifying the types of people most likely to transgress societal norms. In line with his observational approach to research, Trinkaus asked his team to follow these people into the supermarket parking lot and make a note of their gender and the type of vehicle they owned. The result: About 80 percent of the transgressors were female van drivers.

This is not the first time that Trinkaus has uncovered evidence suggesting that female van drivers are especially likely to indulge in antisocial behavior. In 1999, he counted and classified the number of motorists speeding near a school, and noted that 96 percent of female van drivers exceeded the speed limit, compared to just 86 percent of male van drivers.[14] In the same year, he had also been counting the number of motorists who failed to come to a complete stop at stop signs.[15] In total, 94 percent of motorists failed to comply with the sign, versus 99 percent of female van drivers. In 2001, he spent thirty-two hours logging two hundred instances in which motorists had failed to keep a boxed intersection clear, and found that 40 percent of incidents involved, yes, you guessed it, women driving vans.[16] A year later, he counted instances of people parking their vehicles in a prohibited fire zone at a shopping center. Again, female van drivers were the least compliant, accounting for about 35 percent of all violations.

Trinkaus has put forward two explanations to account for this aspect of his data. First, he has speculated that "women Chevy drivers are inadvertently carrying over from the workplace the now 'in' concept of empowerment." According to this approach, women are still getting used to their newfound power in society, and may have developed an unconscious need to outdo behaviors previously associated with men, such as breaking speed limits, parking in restricted areas, and ignoring traffic signs. Alternatively, notes Trinkaus, these drivers may be ahead of the game when it comes to the moral decline of society, and are acting as an omen of things to come.

Testing the Honesty of a Nation

In 1997, *U.S. News and World Report* conducted a poll in which they asked Americans who was "somewhat likely" to go to heaven.[17] Bill Clinton didn't do too badly, with 52 percent of respondents thinking that he would be welcome at the pearly gates. Diana, Princess of Wales, fared a little better with 60 percent of the vote, and in second place came Mother Teresa with 79 percent. But who won the poll, scoring a massive 87 percent? Most people placed *themselves* on top of the heavenly A-list. Do we really live in communities and countries populated almost entirely by potential saints?

A few years ago, I was asked by the producers of a British television program called *World in Action* to help devise several tests that would examine the honesty of the nation. Rather than adopt Trinkaus's approach of observing people carrying out minor transgressions, we decided to be more proactive and focus on serious acts of selfishness. Many of the tests took place in the most innocent of places, and most of the participants are still completely unaware that they have taken part in a scientific study.

Imagine that you walk up to an ATM. You are just about to place your card in the machine, and out pops £10. Would you take the money and run, or would you return it to the bank?

The first experiment was designed to discover how a random sample of people would react to this situation. The producers obtained special permission to take over the ATM of a well-known British bank for the day. They had an engineer remove all the normal machinery and replace it with a device that dispensed £10 whenever people stood in front of the machine. Our first unsuspecting customer walked up to the machine, and, on cue, out popped £10. Secret cameras recorded her every move. The woman proved to be remarkably honest. She immediately took the money into the bank, handed it to the bemused cashier, and explained what had happened. But such honesty proved to be the exception rather than the rule. Two-thirds of the subjects kept the cash, some returning several times to make the most of the opportunity. Our most dishonest participant returned twenty times.

Why had so many people been prepared to take money that didn't belong to them? Perhaps the use of an ATM had skewed the data. People may consider it one thing to retain money given to them by a machine, but quite another to take it from another person. Then there was the fact that people thought they were taking money that belonged to a bank. Perhaps our unsuspecting participants saw the money emerging from the ATM as an opportunity to get even with an organization that is seen as making mistakes in its own favor only.

To test these ideas, the producers staged a second experiment. This time, people were given money by a person rather than a machine, and the faceless bank was replaced by a friendly shop.

Imagine that you buy a magazine in a shop, and pay with £5. To your surprise, the cashier gives you change for £10. Would you be honest enough to return the money?

To discover the level of public honesty in this scenario, the producers took over a branch of a national newsagent in the north of England and transformed it into a laboratory for the day. In the first part of the study, the cashier was instructed to give customers too much change. When a customer paid with £5, the cashier returned change for £10; and whenever a customer paid with £10, that person received change for £20. As our first unsuspecting customers entered the shop, the team waited to see whether they would be honest enough to own up to their unexpected windfall. Everyone took the money; many left the shop slyly smiling.

As with all research, it was important to rule out other ways of interpreting the results. Perhaps it wasn't that people had been dishonest but that (despite smiling) they hadn't noticed they had been given too much change. The study was repeated, but this time the cashier was asked to count the change aloud. The next set of customers entered the shop and the cashier carefully counted too much change into their hands. Those paying with £5 were given change for £10, and those handing over £10 received change for £20. All the customers took the money without saying a word.

To further emphasize the mistake, in a penultimate part of the experiment, the cashier was asked to count the excess change into the customer's hand, look slightly confused, and then ask the customer the value of the note he or she had used. Surely this time people would be honest enough to own up? Almost no one told the truth. Interestingly, the shoppers often didn't lie straight away but checked that the cashier had no way of knowing which denomination they had used ("Can't you look in the drawer?") before calling the situation in their favor. Only one person pointed out the cashier's error. In an interview afterward, he said that he was a Christian and that Jesus wouldn't have been pleased if he had held onto the cash. Try as they might, team members could not come up with a way of testing his claim.

In the final part of the study, one member of the team stood outside the shop and posed as a market researcher. When customers who had accepted too much change emerged from the shop, they were asked a few questions about honesty. Did they think journalists were honest? Could the Queen be trusted? Finally, the most important question of all: "If you were given too much change in a shop, would you own up and return the money?" Until the final question, everyone's answers were fast and clear. No, they didn't trust journalists. Yes, they thought the Queen was honest. Then people suddenly became evasive. Even though they had just committed the dishonest act in question, they produced much longer and vaguer answers: "I can't remember the last time that happened to me," "I don't usually look at my change," and "I never really check my change." People couldn't even bring themselves to be honest in an anonymous survey.

The findings presented a fascinating, but depressing, view of human nature. Unethical behavior was alive and well in modern-day Britain. Although the vast majority of people claim to be upstanding citizens, most of us are more than capable of dishonesty if the situation is right.

However, it was not all so disheartening. A third and final set of studies revealed that when it comes to being selfish or selfless, small and subtle changes make a big difference. The first stage of the newsagent experiment was repeated, but rather than a branch of a large chain of newsagents, the location chosen was a small corner shop. Like the cashier in the newsagents, the owner of the shop was asked systematically to give his customers too much change—if they paid with £5, they were given change for £10, and if they paid with £10, they were given change for £20. This time, the results were very different. Whereas before, everyone had taken the money and said nothing, now half of the people instantly returned the excess change. It appeared to be acceptable to take money from a large company but not from a small local shop. When interviewed afterward, many of the honest customers said that it simply wasn't right to steal from someone who was like them. Their comments provide support for one of the key theories that influences when we give and when we take. It is all to do with the psychology of similarity.

NIXON, HORN-HONKING, AND THE MAD MONK OF RUSSIA

Richard Nixon made several inadvertent contributions to psychology. In 1960, he took part in the first-ever televised presidential debate. Radio listeners thought that Nixon had won, but television viewers gave the verdict to John Kennedy. Why? Because Nixon had refused makeup beforehand and his face appeared pale, sweaty, and anxious throughout the debate. Researchers discovered that television viewers focused on what they saw rather than on what they heard, and so came to a decision opposite to that of radio listeners.[18] Then there is the famed "Nixon effect."[19] When giving his resignation speech after the Watergate scandal, Nixon appeared calm and collected. However, researchers analyzing his facial expressions noticed a "furious rate" of eye blinking (well more than fifty blinks per minute), suggesting extremely high levels of anxiety. Subsequent analyses of blink rates during eight televised presidential debates showed that the candidate who blinked the most frequently lost the forthcoming election in seven instances.[20]

Nixon's presidency also proved extremely helpful to researchers examining the psychology of altruism. His stance on Vietnam resulted in some of the largest peace demonstrations of the era. In April 1971, more than 200,000 protesters descended on Washington to stage a rally. The media focused on the possible impact of the event for international policy, but Peter Suedfield and his colleagues, psychologists from Rutgers University in New Jersey, saw it as an opportunity to carry out a secret study investigating similarity and helping.[21]

A few months before, the researchers had told an actor to grow his hair long and to cultivate a moustache. Toward the start of the rally, they gave him a "Dump Nixon" placard, and they ensured that he was, in the words of their subsequent paper, "attired in hip garb." A female experimenter led the actor into the crowd. At a predetermined moment, the actor suddenly sat on the ground and held his head in his hands, pretending to be sick. The experimenter then approached an unsuspecting genuine protester and started to work her way through a well-rehearsed script.

Initially, she asked the protester to assist her ailing friend. If the protester was willing to lend a helping hand, she then asked for help in moving her friend away from the crowd. Those who agreed were then asked to help take the friend to the nearest first-aid station. If the protester went along with that request, the actor would ask for help in making the seven-mile trip home. Finally, those protesters who indicated that they were prepared to make the trip were asked to provide the necessary bus fare. At this point, the allegedly ill actor made a sudden and unexpected recovery; the protester was thanked and told that his or her assistance was no longer necessary.

To discover the relationship between the help given and similarity, the experimenters repeated the study under a different set of circumstances. This time, the actor carried a "Support Nixon" sign, had short hair, didn't sport the moustache, and lost the "hip garb" in favor of more conservative clothing (a sports shirt, slacks, and loafers). The only thing that didn't change was the script—the experimenter and the actor went through exactly the same requests as before.

The two conditions yielded very different levels of help. When the actor looked like a peace protester, the peace protesters appeared to be Good Samaritans. Lots of them offered to help, with many going so far as to offer to finance the actor's bus journey home. Some protesters even offered to drive the actor themselves or, when the protester had no money or car, to accompany the actor on a seven-mile walk to his home. The situation was very different when the actor was clean-shaven and conservatively dressed. Suddenly, the kindly peace protestors were far less willing to help. The need for assistance was exactly the same, but now the actor was one of "the opposition."

The study illustrates a simple but powerful concept. We help people who are like us. Decades of experiments involving ketchup-covered students lying on the street asking for help have shown the same effect time and again. People are at their most altruistic when those in need are similar in age, background, and fashion sense. It all makes sense from an evolutionary viewpoint. People who look and behave like us are more likely than others to be genetically related to us, or at least from the same tribe, and so are seen as being more deserving of our goodwill.

My favorite experiment into this similarity effect, conducted by Joseph Forgas from Oxford University, examined the way different European drivers honked their car horns.[22] Forgas's idea combined the three elements that underlie many quirky ideas; it was brilliant, simple, and slightly strange. He had a man and woman drive around Germany, France, Spain, and Italy in a gray VW Beetle. They drove through various towns of roughly the same size, and tried their best to be at the front of traffic when the traffic lights showed red. As the lights turned green, much to the annoyance of the drivers behind them, they simply sat in the car. Actually, that is not quite true. They carefully noted down how the driver directly behind them used his or her horn, including the time elapsed before the first honk, and the duration of honking. This was dangerous work. In a similar experiment conducted a few years before, several motorists had taken out their frustration by ramming the experimenters' vehicles.[23] However, Forgas and his colleagues lived to tell the tale and, perhaps more important, analyze their data.

The Italians proved the most impatient, honking their horns, on average, after about five seconds. Next were the Spanish at about the six-second mark. The French came in at about seven seconds, and the Germans proved the most patient, at about seven and a half seconds.

In this initial part of the study, the experimenter had been keen to ensure that the motorists were not influenced by the nationality of the stationary drivers. For this reason, the Beetle carried a highly salient Australian insignia. According to the researchers, this "more or less satisfied the requirements of a generic 'foreign' car, representing a nation with a presumably neutral national stereotype." In a second stage of the study, the team sneakily swapped the Australian insignia for a German one, and repeated the procedure. This time, the Italians, Spanish, and French all honked their horns much sooner, the Italians holding off for just three seconds and the Spanish and French venting their anger at about the four-second mark. In Germany, however, the situation was quite different. Here, almost eight seconds passed before honking started. Something as simple as an insignia had instigated feelings of similarity, or dissimilarity, and had a significant impact on the time before drivers started to hit their horns.

Cars—and more specifically, bumper stickers—figured in another study that illustrated the important role that similarity plays in our lives. The summer of 1969 saw a series of bloody encounters between the police and the Black Panther Party, the African American civil rights organization. Frances Heussenstamm was teaching a psychology course at the California State College during this period, and many of her black students mentioned that they were receiving a large number of traffic citations. Heussenstamm noticed that all these students had bumper stickers supporting the Black Panthers on their cars, and she wondered whether the citations were the result of police prejudice or poor driving.[24]

Heussenstamm asked forty-five students with exemplary driving records to participate in an unusual experiment. The students were asked to put Panther Party bumper stickers on their vehicles. All the participants signed a statement saying that they would do nothing to attract the attention of the police, and their cars were carefully inspected and found to be in roadworthy condition. In addition, each morning the students made a pledge to drive safely. The first participant received a ticket for "incorrect lane change" within two hours of starting the experiment. The following day, five more participants received citations for minor offenses, such as "following too closely" and "driving too slowly." The participants paid their fines in person after receiving the citations, and one participant received his second citation on the way to paying his fine for the first one. Within three weeks, the group received a total of thirty-three citations, whereupon the experiment had to be terminated because Heussenstamm ran out of money to pay for the fines. Heussenstamm reports that when she announced the end of the study "the remaining drivers expressed relief and went straight to their cars to remove the stickers." Although the design of the study was far from perfect (Heussenstamm suggests that future work should involve a second group of participants driving around with the bumper sticker "America—Love It or Leave It"), the results illustrate how something as simple as a bumper sticker has a large impact on whether people help or hinder others, even when it is their job to be fair and impartial.

Jerry Burger, a professor at Santa Clara University in California, and his colleagues wondered whether people would take the similarity principle way too far. Could they, for example, be persuaded to help a stranger because the two of them shared a completely meaningless symbol of similarity—the same date of birth? Burger and his team had volunteers visit his laboratory on the pretense of taking part in an experiment on astrology.[25] The experimenter introduced the volunteer to a second participant (an actor working with the experimenter), and handed each a form. The front page of the form asked for various personal details, including name and date of birth. On 50 percent of occasions, when the genuine participant completed his or her date of birth, the actor surreptitiously noted it and then filled in the same date on his own form. For the other 50 percent, the actor deliberately wrote in a different date.

The experimenter then asked "volunteers" to read their dates of birth out loud to ensure that they were given the correct horoscope to assess. Half the participants discovered an amazing coincidence—they shared the same birthday with the other person! (The other half of the participants, of course, found out that the two of them were born on different days.) The participant and actor rated the accuracy of their respective horoscopes and then left the laboratory. The volunteer thought that the experiment was over. In fact, it was just about to begin.

As the two walked along the hallway, the actor pulled a four-page essay from a book-bag and asked the volunteer whether he or she would mind carefully reading it and then writing a critique about how convincing the arguments were. Would those volunteers who believed that they shared a birthday with the actor be more accommodating than those who didn't? About a third of people who thought they did not share a birthday with the actor agreed to help. In the "Wow, we have the same birthday, what a coincidence" group, almost two-thirds agreed. The simple belief in a shared birthday was enough to persuade people to donate a considerable chunk of their valuable time to a complete stranger.

John Finch and Robert Cialdini have even shown that the same effect causes people to turn a blind eye to other people's crimes and misdemeanors.[26] In their study, participants read a biographical sketch describing the terrible crimes committed by Rasputin, the "Mad Monk of Russia," and then rated the degree to which they thought Rasputin sounded like a nice fellow. Unbeknownst to the participants, the experimenters had found out their dates of birth beforehand and had manipulated the text seen by half the volunteers to make sure that Rasputin's date of birth matched their own. When participants thought they shared a birthday with the mad monk, they were prepared to overlook his wrongdoings and evil deeds, and they found him significantly more likeable.

TOM DESMOND, DONATION BOXES, AND *MEDICAL CENTER*

Chapter 3 described how Stanley Milgram's innovative experiments into the "small-world" phenomenon helped explain why people frequently encounter friends of friends. When not conducting these giant games of pass the parcel, Milgram also carried out a considerable amount of research into the psychology of prosocial and antisocial behavior.[27] In the late 1960s, he turned his attention to one of the hottest questions: When it comes to hurting or helping others, to what extent is our behavior influenced by television? In short, do the programs we watch create the society in which we live?

The results of several surveys into the amount of violence on television had emphasized the need for this work. In 1971, one researcher found that violent incidents were shown on prime-time networks at the rate of eight times an hour. Another survey, conducted a few years later, found that children's programming was "saturated with violence" and that 71 percent of shows contained at least one violent act.[28] Times haven't changed. One recent survey estimated that by the time children leave primary schoo,l they will have witnessed an average of 8,000 murders and more than 100,000 acts of other violence on television.[29]

Previous work on the topic had involved small-scale, laboratory-based studies in which experimenters showed children violent cartoons and then carefully counted the number of times the youngsters punched a large inflatable figure that just happened to be behind them. Milgram was determined to carry out a highly realistic piece of mass-participation research examining the possible impact of television on the American nation.

Funded by a large grant from CBS, Milgram persuaded television scriptwriters to pen different endings to an episode of a hugely popular prime-time drama series called *Medical Center* (apparently *Mission Impossible* was considered but rejected because, according to Milgram, it "regularly depicts such a degree of violence that our experimental act would appear trivial by comparison"). During the episode, a hospital orderly named Tom Desmond lost his job and so could not care for his sick wife and child. In one of the alternative endings, Desmond smashed open several fund-raising collection boxes, stole the money they contained, but he was *not* caught by the police. In another version, he stole the money but he *was* caught. As a control, the experimenters used a "neutral" episode of the series that was, according to Milgram, "romantic, sentimental, and entirely devoid of any violence or antisocial behavior." Vincent Sherman, a well-known movie director who had made several successful films with Bette Davis and Errol Flynn, was employed to help make the versions of the episode.

CBS broadcast the three episodes at different times throughout April 1971. Milgram had devised an elaborate, and ingenious, way of assessing the impact of the different programs on people's behavior. Prior to the broadcasts, he mailed letters to thousands of people in New York City and St. Louis stating that they had been selected to take part in a market survey; the participants were asked to watch an episode of *Medical Center* at a designated time. They were then invited to complete a simple questionnaire about the characters in the episode and the commercials shown during the show's breaks. Respondents were told that after the broadcasts they could claim a new radio in return for their participation and were directed to pick it up from a downtown "gift distribution center."

The so-called gift distribution centers were actually fake warehouses staffed with actors and fitted with hidden cameras. When viewers arrived, they walked into an empty office and encountered this notice:

> We have no more transistor radios to distribute.
> This distribution center is closed until further notice.

This apparent lack of radios, combined with the brusque wording of the notice, was designed to elicit a sense of frustration in participants. The same room also contained a charity gift box on one of the walls. The box was overflowing with cash and would have proved a temptation to anyone of dishonest intent. The experimenters had even carefully placed a one-dollar bill dangling from the box to tempt those unwilling actually to break it open. This clever setup allowed Milgram to discover whether those who had seen Desmond steal from the charity box during the television program were more likely to engage in criminal behavior. After a few moments, the participants tried to retrace their steps and leave the building. It was then they discovered that the door that they had used to enter the office was locked, and they thus had to follow a series of exit signs. These signs led the participants into a small room in which they were met by a clerk who explained that the promised radios *were* available and gave the participants their gifts.

Almost 1,000 people came to the distribution centers. In New York City, CBS broadcast the neutral episode of *Medical Center* and the episode in which Tom stole from the charity box and was caught by the police. Nine percent of the people who had seen the *neutral* program took the dangling dollar or broke open the charity box. Did watching Tom steal money and receive punishment for his crimes increase the likelihood of theft? In fact, it seemed to make people slightly more honest, since only about 4 percent of people took the dollar or broke into the box. In St. Louis, CBS broadcast the neutral episode and the episode in which Tom's crimes went unpunished. Only about 2 percent of people who saw the neutral program behaved in a dishonest way, compared to 3 percent of those who had seen Tom steal the money and get away with his crime.

Worried that any potential effect might have been diluted by the relatively long delay between the time people watched the programs and when they arrived at the gift distribution centers, Milgram repeated the experiment but this time eliminated the delay. In this new study, people in New York's Times Square area were offered a "Free Ticket for a Color Television Preview." Those accepting the offer were taken to a room in a nearby building containing just a television set, a chair, and the charity box. Participants were left alone to watch one of the specially filmed episodes of *Medical Center;* they were then secretly observed to see whether they removed money from the charity box. The experiment was not a success. Most of the people accepting the free tickets turned out to be alcoholics, drug addicts, or homeless (several asked whether they were allowed to sleep in the laboratory), and the subsequent levels of antisocial behavior, including urinating on floors and threats to staff, forced the early closure of the experiment. As far as I am aware, this is the only time an experiment examining the psychology of antisocial behavior has been terminated because of antisocial behavior.

Milgram's highly elaborate, expensive, and extensive studies revealed that the television programs had little, if any, impact on public behavior. The findings caused controversy; some argued that they represented conclusive evidence against legislation to control television programming; others criticized Milgram's methods and said the findings promoted the case for censorship.

This mass-participation television experiment was not Milgram's only sojourn into the world of antisocial and prosocial behavior. His other contribution had a much larger impact, and it involved devising a method that is still used by psychologists around the globe. The idea, which was simplicity itself, concerned the innocent act of inadvertently dropping an envelope on the street.[30]

Envelope Dropping, and the Friends of the Nazi Party

In 1963, Milgram and his research assistants secretly wandered around ten districts in New Haven, Connecticut, dropping three hundred envelopes in phone booths, on pavements, and inside shops. The first line of the address on the envelopes read either "Friends of the Nazi Party," "Friends of the Communist Party," or "Medical Research Associates." The remaining address lines on all of the envelopes were identical—a post office box in Connecticut. Milgram figured that people would be far more likely to pick up the envelopes and put them in a mailbox if they felt some level of support for the organization listed in the address. Milgram was right. About 70 percent of the envelopes addressed to the "Medical Research Associates" were returned, compared to just 25 percent of those addressed to either "Friends of the Nazi Party" or "Friends of the Communist Party."

These findings demonstrated that this simple technique could be used to gauge public opinion without ever having to ask people a single question. It was a clever way to find out what people actually thought about an issue, rather than relying on notoriously unreliable surveys and opinion polls.

The technique was not, however, without its problems. Milgram was concerned that scattering so many envelopes addressed to organizations associated with Communists and Nazis might arouse suspicion among both the public and the police. In an attempt to avoid such unwanted and unnecessary attention, he contacted the FBI prior to the study and informed them about the research. It was to little avail. When Milgram telephoned back after the experiment, the FBI agent said that he couldn't remember Milgram's original call; he also hinted that a significant number of agents were now involved in the case. The feds were not the only problem. Milgram also reported that researchers often complained of aching feet after walking the considerable distances needed to ensure a satisfactory distribution of envelopes. The situation was made worse by "helpful" passersby frequently spotting an envelope immediately after it had been dropped, picking it up, and handing it back to an experimenter.

The technique was, however, sufficiently promising for Milgram to devise and test various ways of overcoming these problems. In one instance, he tried distributing the envelopes from a moving car. To avoid arousing suspicion, this had to happen at night, but the envelopes frequently landed face down in unintended, and inappropriate, places. Undeterred, on another occasion Milgram hired a light aircraft and dropped hundreds of envelopes over Worcester, Massachusetts. Again, the method proved unsuccessful. Many of the envelopes became stuck in trees or landed on rooftops. Worse still, others were swept into the aircraft's wing flaps, endangering the safety of both the pilot and the researcher.

Despite these setbacks, Milgram was to employ the envelope-dropping procedure in several additional studies. In one, he measured the levels of racial prejudice in predominately white and black neighborhoods in North Carolina. In another, the technique was successfully used to predict the outcome of the 1964 presidential election race between Barry Goldwater and Lyndon B. Johnson (albeit dramatically underestimating the margin of Johnson's subsequent victory). Milgram also attempted to export the technique to the Far East to investigate the percentage of pro-Mao and pro-Nationalist people living in Hong Kong, Singapore, and Bangkok. Unfortunately, this ambitious project was besieged by unforeseen problems. The experimenter Milgram sent to conduct the study in Singapore was placed on a return plane immediately after arriving in the country because of widespread rioting, and the researcher hired in Hong Kong promptly absconded with Milgram's research funds.

The technique is still used by social psychologists today, and it has been employed to examine public opinion about a diverse range of issues, including Bill Clinton's impeachment,[31] gay and lesbian issues, abortion, Arab-Israeli relationships,[32] and the attitudes of Catholics and Protestants toward one another in Northern Ireland. In 1999, a student named Lucas Hanft carried out one of the largest studies, dropping 1,600 letters addressed to various fictitious organizations in Manhattan and Nassau County that were for and against gay marriage. The results revealed that those living in the city were more liberal than suburbanites. Hanft also experienced many of the same types of problems encountered by Milgram, including, for example, being threatened with arrest for littering.

Over the years, psychologists have employed a modified version of the envelope-dropping technique to measure levels of altruism in different communities and countries. The results of these subsequent studies have helped identify who helps, and when. Some of the most intriguing experiments have investigated a group of people who are often perceived as highly helpful: the deeply religious.

THE PARABLE OF THE GOOD SAMARITAN, AND OTHER RELIGIOUS MYTHS

Results from work examining religion and altruism suggest that, in general, religious people often give to those in need.[33] However, some of the more quirky research into the subject has questioned whether such altruism is always present.

In the 1970s, Gordon Forbes and his colleagues, psychologists from Millikin University in Illinois, wanted to discover which religious groups were the most, and least, helpful.[34] There seemed little point in simply asking different sets of churchgoers whether they were good people because everyone was likely to say yes. Instead, the researchers asked a knowledgeable theologian to identify the ten most liberal and ten most conservative churches in the region. During Sunday services at these churches, the experimenters tiptoed around the outside of the building and dropped letters in doorways and parking lots. They then repeated the procedure at local Catholic churches during mass.

The letters were all sealed and unstamped, and they were addressed to local residents "Mr. and Mrs. Fred Guthrie." Rather sneakily, the experimenters had made sure that letters dropped in the liberal, conservative, and Catholic churches, respectively, could be identified on the basis of Fred's alleged middle initial. Roughly 40 percent of letters were returned from each of the three types of church. None of the letters bore a stamp, and thus people picking up the letters faced a choice. They could either place a stamp on the letter and drop it in a mailbox or send it postage due. The Catholics and liberals came out of the study looking most generous, placing stamps on 89 percent and 87 percent of the envelopes, respectively. However, only 42 percent of those at the conservative churches were prepared to indulge in this act of kindness, the remaining being returned postage due. As noted by the authors: "These findings suggest that members of conservative churches are as willing to help strangers as are members of liberal or Catholic churches; yet they are far less willing to spend a few cents to do so."

Other researchers have also questioned the altruistic intentions of those claiming to be highly religious. In 1973, Princeton psychologists John Darley and C. Daniel Batson reported a remarkable study on religion and helping.[35] At the beginning of their experiment, a group of trainee ministers at one of the world's leading institutions for theological education were asked to prepare sermons based on the parable of the Good Samaritan. According to this well-known biblical story, a man is beaten up by thieves and left lying in the street. Various priests come across the man, but walk by. Eventually, a Good Samaritan goes out of his way to provide assistance, and the parable ends by urging others to help those in need. After they had made their preparations, the trainee ministers were told that their sermons would be filmed in another building, were given directions to the new location, and sent on their way. Although they didn't realize it, every step of their journey was being secretly observed by the experimenters.

On the short trip between the two buildings, each participant came across a man (an actor) who was in need of assistance. He was slumped against a doorway, his head down and eyes closed. As each participant walked past, the actor gave a well-rehearsed groan and two coughs. The experimenters wanted to know whether the trainee ministers would practice what they preached and help the man. Even though they were on their way to deliver a sermon about the importance of being a Good Samaritan, more than half the participants walked straight past the man. Some of them actually stepped *over* him. In a slightly modified version of the study, the experimenters told another group of trainee ministers that they needed to get to the second building as soon as possible. Under these circumstances, the level of helping dropped to just 10 percent. The experiment reveals a great deal about human nature, including the dramatic difference between people's words and actions, and how a fast pace of life can help create an uncaring culture.

Earlier in this chapter, I described a series of studies, conducted by the *World in Action* program, examining the honesty of the nation. The producers also carried out a study comparing the honesty of two groups of the most, and least, trusted people in society: priests and used-car dealers. According to the results of a recent Gallup poll, 59 percent of people rate the clergy as honest, versus only 5 percent for car salesmen. But do these beliefs really reflect honesty? To find out, the team members set up a fictitious furniture company called "Honesty," and then they sent a group of priests and used-car dealers a letter from our newly formed organization. The letter thanked them for their recent purchase; it also contained a check for about £10 as a refund. All the recipients would have known that they hadn't bought anything from the company, but how many of them would be dishonest enough to cash the check? There was very little difference between the two groups, with both the priests and car dealers cashing about 50 percent of the checks.

City Living

A slight variant of Milgram's envelope-dropping technique has also been used by Robert Levine, from California State University, to assess kindness across the world.

Levine's initial work investigated whether people helped or not in thirty-six major cities across the United States.[36] Instead of dropping envelopes in the street, Levine and his team placed stamped, addressed envelopes on the windshields of randomly selected cars parked in shopping centers; they also left a neat handwritten note: "I found this next to your car." They wanted to find out how many of the letters would be returned from each area. This test of helping was supplemented by several others. As experimenters walked in front of randomly selected people, they dropped pens and then counted how many people picked them up and returned them. A concealed experimenter observed the response of the public as a perfectly healthy experimenter who had donned a large leg brace stood on the street and struggled to pick up a pile of magazines that he had dropped. The same experimenter also put on dark glasses, held a white cane, and took note of how many passersby helped him cross a busy street.

Levine invested a great deal of time and effort in making these tests as scientific as possible. In the pen-dropping task, for instance, researchers made sure that they were able to walk consistently at a standard speed (1.5 paces per second) toward someone moving in the opposite direction; they also rehearsed naturally reaching into a pocket and, without appearing to notice, dropping a pen. When pretending to be blind, the researchers located themselves on street corners that had "crosswalks, traffic signals and moderate, steady pedestrian flow." Stepping up to the corner when the lights turned green, the experimenters secretly timed how long it was before someone helped them cross the street.

Overall, they found that people in small towns in the Southeast were the most helpful, whereas those living in large towns in the Northeast were least likely to assist. Top of the "helping" list came Rochester, New York; Houston, Texas, was a close second; Nashville, Tennessee, third; and Memphis, Tennessee, fourth. The least helpful in the United States can be found in Patterson, New Jersey, and the second- and third-lowest positions go to New York and Los Angeles, respectively.

The results from the lost-letter test proved especially interesting. In New York, the letters were sometimes returned with angry and abusive comments scrawled on them. As Levine notes when describing the experiment in his book *The Geography of Time:* "Only from New York did I receive an envelope which had its entire side ripped and left open. On the back of the letter the helper had scribbled, in Spanish: '*Hijo de puta iresposable*'—which, translated, makes a very nasty accusation about my mother. Below that was a straightforward English-language 'F____ You.'"

In Rochester it was different. One anonymous Good Samaritan wrote a very pleasant note to accompany the lost letter, adding a postscript that is reminiscent of Milgram's original work into small worlds. The envelope asked Levine: "Are you related to any Levines in New Jersey or Long Island?"

Flushed by the success of their national study, Levine and his colleagues decided to go global.[37] They traveled the world, visiting capital cities in twenty-three countries. They dropped more than four hundred pens, donned the leg braces more than five hundred times, and lost about eight hundred letters. The lost-letter technique proved a cross-cultural nightmare. In Tel Aviv, packages and letters lying on the ground, or placed on car windshields, are often associated with bombs, and so were given a wide berth by almost everyone. In El Salvador, they generated suspicion because they often form part of a well-known scam in which, as soon as someone picks up the letter, a man approaches and claims that the letter is his, that it contains some money, that the money is now missing, and so would the finder like to hand over his or her own hard-earned cash? Some other countries had no mailboxes or, as in Albania, no reliable postal system. However, despite the difficulties, the researchers persevered and eventually produced the international helping poll.

It proved to be good news for Latin America, with Rio de Janeiro (Brazil) and San Jose (Costa Rica) heading the list of highly helpful countries. Lilongwe (Malawi) in Africa came in third. Singapore (Singapore), New York (United States), and Kuala Lumpur (Malaysia) filled the bottom three places. The differences were far from trivial. In Rio de Janeiro and Lilongwe, "blind" experimenters were helped across the street on every occasion, whereas in Singapore and Kuala Lumpur they encountered only a 50 percent success rate. In San Jose, 95 percent of people helped the experimenter sporting a leg brace to pick up the dropped magazines. In New York, the figure fell to just 28 percent.

Looking deeper into his data on helping in U.S. cities, Levine and his colleagues discovered that population density provided one of the best predictors of helping. Why should higher-population densities lead to less helping? According to one theory, developed by Milgram, people in high-population cities tend to experience a greater amount of "sensory overload."[38] They are constantly being bombarded with information from other people, their cell phones, traffic, and advertising. As a result, they do what all systems tend to do when receiving too much information—they set priorities, and they spend less time dealing with the sources competing for their attention. Milgram believed that situations are created in which people will walk past those in need of help, thus diverting onto others the responsibility to assist such individuals. All this creates a paradox: The greater the number of people occupying a space, the greater the sense of loneliness and isolation.

But Levine wasn't just curious about the relationship between the size of a city and the help that citizens provided. He wondered whether helping or not is also determined by the speed of life in the city.

MEASURING THE PACE OF LIFE

Eager to put numbers to these seemingly elusive factors, Levine and his coworkers visited thirty-one countries and took three indicators of the speed of life.[39]

He measured the average walking speed of randomly selected pedestrians over a sixty-foot stretch of pavement, visited post offices and secretly timed how long it took them to serve a customer buying a single stamp, and took note of the accuracy of the clocks in fifteen randomly selected downtown banks.

The work was highly methodical. When measuring walking speed, the investigators ensured that all the locations were flat, free from obstruction, and not especially crowded. Children, those with obvious physical disabilities, and window-shoppers were excluded from the analyses. When timing the speed of service in post offices, the experimenters handed clerks a note written in the native language to help minimize potential cross-cultural confusion. Analyses showed that the three measures were all related to one another, suggesting that they did indeed provide an indicator of a city's speed of life.

Levine combined the different indicators into a single measure of speed. The results revealed that Switzerland has the fastest pace of life in the world (Swiss bank clocks showed a discrepancy of just nineteen seconds); Ireland was second and Germany third. Interestingly, eight of the nine fastest countries were from Western Europe (Japan broke the total domination of the poll positions by coming in fourth). England was fifth, and had the fourth-highest walking speed of the entire list. The only Western European country involved in the study not to make it into the top ten was France (it came in eleventh, just behind Hong Kong), a result that Levine attributes to the measurements being taken at a time when the country was experiencing one of its hottest summers on record. The three slowest countries were Brazil, Indonesia, and Mexico. The bottom eight positions were all held by countries in Africa, Asia, the Middle East, and Latin America. Within the United States, Boston proved to be the speediest (just beating New York to poll position), and Los Angeles the most laid back. The study also revealed more evidence of New Yorkers' rudeness: It was only one of two cities where the experimenters were insulted by postal clerks (the other was Budapest).

Levine found some evidence that cities with a slower pace of life are more helpful. As predicted by Milgram's "sensory overload" theory, the more people rush around, the less time they have to devote to factors that are peripheral to their main goals.

This is not the only downside of living in a fast-paced society. In the late 1980s, Levine and his team visited thirty-six cities across the United States to compare the pace of life with the city's rate of death from coronary heart disease.[40] The hypothesis was simple. People living in faster-paced cities were more likely to resemble the so-called Type A personality. This cluster of traits places great emphasis on urgency, competitiveness, and a general rushing around trying to achieve a great deal in very little time. Type A's tend to talk fast and to complete other people's sentences for them. They are often the first to finish at the dinner table, and they glance at their watches more frequently than most. Some researchers believe that this mode of living places a large number of stresses and strains on the body. Levine's work showed that cities living life in the fast lane had higher numbers of smokers and increased rates of coronary heart disease. Further analyses showed that the speed of walking, and the percentage of people wearing watches in each city, were especially good predictors of the problem. Why is there such an unhealthy relationship between these factors? Perhaps Type A's are attracted to fast-paced cities. Perhaps living in such speedy places causes people to become Type A's. Perhaps it is a combination of the two. Whatever the explanation, the message is clear: In addition to making people less helpful to others, speed kills.

ALL TOGETHER NOW

Levine's global measures of magazine, pen, and letter dropping suggest that population density and speed of life are not the only factors that influence levels of helping. Do you care about others or are you out for yourself? Some psychologists believe that the way in which people answer this question is, to a large extent, culturally determined. Some communities and countries have adopted a set of values that researchers refer to as "individualism." These societies stress the needs and rights of the individual and place less emphasis on rewarding activities that benefit groups of people. At the other end of the spectrum is the collectivist approach, in which people view themselves as part of a larger group (be it family, organization, or an entire society), and tend to reward behavior that is for the greater good. Levine's results contain tentative evidence that highly individualistic societies (such as the United States, Britain, and Switzerland) are less caring than collectives (such as Indonesia, Syria, and China). Other work suggests that the effect starts in our early years. When researchers asked four-year-old children to make up stories about their dolls, the narratives produced by Indonesian children included more friendly and helpful characters than those created by children from the United States, Germany, and Sweden.[41]

One of the most dramatic studies demonstrating the impact of living in a caring community was conducted by the social psychologist Philip Zimbardo.[42] Like Stanley Milgram (who carried out the work into obedience, small worlds, envelope dropping, and television violence), Zimbardo's experiments have stood the test of time. He is perhaps best known for his now infamous "prison" study. During this experiment, college students randomly assigned to the role of guards in a mock prison behaved in a highly sadistic way toward fellow students assigned the role of prisoners. Such high-profile research is not the only link between Zimbardo and Milgram. As children, they both attended James Monroe High School in the Bronx, New York, and at one stage even sat next to one another in several classes.[43] Also, like Milgram, Zimbardo was interested in the psychology of helping.

His most striking contribution to the area examined the effects of community on antisocial behavior. Zimbardo secretly filmed what happened when he left a used car unlocked with its hood up on a street opposite New York University. After just ten minutes, a passing car stopped and a family got out. The mother quickly removed items of value from the interior of the car, the father removed the radiator with a hacksaw, and their child rooted through the trunk. About fifteen minutes later, another two men jacked up the car and removed its tires. Over the next few hours, other people stripped the vehicle until nothing of value remained. In just two days, Zimbardo secretly filmed more than twenty instances of destruction (mostly committed by middle-class white adults in broad daylight), and the resulting carnage was so bad that two trucks were required to remove the wrecked car from the street.

Zimbardo then left a similar car (again with its hood raised) in a location that had a much greater sense of community—opposite Stanford University in Palo Alto, California. In stark contrast to the events that took place in New York City, not one instance of vandalism was recorded over the course of a week. When it started to rain, one passerby lowered the car's hood to protect the motor. When Zimbardo eventually went to remove the car, three people called the police to report that an abandoned car was being stolen.

How does one create a sense of social responsibility? How do you stop people from thinking about only their own needs and concerns and encourage them to move toward seeing themselves as part of a larger community? The good news is that work conducted by Jonathan Freedman and Scott Fraser, Stanford University psychologists, suggests that it doesn't take much.[44]

In the first part of their study, a researcher posed as a volunteer worker. They went from door to door in a residential Californian neighborhood and asked people whether they would mind placing a sign in their gardens to help cut speeding in the area. There was just one small problem: It was a very big sign that would completely ruin the look of the person's house and garden. To make the point as vividly as possible, the researcher showed residents a photograph of the large, poorly written sign, which said "DRIVE CAREFULLY," on someone's lawn. It completely dominated the surroundings, concealed much of the front of the house, and completely blocked the doorway. Not surprisingly, few residents took up the offer.

In stage two of the experiment, the researcher approached a second set of residents and asked almost exactly the same question. However, this time the sign was much, much smaller. It was just three inches square and said "BE A SAFE DRIVER." It was a small request and almost everyone accepted. Two weeks later, the researcher returned and now asked them to display the larger sign. This time, 76 percent of people agreed to display the large ugly placard.

Why the dramatic change? Freedman and Fraser believe that agreeing to accept the first small sign had a dramatic effect on how residents saw themselves. Suddenly, they were the type of people who helped out. They were good citizens, people who were prepared to make sacrifices for the greater good. So, when it came to making a decision about the big, horrible sign, they were much more likely to say yes. It is a striking example of how to create cooperation. Get people to agree to the small, and it is much easier to persuade them not to worry about the big.

7 The Pace of Life and Other Quirkological Oddities

The Future of Quirkology

The potential for quirky psychology surrounds us. Take, for example, the simple act of giving a greetings card. To the uninformed eye, it may appear as if one person were sending a simple message of thanks or celebration to another. In reality, however, there is a great deal of psychology underlying the event. The very act of choosing the card says a great deal about your personality. How do I know this? Because I recently teamed up once again with Roger Highfield, the science editor at the *Daily Telegraph,* to conduct the first experiment into what people's choice of greetings card reveals about their personality.

The experiment was conducted toward the end of 2006, and it focused on Christmas cards. More than a thousand members of the public completed a standard personality test, looked at six types of Christmas card—modern, traditional, religious, humorous, cute, and abstract—and checked off the type of card they tended to send. We discovered large relationships between personality and card type (see box). For example, people who are drawn to modern designs tend to be extraverted, easily upset, and highly unconventional. In contrast, those who prefer religious cards are more emotionally stable, sympathetic, and well organized. A very different personality profile emerged for each of the six card types, and many of the findings supported existing theories linking personality and brain functioning. For example, extroverts were drawn to relatively striking modern designs and also to humorous cards, but introverts preferred more sedate-looking traditional cards. Why should this be? Research suggests that each person's brain has a different preset level of arousal, much as a television set has a preset volume when you switch it on. Introverts have a high preset level of arousal, and, as a result, tend to avoid situations that further arouse their already stimulated brains. Because of this, they prefer a quiet evening in with a good book to a night out on the town; they find themselves drawn to Christmas cards showing relaxing traditional scenes because these cards are not overstimulating. The opposite is true of extroverts. Since their brains have a much lower preset level of arousal, they need the continuous stimulation that being with other people gives them; their preferences in Christmas card designs are likely to be the bright and the modern as well as those that make them laugh.

We also discovered that women send about twice as many Christmas cards as men. This pattern could be explained in various ways. Men who didn't send cards scored low on a personality dimension known as "agreeableness"—a measure of the degree to which people are critical of others—and thus might not send cards because they are less bothered about making potential recipients feel good. There again, the data also revealed that

What Does Your Choice of Greeting Card Reveal About Your Personality?

Modern: Extraverted and enthusiastic about life, although somewhat anxious and easily upset, with a tendency to be more creative and unconventional than most.

Humorous: Outgoing and emotionally secure, but with a distinct lack of warmth and sympathy for others.

Traditional: People who prefer reading a good book to a night out on the town, with a tendency to experience extremes of emotions and to follow the rules.

Abstract: Tendency to be disorganized and spontaneous, to be high strung, and to have a low need to surround themselves with others.

Cute: Sympathetic, calm, and open to new experiences, with a tendency to prefer one's own company to others.

Religious: Emotionally stable, sympathetic to the needs of others, and well organized.

women who sent a large number of cards were highly conventional, a result suggesting that excessive card sending might not reflect a genuine concern for others but rather a need to comply with societal norms. The data also helped explain why men and women often fail to impress one another with the cards they choose. They have very different tastes; for example, 30 percent of women like modern cards versus only 16 percent of men, and only 14 percent of women like humorous cards compared to 32 percent of men.

The experiment demonstrates the complex science lurking beneath the seemingly simplest of traditions. These exciting findings have motivated me to continue researching the topic. Next year, for example, I hope to place Santa Claus on the couch and explore the childhood experiences that cause him to feel the need to spend one night of the year rewarding good behavior around the world.

My investigation into the psychology of greeting cards is part of an ongoing program of unusual research. Some of the experiments are conducted online, and others are carried out in everyday settings. Some are small-scale affairs, others are more significant undertakings. My latest, and largest, study involved coordinating teams of researchers all over the world and having them secretly observe hundreds of people as they carried out perhaps the most mundane aspect of everyday behavior—walking down the street.

At the beginning of this book, I described my first quirkology experiment. Conducted in 1985, the study involved approaching people in a railroad station with a hidden stopwatch and having them judge how many seconds had passed since I had introduced myself. Twenty-one years later, I have just carried out my latest piece of research. Like my railroad station experiment, this study also involved unsuspecting passersby and a secret stopwatch. Unlike my earliest work, this was no small-scale affair.

At 1:00 P.M. on August 22, 2006, I found myself standing outside the General Post Office in the center of Dublin. The building's magnificent façade has six large stone columns. As I carefully trundled a surveyor's wheel along the pavement, I discovered that the first and fifth column were exactly sixty feet apart. Leaning against the fifth column, I pretended to be just another tourist enjoying the summer sun. In reality, I had a stopwatch hidden in my left hand and was secretly observing people as they walked in front of the building. I was on the lookout for lone pedestrians. Whenever a person walked past the first pillar, I hit the "start" button on the stopwatch. A few seconds, and exactly sixty feet later, they would pass me, and I stopped the clock. I then furtively glanced at the stopwatch and wrote down the time in the battered notebook that has accompanied me on most of my field trips. Ireland wasn't the only focus of this strange activity that day: Researchers were making exactly the same measurements in thirty-two other countries.

The British Council has offices worldwide, each of which promotes Britain abroad through the arts, education, science, technology, and sporting events. In late 2005, I suggested that we join forces to stage a large-scale cross-cultural experiment examining the pace of life across the globe. Following from Robert Levine's innovative research into the topic (described in chapter 6), we aimed to measure worldwide walking speeds in the twenty-first century, and, by comparing the results with Levine's data from the early 1990s, to discover whether people are moving faster than ever before.

On the same day that I was in Dublin, our research teams around the globe ventured into city centers armed with stopwatches, measuring tape, paper, and pens.[1] Following in the footsteps of Levine, they found a busy street with a wide pavement that was flat, free from obstacles, and sufficiently uncrowded to allow people to walk along at their maximum speeds. Between 11:30 A.M. and 2:00 P.M. local time, they timed how long it took thirty-five men and thirty-five women to walk along a sixty-foot stretch of the pavement. They monitored only unaccompanied adults and ignored anyone talking on a cell phone or struggling with shopping bags.

From Paris to Prague, Singapore to Stockholm, the researchers measured the pace of life in major cities across thirty-two countries. The survey covered many of the cities documented by Levine and several not included in his 1994 study. The overall rankings for the different cities, and countries, are shown in table 1 below.[2]

On the same day, we also sent out teams to each of the capital cities within the United Kingdom. Londoners were moving the fastest, taking an average of 12.17 seconds to cover sixty feet. Next were people in Belfast, who covered the same distance in 12.98 seconds. Third place went to Edinburgh, with an average of 13.29 seconds, and the slowest walkers were found in Cardiff, who clocked up an average time of 16.81 seconds. These differences may seem small, but they all add up. It would take Londoners approximately eleven days of continuous walking to cover the 874 miles from Lands End to John O'Groats, but people from Cardiff would take almost fifteen days to make the same journey.

By comparing the sixteen cities that were in Levine's work and our own, we were able to determine whether the pace of life was increasing. I had traveled to Ireland because in Levine's survey Dubliners proved to be the fastest, covering the sixty-foot distance in an average of 11.13 seconds. In 2006, the situation was roughly the same, with my results showing an average of 11.03 seconds. This pattern was repeated for a few of the other cities toward the top of Levine's table, including Tokyo, New York, London, and Paris. But what about the slower cities in Levine's list? In 1994, people in Bucharest took an average of 16.72 seconds, but in 2006 they completed the distance in an average of 14.36. People in Vienna were now going 2 seconds faster, with their original average time of 14.08 seconds cut to 12.06. The same pattern emerged in Sofia, Prague, Warsaw, and Stockholm. The biggest changes were

RANK	CITY	COUNTRY
1 *(fastest)*	Singapore	Singapore
2	Copenhagen	Denmark
3	Madrid	Spain
4	Guangzhou	China
5	Dublin	Ireland
6	Curitiba	Brazil
7	Berlin	Germany
8	New York	United States of America
9	Utrecht	Netherlands
10	Vienna	Austria
11	Warsaw	Poland
12	London	United Kingdom
13	Zagreb	Croatia
14	Prague	Czech Republic
15	Wellington	New Zealand
16	Paris	France
17	Stockholm	Sweden
18	Ljubljana	Slovenia
19	Tokyo	Japan
20	Ottawa	Canada
21	Harare	Zimbabwe
22	Sofia	Bulgaria
23	Taipei	Taiwan
24	Cairo	Egypt
25	Sana'a	Yemen
26	Bucharest	Romania
27	Dubai	United Arab Emirates
28	Damascus	Syria
29	Amman	Jordan
30	Bern	Switzerland
31	Manama	Bahrain
32	Blantyre	Malawi

Table 1 The 32 Countries in the "Pace of Life" Experiment Ranked by Their Speed of Walking.

found in Guangzhou and Singapore, where people in both cities now take, on average, 4 seconds less to walk 60 feet than in the early 1990s, suggesting that the pace of life there is increasing around four times faster than in many parts of the world. In the early 1990s, the overall average walking speed in the sixteen countries was 13.76 seconds. In 2006, this figure had fallen to 12.49 seconds. Our global walking experiment suggested that people around the world are indeed moving faster than ever.

This increase has taken about ten years. Projected forward, the results suggest that by 2021 people will be covering the same distance in almost no time at all. By 2040, they will arrive at their destinations several seconds *before* they set off. Looked at from the perspective of Milgram's "sensory overload" hypothesis (described in chapter 6), the findings suggest that people in these cities are likely to be less caring, more focused on what matters to them, and more isolated from one another than ever before. Given the important role that these factors play in creating caring communities, some might argue that city dwellers worldwide are now moving faster than the speed of life. It is a chilling thought, especially since the recent United Nations report *State of the World's Cities 2006/7* concluded that, for the first time in history, more people are now living in cities than in the countryside.

After completing my Dublin measurements, I closed my notebook, walked away from the General Post Office (at 5.45 feet per second), and reflected on twenty-one years of examining the quirky side of life. In addition to diverse topics such as testing the lie-detection skills of nations and uncovering the psychology of pick-up lines and personal ads, it has produced many wonderful and highly memorable times, including nights spent in apparently haunted houses, performing unfunny stand-up routines in comedy clubs, having my doctoral students dress as giant chickens, watching a four-year-old child beat the stock market, and feeling the heat emanate from a sixty-foot bed of white-hot coals (we didn't measure the speed of walking during that study, but I suspect it would have made Dubliners look slow).

But no scientific work exists in a vacuum. My research has built upon studies conducted by academics who have also dared to explore the backwaters of human behavior—researchers who have suffered for their science by secreting themselves in supermarkets and bowling alleys, applying voltages to the corpses of murderers, stalling cars at traffic lights, and spending countless hours trawling through millions of death records. Together, quirkologists have given us important insights into many areas of psychology, including deception, superstition, and altruism. Such work has also helped uncover the secret psychology that underlies our everyday lives and, in doing so, has illustrated just how fascinating those everyday lives *really* are. Or as Arthur Conan Doyle so eloquently put it in his book *Study in Scarlet:* "Life is infinitely stranger than anything the mind of man could invent."

For more than a hundred years, a small group of highly dedicated researchers have been studying people like you. To date, their work has only scratched the surface of the fascinating phenomenon that is your life. My hope is that this book will help quirkology move from the margins to the mainstream, and that studying the unusual will become surprisingly commonplace. I hope that my fellow academics will be encouraged to carry out more work that is both interesting and unusual; that they will, for instance, discover whether blondes *really* do have more fun, why we daydream, the relationship between personality and a person's choice of cell phone ringtone, why some people are more likeable than others, whether ventriloquists have multiple personalities, whether wearing school uniforms makes children less creative, and why we cry when we are happy. In short, I dream of a world packed full of researchers examining the more offbeat, and quirky, aspects of life. Next time someone stops you in the street and asks for the correct time, or you are stuck behind a car that has just stalled at a traffic light, or you find a $20 bill on the ground, beware. There may be far more going on than you suspect.

Afterword

How to Pep Up the Dullest of Dinner Parties

Surveys show that 87 percent of the population suffer from the entirely rational fear of being trapped in dull conversations at dinner parties.[1] To help alleviate such suffering, I recently held a series of "experimental" dinner parties. Before being allowed access to food, each of my guests had to rate a long list of factoids derived from the studies described in this book, on a scale of 1 ("Whatever") to 5 ("Really? When does it come out in paperback?"). I then used the data to identify the factoids that were most likely to provoke good conversation at even the dullest of gatherings.

Here are the factoids that took tenth place upward:

10th: People asked to write down a few words describing a university professor subsequently answer more Trivial Pursuit questions correctly than those describing a soccer hooligan.

9th: Women's personal ads would attract more replies if they were written by a man. The opposite is not true of men's ads.

8th: The *Mona Lisa* seems enigmatic because Leonardo da Vinci painted her so that her smile appears more striking when people look at her eyes than at her mouth.

7th: Women van drivers are more likely than others to take more than ten items through the express lane in a supermarket, to break speed limits, and to park in restricted areas. (This one proved especially popular with women.)

6th: Some seemingly ghostly experiences, such as feeling an odd sense of presence, are actually due to low-frequency sound waves produced by the wind blowing across an open window. (This received the top score from men.)

5th: Words containing the *k* sound—such as duck, quack, and Krusty the Clown—are especially likely to make people laugh.

4th: People born during the summer are luckier than those born in the winter—temperature differences around the time of birth make summer-borns more optimistic and open to opportunities.

In third place came work relating to the language of lying:

3rd: The best way of detecting a lie is to listen rather than look—liars say less, give fewer details, and use the word "I" less than people telling the truth.

The factoid that was placed second continued the deception theme and was all about fake smiles:

2nd: The difference between a genuine and a fake smile is all in the eyes—in a genuine smile, the skin around the eyes crinkles; in a fake smile it remains much flatter.

The number one factoid was that curious fact about sweater-wearing and dog feces:

1st: People would rather wear a sweater that has been dropped in dog feces and not washed than one that has been dry-cleaned but used to belong to a mass murderer.

So, next time you go to a dinner party, arm yourself with one or more of these scientifically proven ways of creating interesting conversation. Together, we can terminate tedious talk and pep up the dullest of evenings.

Acknowledgments

This book has its roots in a chance conversation with science writer and *Scientific American* columnist Michael Shermer. In November 2005, Michael kindly arranged for me to speak at the *California Institute of Technology.* While chatting on the way back to my hotel, the idea of my writing a book about my unusual experiments in psychology emerged. Thank you Michael. Without that conversation, this book might never have happened.

Various organizations have funded and helped carry out many of the studies described here. First and foremost, I wish to thank the University of Hertfordshire for supporting my work over the years. I would like to thank Sue Hordijenko, Jill Nelson, Nick Hillier, Craig Brierley, and Paul Briggs from The British Association for the Advancement of Science for their invaluable work during the financial astrology experiment and LaughLab. My thanks also to Simon Gage, Tracy Foster, and Pauline Mullin from The Edinburgh International Science Festival for helping to stage Born Lucky and for conducting the studies exploring the science of smiling and speed dating. Thanks also to Katie Smith and the team from the Cheltenham Festival of Science for helping to arrange the small world study. Similarly, my thanks to Karen Hartshorn, director of The New Zealand International Science Festival, for helping to conduct Born Lucky 2 and for arranging the smiling exhibition-experiment at The Dunedin Public Art Gallery. My thanks to The British Council for funding my trip to New Zealand and to Felicity Connell for doing such a wonderful job of looking after me while I was there. I would also like to thank Michael White from The British Council for organizing the global pace of life study and to the teams of researchers who found the time to measure the speed of walking around the world.

Much of the work described here has involved the media, and I have been lucky enough to work with several talented journalists and programme makers over the years. My thanks to Penny Park and Jay Ingram from *The Daily Planet* for collaborating on so many studies and for persuading my childhood hero, Leslie Nielsen, to participate in one of our experiments. Also, thanks to John Zaritsky and the team for creating many happy memories when we filmed the *No Kidding* documentary on LaughLab, and Isobel Williams from Bite Yer Legs for the surreal experience of watching people offer to pay several pounds for a worthless brass curtain ring. Special thanks are due to Roger Highfield, Science Editor of *The Daily Telegraph*, and writer Simon Singh. Roger, thank you for introducing me to the heady world of science communication and for turning so many of my ideas into reality. As you remind me every time we meet, without you I would be nothing. Simon, thank you for making such a great job of the experiment with Sir Robin Day and for your invaluable advice and expertise over the years. Without you, Roger would be nothing.

Thanks are also due to my colleagues and collaborators. To Matthew Smith, who carried out the lottery experiment and spent lots of time doing secret stuff in the dark during fake séances. To Emma Greening, for sending out all those parcels in the small world study, ghost hunting, exploring the psychology of suggestion, vetting thousands of jokes, and still finding the energy to laugh. To Sarah Woods, for having her brain scanned, measuring the pace of life in London, and not taking the LaughLab blonde jokes personally. To Ciarán O'Keeffe, for dressing up as a giant chicken and for exploring some of Britain's least haunted locations with me. To Adrian Owen, for helping out with brain scanning and finding the origin of the world's funniest joke. To all of the Infrasonic team (Sarah Angliss, Ciarán O'Keeffe, Richard Lord, Dan Simmon, and GéNIA) for managing to have such a good time while carrying out a study that has inspired so many. To Jim Houran and Jayanti Chotai, for sharing your invaluable expertise on ghostly experiences, speed dating, and chronopsychology. To Karen, for helping with the speed-dating experiment and for allowing us to use your photograph on the cover of the book. To Peter, for allowing me to reproduce your wonderfully instructive fake and genuine smiles. To Brian Fischbacher, for taking such great photographs of Karen and Peter. To Clive Jeffries, for spending so much time in the dark during the séance studies and for providing such insightful feedback on the book. And to Andy Nyman, for doing such a convincing job of talking to the dead and for making me laugh so much—you deserve any success that may eventually come your way.

This book would not have been possible without the guidance and expertise of my agents Patrick Walsh and Emma Parry, and editors Jason Cooper, Richard Milner, and Joann Miller.

Special thanks also to my wonderful colleague, and collaborator, Caroline Watt. You have helped design and conduct almost all the studies described here, provided much-needed support when the going got tough, and given far beyond the call of duty. Thank you.

Finally, my thanks to the researchers who have carried out the hundreds of slightly strange studies described here, and the millions of participants who have contributed to this work. Without you, the book would have been completely different, and much shorter.

Notes

Introduction

1. M. Brookes, *Extreme Measures: The Dark Visions and Bright Ideas of Francis Galton* (London: Bloomsbury, 2004).

2. F. Galton, "Statistical Inquiries into the Efficacy of Prayer," *Fortnightly Review* 68 (1872): 125–135.

3. F. Galton, *The Art of Travel* (London: John Murray, 1855), 209.

4. I. Farkas, D. Helbing, and T. Vicsek, "Mexican Waves in an Excitable Medium," *Nature* 419 (2002): 131–132.

5. L. Standing, "Learning 10,000 Pictures," *Quarterly Journal of Experimental Psychology* 25 (1973): 207–222.

6. R. Sommer, "The Personality of Vegetables: Botanical Metaphors for Human Characteristics," *Journal of Personality* 56, no. 4 (1988): 665–683.

7. J. Trinkaus, "Wearing Baseball-Type Caps: An Informal Look," *Psychological Reports* 74, no. 2 (1994): 585–586.

8. R. B. Cialdini and D. A. Schroeder, "Increasing Compliance by Legitimizing Paltry Contributions: When Even a Penny Helps," *Journal of Personality and Social Psychology* 34 (1976): 599–604.

9. R. A. Craddick, "Size of Santa Claus Drawings as a Function of Time Before and After Christmas," *Journal of Psychological Studies* 12 (1961): 121–125.

CHAPTER 1

1. G. Dean, A. Mather, and I. W. Kelly, "Astrology," in *The Encyclopedia of the Paranormal,* ed. G. Stein, 47–99 (Amherst, MA: Prometheus Books, 1996).

2. D. T. Regan, *For the Record: From Wall Street to Washington* (New York: Harcourt Brace, 1988); J. Quigley, *What Does Joan Say? My Seven Years as White House Astrologer to Nancy and Ronald Reagan* (New York: Carol Publishing Group, 1990).

3. J. Chapman, "How a Girl of Four Trounced a Top Investor and a Stargazer at Playing the Stock Market," *Daily Mail* (London), March 21, 2001, 2–3.

4. M. Nichols, "An Investor, an Astrologer, and a Girl, 4, Played the Market. Guess Who Won?" *Scotsman* (Edinburgh), March 24, 2001, 5.

5. T. Teeman, "Girl Shows Money Game Is Child's Play," *Times* (London), March 24, 2001.

6. G. Rollings, "Mcnuggets of Wisdom from the Shares Ace Aged Four," *Sun* (London), March 24, 2001, 50.

7. Ibid.

8. T. Utton, "Girl of Five Beats the Stock Market Experts (Again)," *Daily Mail* (London), March 14, 2002, 43.

9. J. Mayo, O. White, and H. J. Eysenck, "An Empirical Study of the Relation Between Astrological Factors and Personality," *Journal of Social Psychology* 105 (1978): 229–236.

10. Editorial, "British Scientist Proves Basic Astrology Theory," *Phenomena* (April 1, 1977): 1.

11. H. J. Eysenck and D.K.B. Nias, *Astrology: Science or Superstition?* (London: Pelican, 1988).

12. H. B. Gibson, *Hans Eysenck: The Man and His Work* (London: Peter Owen, 1981), 210.

13. G. Jahoda, "A Note on Ashanti Names and Their Relationship to Personality," *British Journal of Psychology* 45 (1954): 192–195.

14. M. Gauquelin, *Dreams and Illusions of Astrology* (London: Glover & Blair, 1979).

15. G. Dean and I. W. Kelly, "Is Astrology Relevant to Consciousness and Psi?" *Journal of Consciousness Studies* 10, nos. 6–7 (2003): 175–198.

16. For an overview of this work, see Dean, Mather, and Kelly, "Astrology," 47–99.

17. V. Muhrer, "Astrology on Death Row!" *Indian Skeptic* 11 (1989): 13–19.

18. B. R. Forer, "The Fallacy of Personal Validation: A Classroom Demonstration of Gullibility," *Journal of Abnormal Psychology* 44 (1949): 118–121.

19. P. E. Meehl, "Wanted—A Good Cookbook," *American Psychologist* 11 (1956): 263–272.

20. D. H. Dickson and I. W. Kelly, "The 'Barnum Effect' in Personality Assessment: A Review of the Literature," *Psychological Reports* 57 (1985): 367–382.

21. Gauquelin, *Dreams and Illusions of Astrology.*

22. S. J. Blackmore, "Probability Misjudgment and Belief in the Paranormal: A Newspaper Survey," *British Journal of Psychology* 88 (1997): 683–689.

23. M. Hamilton, "Who Believes in Astrology? Effects of Favorableness of Astrology Derived Personality Descriptions on Acceptance of Astrology," *Personality and Individual Differences* 31 (2001): 895–902.

24. M. Siffre, *Beyond Time* (New York: McGraw-Hill, 1964).

25. S. S. Campbell and P. J. Murphy, "Extraocular Circadian Phototransduction in Humans," *Science* (1998): 279, 396. This finding has been challenged in the following paper: K. P. Wright and C. A. Czeisler, "Absence of Circadian Phase Resetting in Response to Bright Light Behind the Knees," *Science* (2002): 297, 571.

26. A. Dudink, "Birth Date and Sporting Success," *Nature* (1994): 368, 592.

27. R. H. Barnsley, A. H. Thompson, and P. E. Barnsley, "Hockey Success and Birthdate: The Relative Age Effect," *Canadian Association for Health, Physical Education, and Recreation Journal* 51 (1985): 23–28; S. Edwards, letter to the editor, *Nature* 370 (1994): 186; J. Musch and R. Hay, "The Relative Age Effect in Soccer: Cross-Cultural Evidence for a Systematic Discrimination Against Children Born Late in the Competition Year," *Sociology of Sport Journal* 16 (1999): 54–64; A. H. Thompson, R. H. Barnsley, and G. Stebelsky, "Born to Play Ball: The Relative Age Effect and Major League Baseball," *Sociology of Sport Journal* 8 (1991): 146–151.

28. This work is summarized in R. Wiseman, *The Luck Factor* (London: Random House, 2004).

29. J. Chotai and R. Wiseman, "Born Lucky? The Relationship Between Feeling Lucky and Month of Birth," *Personality and Individual Differences* 39 (2005): 1451–1460.

30. J. Chotai et al., "Season of Birth Variations in the Temperament and Character Inventory of Personality in a General Population," *Neuropsychobiology* 44 (2001): 19–26.

31. S. Dickert-Conlin and A. Chandra, "Taxes and the Timing of Births," *Journal of Political Economy* 107, no. 1 (1999): 161–177.

32. A. A. Harrison, N. J. Struthers, and M. Moore, "On the Conjunction of National Holidays and Reported Birthdates: One More Path to Reflected Glory?" *Social Psychology Quarterly* 51, no. 4 (1988): 365–370.

33. Eysenck and Nias, *Astrology.*

34. For a readable introduction to this controversy, see G. Dean, "Is the Mars Effect a Social Effect? A Re-analysis of the Gauquelin Data Suggests That Hitherto Baffling Planetary Effects May Be Simple Social Effects in Disguise," *Skeptical Inquirer* 26, no. 3 (2002): 33–38; S. Ertel, "The Mars Effect Cannot Be Pinned on Cheating Parents—Follow-Up," *Skeptical Inquirer* 27, no. 1 (2003): 57–58; G. Dean, "Response to Ertel," *Skeptical Inquirer* 27, no. 1 (2003): 59–60, 65.

35. D. P. Phillips and D. G. Smith, "Postponement of Death Until Symbolically Meaningful Occasions," *Journal of the American Medical Association* 263 (1990): 1947–1951.

36. D. P. Phillips, C. A. Van Voorhees, and T. E. Ruth, "The Birthday: Lifeline or Deadline?" *Psychosomatic Medicine* 54 (1992): 532–542.

37. For a review of this data and debate, see J. A. Skala and K. E. Freedland, "Death Takes a Raincheck," *Psychosomatic Medicine* 66 (2004): 382–386.

38. S. A. Everson et al., "Hopelessness and Risk of Mortality and Incidence of Myocardial Infarction and Cancer," *Psychosomatic Medicine* 58 (1996): 113–121.

39. W. Kopczuk and J. Slemrod, "Dying to Save Taxes: Evidence from Estate-Tax Returns on the Death Elasticity," *Review of Economics and Statistics* 85, no. 2 (2003): 256–265.

CHAPTER 2

1. M. D. Morris, "Large Scale Deceit: Deception by Captive Elephants?" in *Deception: Perspectives on Human and Nonhuman Deceit,* ed. R. W. Mitchell and N. S. Thompson, 183–192 (New York: State University of New York Press, 1986).

2. Information about Koko and Michael can be found at www.koko.org.

3. A full transcript of this conversation is available at www.koko.org/world/talk_aol.html. OnlineHost content: Copyright 1998–2006 AOL LLC. Used with permission.

4. H. L. Miles, "How Can I Tell a Lie? Apes, Language, and the Problems of Deception," in Mitchell and Thompson, *Deception,* 245–266.

5. M. Lewis, "The Development of Deception," in *Lying and Deception in Everyday Life,* ed. M. Lewis and C. Saarni, 90–105 (New York: The Guilford Press, 1993).

6. P. Ekman, *Telling Lies: Clues to Deceit in the Marketplace, Politics, and Marriage* (New York: W. W. Norton, 1985).

7. R. Highfield, "How Age Affects the Way We Lie," *Daily Telegraph* (London), March 25, 1994, 26.

8. This work is reviewed in A. Vrij, *Detecting Lies and Deceit* (Chichester, UK: John Wiley & Sons, 2000).

9. R. G. Hass, "Perspective-Taking and Self-Awareness: Drawing an *E* on Your Forehead," *Journal of Personality and Social Psychology* 46 (1984): 788–798.

10. R. Wiseman, "The Megalab Truth Test," *Nature* (1995): 373, 391.

11. This work is reviewed in Vrij, *Detecting Lies and Deceit.*

12. Cited in B. M. DePaulo and W. L. Morris, "Discerning Lies from Truths: Behavioural Cues to Deception and the Indirect Pathway of Intuition," in *The Detection of Deception in Forensic Contexts,* ed. P. A. Granhag and L. A. Stromwall, 15–40 (Cambridge: Cambridge University Press, 2004).

13. P. Ekman and M. O'Sullivan, "Who Can Catch a Liar?" *American Psychologist* 46, no. 9 (1991): 913–920.

14. The Global Deception Research Team, "A World of Lies," *Journal of Cross-Cultural Psychology* 37, no. 1 (2006): 60–74.

15. This work is reviewed in Vrij, *Detecting Lies and Deceit,* and in DePaulo and Morris, "Discerning Lies from Truths," 15–40.

16. G. Littlepage and T. Pineault, "Verbal, Facial, and Paralinguistic Cues to the Detection of Truth and Lying," *Personality and Social Psychology* 4, no. 3 (1978): 461–464.

17. R. E. Kraut and R. E. Johnston, "Social and Emotional Messages of Smiling: An Ethological Approach," *Journal of Personality and Social Psychology* 37 (1979): 1539–1553.

18. The photographs used in this study were originally taken for a similar online experiment carried out in collaboration with the Edinburgh International Science Festival.

19. C. Landis, "Studies of Emotional Reactions: II. General Behavior and Facial Expression," *Journal of Comparative Psychology* 4 (1924): 447–509.

20. M. S. Livingstone, "Is It Warm? Is It Real? Or Just Low Spatial Frequency?" *Science* 290 (2000): 1299.

21. A. Parent, "Giovanni Aldini: From Animal Electricity to Human Brain Stimulation," *Canadian Journal of Neurological Sciences* 31 (2004): 576–584.

22. G. T. Crook, *The Complete Newgate Calendar,* vol. 4 (London: The Navarre Society, 1926).

23. "Horrible Phenomena!—Galvanism," *Scotsman* (Edinburgh), February 11, 1819.

24. G. B. Duchenne de Boulogne, *The Mechanism of Human Facial Expression* (1862; reprint, New York: Cambridge University Press, 1990).

25. P. Ekman and W. V. Friesen, *The Facial Action Coding System* (Palo Alto, CA: Consulting Psychologists Press, 1978).

26. D. D. Danner, D. A. Snowdon, and W. V. Friesen, "Positive Emotions in Early Life and Longevity: Findings from the Nun Study," *Journal of Personality and Social Psychology* 80 (2001): 804–813.

27. L. A. Harker and D. Keltner, "Expressions of Positive Emotion in Women's College Yearbook Pictures and Their Relationship to Personality and Life Outcomes Across Adulthood," *Journal of Personality and Social Psychology* 80 (2001): 112–124.

28. E. F. Loftus, *Eyewitness Testimony* (Cambridge, MA: Harvard University Press, 1979).

29. K. A. Wade et al., "A Picture Is Worth a Thousand Lies: Using False Photographs to Create False Childhood Memories," *Psychonomic Bulletin and Review* 9 (2002): 597–603.

30. K. A. Braun, R. Ellis, and E. F. Loftus, "Make My Memory: How Advertising Can Change Our Memories of the Past," *Psychology and Marketing* 19 (2002): 1–23.

31. E. F. Loftus and J. E. Pickrell, "The Formation of False Memories," *Psychiatric Annals* 25 (1995): 720–725.

32. I. E. Hyman, T. H. Husband, and F. J. Billings, "False Memories of Childhood Experiences," *Applied Cognitive Psychology* 9 (1995): 181–195.

33. J. Jastrow, "Psychological Notes Upon Sleight-of-Hand Experts," *Science* (May 8, 1896): 685–689.

34. R. Wiseman and E. Greening, "'It's Still Bending': Verbal Suggestion and Alleged Psychokinetic Metal Bending," *British Journal of Psychology* 96, no. 1 (2005): 115–127.

35. R. Wiseman, E. Greening, and M. Smith, "Belief in the Paranormal and Suggestion in the Séance Room," *British Journal of Psychology* 94, no. 3 (2003): 285–297.

CHAPTER 3

1. N. Lachenmeyer, *13: The World's Most Popular Superstition* (London: Profile Books, 2004).

2. J. McCallum, "Green Cars, Black Cats, and Lady Luck," *Sports Illustrated* 68 (February 8, 1988): 86–94.

3. D. W. Moore, "One in Four Americans Superstitious," Gallup Poll News Service, October 13, 2000.

4. S. Epstein, "Cognitive-Experiential Self Theory: Implications for Developmental Psychology," in *Self-Processes and Development: Minnesota Symposia on Child Psychology*, vol. 23, ed. M. Gunnar and L. A. Sroufe, 79–123 (Hillsdale, MI: Erlbaum, 1993).

5. T. Radford, "If You Aren't Born Lucky, No Amount of Rabbits' Feet Will Make a Jot of Difference," *Guardian* (Manchester), March 18, 2003, 15.

6. S. E. Peckham and P. G. Bhagwat, *Number 13: Unlucky/Lucky for Some* (New Milton, Hampshire, UK: Peckwat Publications, 1993).

7. D. P. Phillips et al., "The Hound of the Baskervilles Effect: Natural Experiment on the Influence of Psychological Stress on Timing of Death," *British Medical Journal* 323 (2001): 1443–1446.

8. G. Smith, "Scared to Death?" *British Medical Journal* 325 (2002): 1442–1443; N. S. Panesar et al., "Is Four a Deadly Number for the Chinese?" *Medical Journal of Australia* 179, nos. 11/12 (2003): 656–658.

9. T. J. Scanlon et al., "Is Friday the 13th Bad for Your Health?" *British Medical Journal* 307 (1993): 1584–1586.

10. S. Näyhä, "Traffic Deaths and Superstition on Friday the 13th," *American Journal of Psychiatry* 159 (2002): 2110–2111.

This work has generated the following debate: I. Radun and H. Summala, "Females Do Not Have More Injury Road Accidents on Friday the 13th," *BMC Public Health* 4, no. 1 (2004): 54; D. F. Smith, "Traffic Accidents and Friday the 13th," *American Journal of Psychiatry* 161, no. 11 (2004): 2140; and S. Näyhä, "Dr. Näyhä Replies," *American Journal of Psychiatry* 161 (2004): 2140.

11. K. Kaku, "Increased Induced Abortion Rate in 1966: An Aspect of a Japanese Folk Superstition," *Annals of Human Biology* 2, no. 2 (1975): 111–115.

12. K. Kaku and Y. S. Matsumoto, "Influence of a Folk Superstition on Fertility of Japanese in California and Hawaii, 1966," *American Journal of Public Health* 65, no. 2 (1966): 170–174.

13. K. Kaku, "Were Girl Babies Sacrificed to a Folk Superstition in 1966 in Japan?" *Annals of Human Biology* 2, no. 4 (1975): 391–393.

14. K. Hira et al., "Influence of Superstition on the Date of Hospital Discharge and Medical Cost in Japan: Retrospective and Descriptive Study," *British Medical Journal* 317 (1998): 1680–1683.

15. D. O'Reilly and M. Stevenson, "The Effect of Superstition on the Day of Discharge from Maternity Units in Northern Ireland: A Saturday Flit Is a Short Sit," *Journal Of Obstetrics and Gynecology* 20 (2000): 139–141; E. M. Keane, P. O'Leary, and J. B. Walsh, "Saturday Flit, Short Sit: A Strong Influence of a Superstition on the Timing of Hospital Discharges?" *Irish Medical Journal* 90 (1997): 28.

16. P. Haining, *Superstitions* (London: Sidgwick and Jackson, 1979).

17. M. D. Smith, R. Wiseman, and P. Harris, "Perceived Luckiness and the UK National Lottery" (proceedings of the 40th Annual Convention of the Parapsychological Association, England, UK, 1997), 387–398.

18. M. Levin, *Do Black Cats Cause Bad Luck?* (winner of the Joel Serebin Memorial Essay Contest organized by the New York Area Skeptics, http://www.petcaretips.net/black_cat_luck).

19. W. Coates, D. Jehle, and E. Cottington, "Trauma and the Full Moon: A Waning Theory," *Annals of Emergency Medicine* 18 (1989): 763–765.

A review of other potential lunacy effects can be found in J. Rotton and I. W. Kelly, "Much Ado About the Full Moon: A Meta-Analysis of Lunar-Lunacy Research," *Psychological Bulletin* 97, no. 2 (1985): 286–306.

20. D. F. Danzl, "Lunacy," *Journal of Emergency Medicine* 5, no. 2 (1987): 91–95.

21. A. Ahn, B. K. Nallamothu, and S. Saint, "'We're Jinxed': Are Residents' Fears of Being Jinxed During an On-Call Day Founded?" *American Journal of Medicine* 112, no. 6 (2002): 504.

22. P. Davis and A. Fox, "Never Say the 'Q' Word," *StudentBMJ* 10 (2002): 353–396.

23. Much of the information in this section is discussed in N. Lachenmeyer, *13: The World's Most Popular Superstition* (New York: Shoemaker & Hoard, 2004).

24. R. G. Ingersoll, "The Superstitions of Public Men" (toast, Thirteen Club dinner, New York, December 13, 1886).

25. B. Malinowski, *Argonauts of the Western Pacific* (New York: E. P. Dutton, 1922).

26. V. R. Padgett and D. O. Jorgenson, "Superstition and Economic Threat: Germany, 1918–1940," *Personality and Social Psychology Bulletin* 8 (1982): 736–774.

27. G. Keinan, "Effects of Stress and Tolerance of Ambiguity on Magical Thinking," *Journal of Personality and Social Psychology* 67, no. 1 (1994): 48–55.

28. C. Nemeroff and P. Rozin, "The Contagion Concept in Adult Thinking in the United States: Transmission of Germs and Interpersonal Influence," *Ethos* 22 (1994): 158–186. Quotation reprinted with permission of the American Psychological Association.

Related work is described in P. Rozin, L. Millman, and C. Nemeroff, "Operation of the Laws of Sympathetic Magic in Disgust and Other Domains," *Journal of Personality and Social Psychology* 50 (1986): 703–712.

29. J. Henry, "Coincidence Experience Survey," *Journal of the Society for Psychical Research* 59, no. 831 (1993): 97–108.

30. S. Milgram, *Obedience to Authority: An Experimental View* (New York: Harper & Row, 1974).

31. C. L. Sheridan and R. G. King Jr., "Obedience to Authority with an Authentic Victim" (proceedings of the 80th Annual Convention of the American Psychological Association, 1972), 165–166.

32. Described in T. Blass, *The Man Who Shocked the World: The Life and Legacy of Stanley Milgram* (New York: Basic Books, 2004).

33. S. Milgram, "The Small-World Problem," *Psychology Today* 1 (1967): 61–67; J. Travers and S. Milgram, "An Experimental Study of the Small World Problem," *Sociometry* 32 (1969): 425–443.

34. D. Watts, *Small Worlds: The Dynamics of Networks Between Order and Randomness* (Princeton, NJ: Princeton University Press, 1999).

35. J. A. Paulos, *A Mathematician Reads the Newspaper* (London: Penguin Books, 1995).

36. R. Wiseman, "It Really Is a Small World That We Live In," *Daily Telegraph* (London), June 4, 2003, 16.

37. D. Derbyshire, "Physics Too Hot for a Fire Walker's Feat," *Daily Telegraph* (London), March 23, 2000, 17.

38. R. Wiseman et al., "An Investigation into Alleged 'Hauntings,'" *British Journal of Psychology* 94 (2003): 195–211.

39. R. Lange and J. Houran, "Context-Induced Paranormal Experiences: Support for Houran and Lange's Model of Haunting Phenomena," *Perceptual and Motor Skills* 84 (1997): 1455–1458.

40. V. Tandy and T. Lawrence, "The Ghost in the Machine," *Journal of the Society for Psychical Research* 62 (1998): 360–364.

41. S. Angliss et al., "Soundless Music," in *Experiments: Conversations in Art and Science,* ed. B. Arends and D. Thackara, 139–171 (London: The Wellcome Trust, 2003). Quotation is from page 152.

42. A. Watson and D. Keating, "Architecture and Sound: An Acoustic Analysis of Megalithic Monuments in Prehistoric Britain," *Antiquity* 73 (1999): 325–336.

43. P. Devereux, *Stone Age Soundtracks: The Acoustic Archaeology of Ancient Sites* (London: Vega Books, 2002).

CHAPTER 4

1. T. E. Moore, "Subliminal Perception: Facts and Fallacies," *Skeptical Inquirer* 16 (1992): 273–281.

A. Pratkanis, "The Cargo Cult Science of Subliminal Persuasion," *Skeptical Inquirer* 16 (1992): 260–272.

2. S. A. Lowery and M. L. DeFleur, *Milestones in Mass Communication Research: Media Effects,* 3rd ed. (White Plains, NY: Longman, 1995). The information in this section is from the chapter "Project Revere: Leaflets as a Medium of Last Resort."

3. M. L. DeFleur and R. M. Petranoff, "A Televised Test of Subliminal Persuasion," *Public Opinion Quarterly* 23 (1959): 168–180.

4. B. Beyerstein, "Subliminal Self-Help Tapes: Promises, Promises . . . ," *Rational Enquirer* 6, no. 1 (1993): 12–15.

5. E. Eich and R. Hyman, "Subliminal Self-Help," in *In the Mind's Eye: Enhancing Human Performance,* ed. D. Druckman and R. Bjork, 107–119 (Washington, DC: National Academy Press, 1991).

6. P. M. Merikle and H. Skanes, "Subliminal Self-Help Audio Tapes: A Search for Placebo Effects," *Journal of Applied Psychology* 7 (1992): 772–776.

7. S. Lenz, "The Effect of Subliminal Auditory Stimuli on Academic Learning and Motor Skills Performance Among Police Recruits" (PhD diss., California School of Professional Psychology, Los Angeles, California, 1989).

8. B. Buchanan and J. L. Bruning, "Connotative Meanings of First Names and Nicknames on Three Dimensions," *Journal of Social Psychology* 85 (1971): 143–144.

9. A. A. Hartman, R. C. Nicolay, and J. Hurley, "Unique Personal Names as a Social Adjustment Factor," *Journal of Social Psychology* 75

(1968): 107–110. Heldref Publications; quotation reproduced with permission.

10. H. Harari and J. W. McDavid, "Name Stereotypes and Teachers' Expectations," *Journal of Educational Psychology* 65 (1973): 222–225.

11. W. F. Murphy, "A Note on the Significance of Names," *Psychoanalytical Quarterly* 26 (1957): 91–106.

12. N. Christenfeld, D. P. Phillips, and L. M. Glynn, "What's in a Name: Mortality and the Power of Symbols," *Journal of Psychosomatic Research* 47, no. 3 (1999): 241–254.

13. G. Smith and S. Morrison, "Monogrammic Determinism?" *Psychosomatic Medicine* 67 (2005): 820–824.

14. R. L. Zweigenhaft, "The Other Side of Unusual Names," *Journal of Social Psychology* 103 (1977): 291–302. Heldref Publications; quotation reproduced with permission.

15. B. W. Pelham, M. C. Mirenberg, and J. K. Jones, "Why Susie Sells Seashells By the Seashore: Implicit Egotism and Major Life Decisions," *Journal of Personality and Social Psychology* 82 (2002): 469–487.

16. J. T. Jones et al., "How Do I Love Thee? Let Me Count the Js: Implicit Egotism and Interpersonal Attraction," *Journal of Personality and Social Psychology* 87, no. 5 (2004): 655–683.

17. L. Casler, "Put the Blame on Name," *Psychological Reports* 36 (1975): 467–472.

18. J. A. Bargh, M. Chen, and L. Burrows, "Automaticity of Social Behavior: Direct Effects of Trait Construct and Stereotype Priming on Action," *Journal of Personality and Social Psychology* 71 (1996): 230–244.

19. A. Dijksterhuis and A. van Knippenberg, "The Relation Between Perception and Behavior, or How to Win a Game of Trivial Pursuit," *Journal of Personality and Social Psychology* 74, no. 4 (1998): 865–877.

20. N. Gueguen, "The Effects of a Joke on Tipping When It Is Delivered at the Same Time as the Bill," *Journal of Applied Social Psychology* 32 (2002): 1955–1963.

21. N. Gueguen and P. Legoherel, "Effect on Tipping of Barman Drawing a Sun on the Bottom of Customers' Checks," *Psychological Reports* 87 (2000): 223–226; K. L. Tidd and J. S. Lockard, "Monetary Signifi-

cance of the Affiliative Smile: A Case for Reciprocal Altruism," *Bulletin of the Psychonomic Society* 11 (1978): 344–346; B. Rind and P. Bordia, "Effect of Server's 'Thank You' and Personalization on Restaurant Tipping," *Journal of Applied Social Psychology* 25, no. 9 (1995): 745–751.

22. M. R. Cunningham, "Weather, Mood, and Helping Behavior: Quasi Experiments with the Sunshine Samaritan," *Journal of Personality and Social Psychology* 37 (1979): 1947–1956; B. Rind and D. Strohmetz, "Effects of Beliefs About Future Weather Conditions on Tipping," *Journal of Applied Social Psychology* 31, no. 2 (2001): 2160–2164.

23. K. Garrity and D. Degelman, "Effect of Server Introduction on Restaurant Tipping," *Journal of Applied Social Psychology* 20 (1990): 168–172; K. M. Rodrigue, "Tipping Tips: The Effects of Personalization on Restaurant Gratuity" (master's thesis, Division of Psychology and Special Education, Emporia State University, 1999).

24. A. H. Crusco and C. G Wetzel, "The Midas Touch: The Effects of Interpersonal Touch on Restaurant Tipping," *Personality and Social Psychology Bulletin* 10 (1984): 512–517.

25. C. S. Areni and D. Kim, "The Influence of Background Music on Shopping Behavior: Classical Versus Top-Forty Music in a Wine Store," *Advances in Consumer Research* 20 (1993): 336–340.

26. J. N. Rogers, *The Country Music Message* (Fayetteville: University of Arkansas Press, 1989).

27. S. Stack and J. Gundlach, "The Effect of Country Music on Suicide," *Social Forces* 71, no. 1 (1992): 211–218.

28. This controversial finding has been discussed in the following papers: E. R. Maguire and J. B. Snipes, "Reassessing the Link Between Country Music and Suicide," *Social Forces* 72, no. 4 (1994): 1239–1243; S. Stack and J. Gundlach, "Country Music and Suicide: A Reply to Maguire and Snipes," *Social Forces* 72, no. 4 (1994): 1245–1248; G. W. Mauk et al., "Comments on Stack and Gundlach's 'The Effect of Country Music on Suicide': An 'Achy Breaky Heart' May Not Kill You," *Social Forces* 72, no. 4 (1994): 1249–1255; S. Stack and J. Gundlach, "Psychological Versus Sociological Perspectives on Suicide: A Reply to Mauk, Taylor, White, and Allen," *Social Forces* 72, no. 4 (1994):

1257–1261; J. B. Snipes and E. R. Maguire, "Country Music, Suicide, and Spuriousness," *Social Forces* 74, no.1 (1995): 327–329; S. Stack and J. Gundlach, "Country Music and Suicide—Individual, Indirect, and Interaction Effects: A Reply to Snipes and Maguire," *Social Forces* 74, no. 1 (1995): 331–335.

29. D. P. Phillips, "The Influence of Suggestion on Suicide: Substantive and Theoretical Implications of the Werther Effect," *American Sociological Review* 39 (1974): 340–354; D. P. Phillips, "Motor Vehicle Fatalities Increase Just After a Publicized Suicide Story," *Science* 196 (1977): 1464–1465; D. P. Phillips, "Airplane Accident Fatalities Increase Just After Newspaper Stories About Murder and Suicide," *Science* 201 (1978): 748–750; D. P. Phillips, "Suicide, Motor Vehicle Fatalities, and the Mass Media: Evidence Towards a Theory of Suggestion," *American Journal of Sociology* 84 (1979): 1150–1174; D. P. Phillips, "Airplane Accidents, Murder, and the Mass Media: Towards a Theory of Imitation and Suggestion," *Social Forces* 58, no. 4 (1980): 1000–1024; D. P. Phillips, "The Impact of Fictional Television Stories on U.S. Adult Fatalities: New Evidence on the Effect of the Mass Media on Violence," *American Journal of Sociology* 87, no. 6 (1982): 1340–1359; D. P. Phillips, "The Impact of Mass Media Violence on U.S. Homicides," *American Sociological Review* 48 (1983): 560–568.

30. S. Stack, "Media Coverage as a Risk Factor in Suicide," *Journal of Epidemiology and Community Health* 57 (2003): 238–240.

31. L. F. Martel and H. B. Biller, *Stature and Stigma* (Lexington, MA: Lexington Books, 1987).

32. B. Pawlowski, R. I. Dunbar, and A. Lipowicz, "Tall Men Have More Reproductive Success," *Nature* 403, no. 6766 (2000): 156.

33. T. Gregor, *The Mehinaku: The Dream of Daily Life in a Brazilian Indian Village* (Chicago: University of Chicago Press, 1977).

34. T. A. Judge and D. M. Cable, "Effect of Physical Height on Workplace Success and Income: Preliminary Test of a Theoretical Model," *Journal of Applied Psychology* 89, no. 3 (2004): 428–441.

35. P. R. Wilson, "Perceptual Distortion of Height as a Function of Ascribed Academic Status," *Journal of Social Psychology* 74 (1968): 97–102.

36. H. H. Kassarjian, "Voting Intentions and Political Perception," *Journal of Psychology* 56 (1963): 85–88.

37. P. A. Higham and W. D. Carment, "The Rise and Fall of Politicians: The Judged Heights of Broadbent, Mulroney and Turner Before and After the 1988 Canadian Federal Election," *Canadian Journal of Behavioral Science* 24 (1992): 404–409.

38. R. Highfield, "Politicians: This Is How We See Them," *Daily Telegraph* (London), March 21, 2001, 22–23; R. Wiseman, "A Short History of Stature," *Daily Telegraph* (London), March 21, 2001, 22.

39. R. J. Pellegrini, "Impressions of the Male Personality as a Function of Beardedness," *Psychology* 10 (1973): 29–33.

40. A. Todorov et al., "Inferences of Competence from Faces Predict Election Outcomes," *Science* 308 (2005): 1623–1626.

41. J. E. Stewart II, "Defendants' Attractiveness as a Factor in the Outcome of Trials," *Journal of Applied Social Psychology* 10 (1980): 348–361.

42. R. B. Cialdini, *Influence: Science and Practice* (Needham Heights, MA: Allyn & Bacon, 2001).

43. S. M. Smith, W. D. McIntosh, and D. G. Bazzini, "Are the Beautiful Good in Hollywood? An Analysis of Stereotypes on Film," *Basic and Applied Social Psychology* 21 (1999): 69–81.

44. D. G. Dutton and A. P. Aron, "Some Evidence for Heightened Sexual Attraction Under Conditions of High Anxiety," *Journal of Personality and Social Psychology* 30 (1974): 510–517.

45. C. Bale, R. Morrison, and P. G. Caryl, "Chat Up Lines as Male Sexual Displays," *Personality and Individual Differences* 40 (2006): 655–664.

46. B. Fraley and A. Aron, "The Effect of a Shared Humorous Experience on Closeness in Initial Encounters," *Personal Relationships* 11 (2004): 61–78.

47. J. E. Smith and V. A. Waldorf, "Single White Male Looking for Thin, Very Attractive . . . ," *Sex Roles* 23 (1990): 675–685.

CHAPTER 5

1. H. R. Pollio and J. W. Edgerly, "Comedians and Comic Style," in *Humor and Laughter: Theory, Research, and Applications,* ed. A. J. Chapman and H. C. Foot, 215–244 (New Brunswick, NJ: Transaction Publishers, 1996).

2. C. Davies, "Jewish Jokes, Anti-Semitic Jokes and Hebredonian Jokes," in *Jewish Humour,* ed. A. Ziv, 59–80 (Tel Aviv: Papyrus Publishing House, 1986).

3. H. A. Wolff, C. E. Smith, and H. A. Murray, "The Psychology of Humor: 1. A Study of Responses to Race-Disparagement Jokes," *Journal of Abnormal and Social Psychology* 28 (1934): 345–365.

4. J. Morreall, *Taking Laughter Seriously* (Albany: State University of New York Press, 1983).

5. G. R. Maio, J. M. Olson, and J. Bush, "Telling Jokes That Disparage Social Groups: Effects on the Joke Teller's Stereotypes," *Journal of Applied and Social Psychology* 27, no. 22 (1997): 1986–2000.

6. B. Seibt and J. Förster, "Risky and Careful Processing Under Stereotype Threat: How Regulatory Focus Can Enhance and Deteriorate Performance When Self Stereotypes Are Active," *Journal of Personality and Social Psychology* 87 (2004): 38–56.

7. R. Provine, *Laughter: A Scientific Investigation* (New York: Viking, 2000).

8. M. Middleton and J. Moland, "Humor in Negro and White Subcultures: A Study of Jokes Among University Students," *American Sociological Review* 24 (1959): 61–69.

9. P. J. Castell and J. H. Goldstein, "Social Occasions of Joking: A Cross Cultural Study," in *It's a Funny Thing, Humour,* ed. A. J. Chapman and H. C. Foot, 193–197 (Oxford: Pergamon Press, 1976).

10. J. B. Levine, "The Feminine Routine," *Journal of Communication* 26 (1976): 173–175.

11. L. La Fave, J. Haddad, and W. A. Maesen, "Superiority, Enhanced Self-Esteem, and Perceived Incongruity Humour Theory," in Chapman and Foot, *Humor and Laughter*, 63–91. Copyright 1996 by Transaction Publishers. Reprinted with permission of the publisher.

12. Sir Harry Kroto originally presented us with a version of the joke in broad Glaswegian. As we knew that the material in LaughLab would be read by people throughout the world, we created a version that would allow a much larger number of people to appreciate the joke. Sir Harry Kroto's original entry, which he much prefers, is reproduced here:

> A guy is walking along the road in Glasgow and sees a man with a humungous great dog on the other side of the street. He goes over and says, "Hey, Jimmy, dis yer dawg byte?"
>
> The man says, "Nu."
>
> So the guy pats the dog on the head, whereupon the dog snaps, and bites off a couple of fingers. "Grrrrwrwrwrwrrfraarrrrrrrrgggggggklle . . . umph."
>
> The guy screams, "Aaaghgee" as blood streams from his hand, and shouts, "A tawt yer said yer dawg dusna byte."
>
> The man says quietly with a look of calm diffidence, "Sna ma dawg."

13. K. Binsted and G. Ritchie, "Computational Rules for Punning Riddles," *Humor: International Journal of Humor Research* 10, no. 1 (1997): 25–76.

14. M. Le Page, "Women's Orgasms Are a Turn-Off for the Brain," *New Scientist* 14 (June 25, 2005).

15. H. H. Brownell and H. Hardner, "Neuropsychological Insights into Humour," in *Laughing Matters: A Serious Look at Humour*, ed. J. Durant and J. Miller, 17–35 (Harlow, Essex, UK: Longman, 1988).

16. T. Friend, "What's So Funny?" *New Yorker,* November 11, 2002, 78–93.

17. D. Barry, "Send in Your Weasel Jokes," *International Herald Tribune* (Paris), January 19–20, 2002.

18. D. Barry, *Dave Barry Talks Back* (New York: Crown Publishers, 1991). See chapter titled "Introducing: Mr. Humor Person."

19. F. Strack, L. L. Martin, and S. Steppa, "Inhibiting and Facilitating Conditions of the Human Smile: A Nonobstrusive Test of the Facial Feedback Hypothesis," *Journal of Personality and Social Psychology* 54, no. 5 (1988): 768–777.

20. V. B. Hinsz and J. A. Tomhave, "Smile and (Half) the World Smiles with You, Frown and You Frown Alone," *Personality and Social Psychology Bulletin* 17, no. 5 (1991): 586–592.

21. A. M. Rankin and P. J. Philip, "An Epidemic of Laughing in the Bukoba District of Tanganyika," *Central African Journal of Medicine* 9 (1963): 167–170.

22. S. S. Janus, "The Great Comedians: Personality and Other Factors," *American Journal of Psychoanalysis* 35 (1975): 169–174. Quotation reproduced with kind permission of Springer Science and Business Media.

23. S. Fisher and R. L. Fisher, *Pretend the World Is Funny and Forever: A Psychological Analysis of Comedians, Clowns, and Actors* (Hillsdale, MI: Erlbaum, 1981). Quotations reproduced with kind permission of Springer Science and Business Media.

24. J. Rotton, "Trait Humor and Longevity: Do Comics Have the Last Laugh?" *Health Psychology* 11, no. 4 (1992): 262–266.

25. H. M. Lefcourt, "Humor," in *Handbook of Positive Psychology,* ed. C. R. Snyder and S. J. Lopez, 619–631 (Oxford: Oxford University Press, 2005).

26. H. Lefcourt, K. Davidson-Katz, and K. Kueneman, "Humor and Immune System Functioning," *International Journal of Humor Research* 3 (1990): 305–321.

27. J. Rotton and M. Shats, "Effects of State Humor, Expectancies, and Choice on Postsurgical Mood and Self-Medication: A Field Experiment," *Journal of Applied Social Psychology* 26 (1996): 1775–1794.

28. H. M. Lefcourt et al., "Perspective-Taking Humor: Accounting for Stress Moderation," *Journal of Social and Clinical Psychology* 14 (1995): 373–391.

29. D. Keltner and G. A. Bonanno, "A Study of Laughter and Dissociation: Distinct Correlates of Laughter and Smiling During Bereavement," *Journal of Personality and Social Psychology* 73 (1997): 687–702; G. A. Bonanno and D. Keltner, "Facial Expressions of Emotion and the Course of Conjugal Bereavement," *Journal of Abnormal Psychology* 106 (1997): 126–137.

30. V. Saroglou, "Sense of Humor and Religion: An A Priori Incompatibility? Theoretical Considerations from a Psychological Perspective," *Humor: International Journal of Humor Research* 15 (2002): 191–214.

31. V. Saroglou, "Religiousness, Religious Fundamentalism, and Quest as Predictors of Humor Creation," *International Journal for the Psychology of Religion* 12 (2002): 177–188.

32. V. Saroglou and J. M. Jaspard, "Does Religion Affect Humour Creation? An Experimental Study," *Mental Health, Religion, and Culture* 4 (2001): 33–46.

33. H. J. Eysenck, "National Differences in 'Sense of Humor': Three Experimental and Statistical Studies," *Journal of Personality* 13, no. 1 (1944): 37–54.

34. T. Radford, "Don't Gag on It, but This Is What Has Us All in Stitches," *Guardian* (Manchester), October 4, 2002, 6.

CHAPTER 6

1. R. T. LaPiere, "Attitudes Versus Actions," *Social Forces* 13, no. 2 (1934): 230–237.

2. J. Trinkaus, "Color Preference in Sport Shoes: An Informal Look," *Perceptual and Motor Skills* 73 (1991): 613–614.

3. J. Trinkaus, "Television Station Weather-Persons' Winter Storm Predictions: An Informal Look," *Perceptual and Motor Skills* 79 (1994): 65–66.

4. J. Trinkaus, "Wearing Baseball-Type Caps: An Informal Look," *Psychological Reports* 74, no. 2 (1994): 585–586.

5. J. Trinkaus, "The Demise of 'Yes': An Informal Look," *Perceptual and Motor Skills* 84 (1997): 866.

6. J. Trinkaus, "Preconditioning an Audience for Mental Magic: An Informal Look," *Perceptual and Motor Skills* 51 (1980): 262.

7. J. Trinkaus, "The Attaché Case Combination Lock: An Informal Look," *Perceptual and Motor Skills* 72 (1991): 466.

8. R. P. Feynman, *Surely You're Joking, Mr. Feynman!* (London: Random House, 1992).

9. J. Trinkaus, "Gloves as Vanishing Personal 'Stuff': An Informal Look," *Psychological Reports* 84 (1999): 1187–1188.

10. M.S.C. Lim, M. E. Hellard, and C. K. Aitken, "The Case of the Disappearing Teaspoons: Longitudinal Cohort Study of the Displacement of Teaspoons in an Australian Research Institute," *British Medical Journal* 331 (2005): 1498–1500.

11. B. Herer, "Disappearing Teaspoons," *British Medical Journal* 332 (2006): 121.

12. J. Trinkaus, "Compliance with the Item Limit of the Food Supermarket Express Checkout Lane: An Informal Look," *Psychological Reports* 73 (1993): 105–106.

13. J. Trinkaus, "Compliance With the Item Limit of the Food Supermarket Express Checkout Lane: Another Look," *Psychological Reports* 91 (2002): 1057–1058.

14. J. Trinkaus, "School Zone Limit Dissenters: An Informal Look," *Perceptual and Motor Skills* 88 (1999): 1057–1058.

15. J. Trinkaus, "Stop Sign Compliance: An Informal Look," *Psychological Reports* 89 (1999): 1193–1194.

16. J. Trinkaus, "Blocking the Box: An Informal Look," *Psychological Reports* 89 (2001): 315–316.

17. "Oprah: A Heavenly Body? Survey Finds Talk-Show Host a Celestial Shoo-In," *U.S. News and World Report,* March 31, 1997, 18.

18. S. A. Hellweg, M. Pfau, and S. B. Brydon, *Televised Presidential Debates: Advocacy in Contemporary America* (New York: Praeger, 1992).

19. P. Jaret, "Blinking and Thinking," *In Health* 4, no. 4 (1990): 36–37.

20. J. J. Tecce, "Body Language in Presidential Debates as a Predictor of Election Results: 1960–2004" (unpublished report, Boston College, 2004).

21. P. Suedfeld, S. Bochner, and D. Wnek, "Helper-Sufferer Similarity and a Specific Request for Help: Bystander Intervention During a Peace Demonstration," *Journal of Applied Social Psychology* 2 (1972): 17–23.

22. J. P. Forgas, "An Unobtrusive Study of Reactions to National Stereotypes in Four European Countries," *Journal of Social Psychology* 99 (1976): 37–42.

23. A. N. Doob and A. E. Gross, "Status of Frustrator as an Inhibitor of Horn-Honking Responses," *Journal of Social Psychology* 76 (1968): 213–218.

24. F. K. Heussenstamm, "Bumper Stickers and the Cops," *Transaction* 8 (1971): 32–33.

25. J. M. Burger et al., "What a Coincidence! The Effects of Incidental Similarity on Compliance," *Personality and Social Psychology Bulletin* 30 (2004): 35–43.

26. J. F. Finch and R. B. Cialdini, "Another Indirect Tactic of (Self-)Image Management," *Personality and Social Psychology Bulletin* 15 (1989): 222–232.

27. S. Milgram and R. L. Shotland, *Television and Antisocial Behaviour: Field Experiments* (New York: Academic Press, 1973).

28. Ibid.

29. A. Huston et al., *Big World, Small Screen: The Role of Television in American Society* (Lincoln: University of Nebraska Press, 1992).

30. S. Milgram, "The Lost-Letter Technique," *Psychology Today* 3, no. 3 (1969): 32–33, 66, 68.

31. F. S. Bridges and P. C. Thompson, "Impeachment Affiliation and Levels of Response to Lost Letters," *Psychological Reports* 84 (1999): 828–831.

32. B. J. Bushman and A. M. Bonacci, "You've Got Mail: Using E-Mail to Examine the Effect of Prejudiced Attitudes on Discrimination Against Arabs," *Journal of Experimental Social Psychology* 40 (2004): 753–759.

33. V. Saroglou et al., "Prosocial Behavior and Religion: New Evidence Based on Projective Measures and Peer Ratings," *Journal for the Scientific Study of Religion* 44 (2005): 323–348.

34. Quotation reproduced with permission from authors and publisher: G. B. Forbes, R. K. TeVault, and H. F. Gromoll, "Willingness to Help Strangers as a Function of Liberal, Conservative or Catholic Church Membership: A Field Study with the Lost-Letter Technique," *Psychological Reports* 28 (1971): 947–949. © Psychological Reports 1971.

35. J. M. Darley and C. D. Batson, "'From Jerusalem to Jericho': A Study of Situational and Dispositional Variables in Helping Behavior," *Journal of Personality and Social Psychology* 27 (1973): 100–108.

36. R. V. Levine et al., "Helping in 36 US Cities," *Journal of Personality and Social Psychology* 67 (1994): 69–81.

37. R. V. Levine, A. Norenzayan, and K. Philbrick, "Cross-Cultural Differences in Helping Strangers," *Journal of Cross-Cultural Psychology* 32 (2001): 543–560.

38. S. Milgram, "The Experience of Living in Cities," *Science* 167 (1970): 1461–1468.

39. R. V. Levine and A. Norenzayan, "The Pace of Life in 31 Countries," *Journal of Cross-Cultural Psychology* 30 (1999): 178–205.

40. R. V. Levine et al., "The Type A City: Coronary Heart Disease and the Pace of Life," *Journal of Behavioral Medicine* 12 (1989): 509–524.

41. J.A.M. Farver et al., "Toy Stories: Aggression in Children's Narratives in the United States, Sweden, Germany, and Indonesia," *Journal of Cross-Cultural Psychology* 28, no. 4 (1997): 393–420.

42. P. G. Zimbardo, "The Human Choice: Individuation, Reason, and Order Versus Deindividuation, Impulse, and Chaos," in *1969 Nebraska*

Symposium on Motivation, ed. W. J. Arnold and D. Levine, 237–307 (Lincoln: University of Nebraska Press, 1970).

43. P. G. Zimbardo, foreword to *The Individual in the Social World: Essays and Experiments,* 2nd ed., ed. S. Milgram, J. Sabini, and M. Silver, ix–xi (New York: McGraw-Hill, 1992).

44. J. L. Freedman and S. C. Fraser, "Compliance Without Pressure: The Foot-in-the-Door Technique," *Journal of Personality and Social Psychology* 4 (1966): 196–202.

CHAPTER 7

1. Due to logistical issues, the measurements in New York and Croatia were taken between 11:30 A.M. and 2:00 P.M. on October 1, 2006, and September 5, 2006, respectively.

2. The mean walking times (in seconds) were as follows: Singapore: 10.55; Copenhagen: 10.82; Madrid: 10.89; Guangzhou: 10.94; Dublin: 11.03; Curitiba: 11.13; Berlin: 11.16; New York: 12.00; Utrecht: 12.04; Vienna: 12.06; Warsaw: 12.07; London: 12.17; Zagreb: 12.20; Prague: 12.35; Wellington: 12.62; Paris: 12.65; Stockholm: 12.75: Ljubljana: 12.76; Tokyo: 12.83; Ottawa: 13.72; Harare: 13.92; Sofia: 13.96; Taipei: 14.00; Cairo: 14.18; Sana'a: 14.29; Bucharest: 14.36; Dubai: 14.64; Damascus: 14.94; Amman: 15.95; Bern: 17.37; Manama: 17.69; and Blantyre: 31.60.

AFTERWORD

1. I made this bit up.

Index

Abortion, 95, 96, 252
Acceptance, comedians' need for, 212
Actions vs. words, 227–29
Adams, John, 42
"Adventure of the Blue Carbuncle, The" (Doyle), 108–9
Advertisements, subliminal, 129–34
Advertising Age (magazine), 132–33
Affirmative answers, words used to express, 230
Age
  jokes that appeal to different age groups, 195–96, 224
  lying about, 36–37
Agreeableness and sending greeting cards, 266–67
Ahn, Andrew, 100
Airplane (movie), 62
Aitken, Campbell, 232–33
Aldini, Giovanni, 70–71, 72
"All about you" in personal ads, 170–71
Allen, Gracie, 37
Allen, Woody, 209, 212
Altruism, 240, 241, 253, 254
Ambrose, Marie, 84–85
American Bar Association, 139
American Dental Association, 139
American Journal of Medicine, 100
American sense of humor, 207–8, 220, 221–22
American Sign Language, 47–49
Amy (gorilla), 48
Anagrams, 109
Anandappa, Geoff, 191, 222
Angliss, Sarah, 122
Animals
  ability to lie, 47–49
  animals as source of humor, 121, 199, 203–4
Anti-Scottish jokes, 186–87
Antisocial behavior, 233, 263
  impact of media on, 246–50
  and prosocial behavior, 246, 250
  of women van drivers, 233–35, 276
Anxiety, 212–13, 239–40
Anxious personalities, 31, 267
Aquarius (astrological sign), 14, 26
Areni, Charles, 144
Argonauts of the Western Pacific (Malinowski), 103
Aries (astrological sign), 14, 26
Aristotle, 181, 185, 186
Aron, Arthur, 163–64, 168
Around the World in 80 Days (movie), 161
Ashanti people, 16–17
Assistance. *See* Help, provision of
Astrology, 7–8, 26, 28–29, 104, 244. *See also* Birth dates; Chronopsychology
  accuracy of predictions, 14–16
  analysis of mass-murderers, 19–20, 24–25
  financial astrology, 8–12
  "Mars Effect" and, 40–41
  "time twins" experiment, 17–19

"Astrology on Death Row!" (Muhrer), 19
Attitudes studies, 252
Attraction, signals of, 175–76
Authoritarianism as a trait of Republicans, 154, 157
Authority, obedience to, 110–11

BAAS. *See* British Association for the Advancement of Science
"baby-faced" appearance, 154, 159, 160
Bad luck. *See* Unlucky
Ball, Lucille, 36
Balloon ride as a false memory, 77–79
Bananas (movie), 215
Bangkok, attitudes in, 252
Bargh, John, 141–42
Barclays Stockholders (company), 9, 11, 12
"Barnum Effect," 23–24
Barry, Dave, 180, 203, 222
Baseball caps, direction worn, 3, 230
Baskerville effect, 93
"Basking in Reflected Glory" effect, 38
Batson, C. Daniel, 254
Battle of the sexes, jokes about, 189–90
BBC, 53, 54, 60, 97, 115–16, 158
Beards, people's perceptions of, 152–53
"Beauty Map," 2
Beetlejuice (movie), 161
Behavior differing from opinion, 227–29
Belladonna, 175–76
Belushi, John, 209
Benny, Jack, 212
Bentine, Michael, 224–25
Bereavement counselors and laughter, 215
Berliner Illustrierte (magazine), 220
"Big men," 147
Bigoted attitudes toward Orientals, 227–29
Biller, Henry, 147
Bingham, Powell, and Bingham-Powell, 107
Binsted, Kim, 198
Biological clock, 27–29
BIRG effect, 38
Birth dates, 4, 13–20, 24–26, 31–33
  helping those with similar, 244–45
  impact of "Mars Effect," 40–41
  manipulation of date of birth, 35–39
  near holidays, 37–39
  and sporting success, 28–29
  tax benefits of December birth, 35–36
  and time of death, 41–43
  unlucky dates, 92–93, 94–95
Birth rates of girls born in year of the Fire-Horse, 95
Black cat, 89–90, 99, 107
Black Panther bumper stickers, 243–44
Blackmore, Susan, 25
Blair, Tony, 151
Blink rates as measure of anxiety, 239–40
Blinko the Clown, 210
Blue, Vida, 137
Body language, 60, 65
Bohr, Niels, 91
Bond, Charles, 57–58
Borge, Victor, 221
"Born Lucky" experiments, 33–35, 66
Boston, Massachusetts, pace of life in, 260
Bowels and low-frequency sounds. *See* "Brown note"
Bowling alley study on smiling, 65–66
Boxing matches and rate of murders, 146
Brain damage and perception of humor, 202
Brain scans, 200–203
Brass ring, special powers of, 86–87
Brazil, 148, 260
Brewster, David, 8
Britain. *See also* England; United Kingdom
  British sense of humor, 207–8, 220, 221
  and caring communities, 262
British Association for the Advancement of Science, 8, 180, 181, 193, 223
British Council, 269
British Medical Journal, 92
British Meteorological Office, 140
Broadbent, Ed, 150

Brooks, Mel, 214
Brown, Derren, 83–85
"Brown note," 121, 125
Bruce, Lenny, 209
Bruning, James, 134
Buchanan, Barbara, 134
Budapest, rudeness in, 260
Bumper stickers and traffic citations, 243–44
Burger, Jerry, 244–45
Burns, George, 37
Bush, George H. W., 149, 155
Bush, George W., 139, 155, 156
Butsumetsu, 96

Cable, Daniel, 148
Caesar, Sid, 210
Calhoun, Cory, 109
Calm personalities, 14
Campbell, Scott, 27–28
Canadian Broadcasting Company, 132
Canadian Discovery Channel, 62
Canadian sense of humor, 221
Cancer (astrological sign), 11, 14, 26
Capilano River bridges, 163–64
Capricorn (astrological sign), 14, 26
Captain Fearless (magic show), 200
Cardiff, Wales, pace of life in, 270
Caring and communities, 262
Caring and open-mindedness as traits of Democrats, 157
Carment, William, 150
Cars, 77, 107
  bumper stickers and traffic citations, 243–44
  horn-honking, 4, 242–43
  treatment of abandoned used car, 263
Carter, Jimmy, 155
Casablanca (movie), 215
Casler, Lawrence, 140
Catch Me If You Can (movie), 61–62
Catholic churches, helpfulness of, 253–54
CBS (TV), 247, 249
Chacque, Paul, 18
Chamberlain, Neville, 50–51
Chandra, Amitabh, 36
Charity gift boxes, theft from, 247–49
Cheating on spouse. *See* Romantic deception
Cheltenham Science Festival, 112, 114
Chicken costume, 182, 223
Children, 50, 246, 262
  childhood memories, 77–81
  manipulating birth dates of, 35–39
  naming of, 16–17, 135, 138
China
  and caring communities, 262
  superstition about number 4, 92
Chinese couple, prejudice against, 227–29
Chinese Harvest Moon Festival, 42–43
Chopin, Frédéric François, 144
Chotai, Jayanti, 31–33
Christenfeld, Nicholas, 136
Christmas, 4
  Christmas cards, 265–67
  number of reported deaths, 42
  people born around, 37–39
Chronopsychology, 26–29
  and date of death, 41–44
  judging passage of time, 1, 27
  and luck, 31–35
  and manipulation of birth dates, 35–39
Church organs and low-frequency sound waves, 126
Churchill, Winston, 90
Cialdini, Robert, 160, 245
Cigars and jokes, 192
Cities
  measuring helpfulness found in, 257–58
  measuring pace of life in, 268–72
"Class clown," 211
Clean-shaven, people's perceptions of, 152
Clergy
  desire to be born near Christmas, 38–39
  Good Samaritan test, 254–55
Clinton, Bill, 109, 149, 155, 156, 235, 252

Close-Up (TV show), 132
Clothing, superstitious behavior toward, 106, 277
Clowns, 19, 209, 210, 211, 213
  Krusty the Clown, 204, 276
  in Sigmund Freud's office, 192, 193–94
Clumsiness and unlucky people, 31
Cobb, Ty, 137
Code Book, The (Singh), 54
Coincidences, 107–15
Coins
  coin tossing, 99, 108
  disappearing coin, 45–46
Collectivist approach and caring, 262
Combinations for locks, 231
Comedians, 208–12, 213
Communist Party, Friends of, 250–51
Computers as source of humor, 198–99
Concert to test impact of low-frequency sound, 122–25
Congo (Crichton), 48
Congressional Medal of Honor Society, 80
Conservative churches, helpfulness of, 253–54
Conservative Party, 151
Contributions, reactions to requests for, 3–4
Controlling personalities, 14
Conversational topics for dull dinner parties, 275–77
Cooper, Gary, 161–62
Copycat suicides, 145–46
"Corpsing," 72
Cosby, Bill, 214
Country music and suicide rates, 4–5, 144–45
Crichton, Michael, 48
Cronkite, Walter, 53
Crook, G. T., 70–71
Crossing fingers, 91, 96, 103
Cruscoe, April, 143
Curtis, Tony, 55, 59
Czechoslovakia, German invasion of, 50–51

Daily Planet, The (TV show), 62
Daily Telegraph (newspaper), 51, 60, 112, 113, 151, 265
Danger and superstitious beliefs, 104–5
Danish sense of humor, 197
Danner, Deborah, 75
Darley, John, 254
Date of birth. *See* Birth dates
Dating, 163–64
  love at first sight, 173–77
  personal ads, 169–73
  pick up lines, 164–69
Davis, Bette, 247
Davis, Patrick, 100
Day, Robin, 53–56, 59–60, 61, 62, 65, 158
Dean, Geoffrey, 17–20, 40–41
Death, 71, 93, 102, 144–45, 146, 179. *See also* Life expectancy; Longevity; Mortality rate; Suicides
  date of birth and time of death, 41–43
  electric shocks used to reanimate corpses, 70–72
  tax liability influencing time of death, 43–44
Deception, 4, 45–87. *See also* Lying
  elephants acting deceptively, 46–47
  fake memories, 77–81
  power of suggestion, 81–87
  self-deception, 229
Decision making, 4, 127–79
DeFleur, Melvin, 129–32
Degrees of separation, 111–12, 113–14
Democratic Party, 133, 154, 155, 156
Dennis, Sandy, 162
Desmond, Tom, 247–49
Details and lying, 59–60, 64
Diaconis, Persi, 108
Diana (Princess of Wales), 235
Dickert-Conlin, Stacy, 36
Die Hard II (movie), 215
Dijksterhuis, Ap, 142
Dinner parties, conversational topics for, 275–77
Dirty jokes, 182–83, 197
Disappearing coin trick, 45–46
Disappearing teaspoons, 232–33

Dishonesty, 4, 51, 233–34, 236–38, 248–49, 255–56
misuse of express lane in grocery stores, 4, 233–34
study of reactions to overpayment, 235–39
theft, 232–33, 247–49
Disneyland, 79
Dogs
Dog feces and sweater, 106, 277
Dogs named after Adolf Hitler, 187
Donation boxes, reactions to requests for contributions, 3–4
Doyle, Arthur Conan, 93, 108–9, 273
"Drive Carefully" signs, 264
Dublin, Ireland, 268–69, 270, 272–73
Duchene de Boulogne, Guillaume, 72–73, 75, 76
Dudink, Ad, 28
Dukakis, Michael, 149
Dunbar, Robin, 147
Dunedin Public Art Gallery (New Zealand), 67, 74–75
Dutton, Donald, 163–64
"Dying as a Form of Social Behavior" (Phillips), 41
"Dying to Save Taxes" (Kopczuk and Slemrod), 43–44

Early-warning system of animals, 121
Eastman, George, 91
Eco, Umberto, 185
Economic downturns and superstition, 103–4
Edinburgh, Scotland, 116, 270
Edinburgh International Science Festival, 32, 165
Edwards, Frank, 131–32
Einstein, Albert, 1
Eisenhower, Dwight D., 155
Ekman, Paul, 57
El Salvador, level of helpfulness in, 258
Elderly, jokes that appeal to, 196, 224
Electricity used in psychological studies, 70
Milgram's study of authority, 110–11
studying facial expressions, 67–68, 72–73
used to reanimate corpses, 70–72
Elephants and deceptive activities, 46–47, 49
Elizabeth II (Queen), 107
Energetic personality and luck, 31
England. *See also* Britain; United Kingdom
pace of life in, 260
Entertainment Personalities of the Past (Hoffman), 213
Envelope dropping technique, 250–53, 256–59
Essence of person carried by objects, 105–6
Even numbers, choosing, 230
Everitt, Jed, 190
"Evil" clown, 19
Express lines, misuse of, 4, 233–34
Extroversion, 13–14
and sending greeting cards, 266
Eyes
eye blinking and anxiety, 239–40
fovea and retina, 69–70
pupil size, 175–76
Eysenck, Hans, 13–17, 19, 219–20

Facial appearance, psychological importance of, 151–57, 161–62. *See also* Smiles
"baby-faced" appearance, 154, 159, 160
in court cases, 158–60
facial expression, 65, 67–68, 72–73, 205–6
"Facial Feedback," 204
facial hair, 151–53
pupil size, 175–76
study of facial appearance of presidents, 154–57
Fake smiles, 46, 66–70, 72–76, 276–77
False memories, 77–81
Far Side (Larson), 158, 205
Favorites, lying about, 53–56, 62–64
FBI, 251
Federal Communications Commission, 133
Fermat's Last Theorem (Singh), 54
Feynman, Richard, 231
Fields, W. C., 212

Financial astrology, 8–12
Finch, John, 245
Fire zones, parking in, 234
Fire-Horse, year of, 94–95
Firewalking, 115–16
First names, 134–35, 137–38
Fischer, Seymour, 210–13
Fisher, Rhoda, 210–13
"Flattery effect," 25–26
Fleetwood Mac (music group), 144
Flynn, Errol, 247
fMRI. *See* Functional magnetic resonance imaging
Forbes 100 (richest men), 153
Forbes, Gordon, 253–54
Ford, Gerald, 155
Ford Theater, 107
Forer, Bertram, 20–23
Forgas, Joseph, 242–43
Forgetting and lying, 59–60, 64
Fortune 500, 148
Foster, George, 70–71
Four (the number), 92–93
"Four degrees of separation," 113–14
Fovea, 69–70
Fowler, William, 100
Fox, Adam, 100
Fraley, Barbara, 168
France
  honking car horns in, 242–43
  pace of life in, 260
Frankenstein (Shelley), 72
Fraser, Scott, 263–64
Frazer, James, 102, 105–6
Freedman, Jonathan, 263–64
Freud, Sigmund and humor, 181, 192–93, 194–95, 196
Freud Museum (London), 193
Friday the thirteenth, 4–5, 39, 93–94
Friend, Ted, 203
Frowns effecting sense of humor, 204–5
Förster, Jens, 188
Full moon and patient behavior, 99–100
Functional magnetic resonance imaging, 200
Fundamentalism and laughter, 216–19
Funny. *See* Humor

Gable, Clark, 54–55
Gabriel, Peter, 110
Gacy, John (astrological study of), 19–20
Gainsborough, Thomas, 67
Galton, Francis, 2–3, 120–21, 123
Gauquelin, Michel, 24–25, 40
Gehrig, Lou, 161–62
Gemini (astrological sign), 14, 26
Gender differences
  and greeting cards, 266–67
  and jokes, 189, 190, 197, 224
  in movie choices, 166–67
  in personal ads, 171–73, 276
  and sneaker color, 230
GéNIA, 123, 124
Gentiles rating jokes, 186–87
Geography of Time, The (Levine), 257
Germany
  and caring communities, 262
  German sense of humor, 219–20, 221
  honking car horns in, 242–43
  pace of life in, 260
  superstition between two world wars, 104
Ghostbusters (movie), 117
Ghosts and ghostly phenomena, 84–85, 116–20, 122, 125, 276
Global shrinkage. *See* Shrinking world
Gloves, mystery of the vanishing, 231–32
"Gloves as Vanishing Personal 'Stuff': An Informal Look" (Trinkaus), 231
Glynn, Laura, 136
Goethe, Johann Wolfgang von, 145
Gold Shield Coffee Company, 130
Golden Bough, The (Frazer), 102
Goldwater, Barry, 252
Goldwyn, Samuel, 137
Gone With the Wind (movie), 54–55, 56, 59
Good Samaritans, 240–41, 254–55, 257
Goon Show, The (radio show), 224
Gore, Al, 139

Gorillas using sign language to lie, 47–49
Gosall, Gurpal, 222–23
"Grand Inquisitor." *See* Day, Robin
Grant, Cary, 55
Graphology, 20
Greenfield, Susan, 197
Greening, Emma, 112, 182–83, 196, 203
Greeting cards, psychology of, 265–67, 267
Gregor, Thomas, 147–48
Grove, Lefty, 137
Guangzhou, China, pace of life in, 272
Guinness World Record, 221
Gundlach, Jim, 144–45
Gutierrez, Debi, 207–8

Hague, William, 151
Hair, psychological importance of, 151–53
Hamilton, Margaret, 26
Hamlet (Shakespeare), 109
Hampton Court (London), 116
Handel, George Frideric, 25
Handwriting analysis, 20
Hanft, Lucas, 252
Hannin, Harry, 107–8
Happiness, 14, 75, 76, 102, 274
- happy eaters are bigger tippers, 142–43
- and smiling, 65–66, 204–5

Harker, Lee Anne, 76
Harlem Globetrotters, 107
Harris, Peter, 97–98
Harrison, Albert, 37–39
Hartman, Arthur, 135
Harvard, John, 91
Harvard University, 91
Hauntings. *See* Ghosts and ghostly phenomena
Health
- benefits of laughter, 213–16
- and numbers, 92–94

Heart rate and physical attraction, 164
Heaven, people's chances of going to, 235
Height, psychological importance of, 147, 147–51
- estimated based on status of person, 149–51
- in politics, 128, 148–49, 150

Height of Your Life, The (Keyes), 149
Hellard, Margaret, 232–33
Help, provision of, 240–41
- and caring communities, 261–62
- giving aid only to those with similar views, 240–42
- helpful cities, 257, 258
- measuring willingness to help, 256–59
- to those with similar birth dates, 244–45
- treatment of abandoned used car, 263
- by various religious groups, 253–55

Herrmann, Alexander, 81–82
Heussenstamm, Frances, 243–44
Hidden messages, 129–34
Higham, Philip, 150
Highfield, Roger, 60, 112, 151, 265
High-frequency sound waves, 120
Hingis, Martina, 91
Hinsz, Verlin, 205
Hira, Kenji, 95–96
Hitler, Adolf, 50–51, 90, 187
Hoffman, Dustin, 149
Hollywood movies, 128–29
- effects of watching different kinds, 214–15
- gender taste in, 167–68
- influence of Hollywood on stereotyping, 161–62

Holmes, Sherlock (joke about), 191, 222
Honesty. *See also* Deception; Lying
- amount of hair a factor in determining, 152, 154
- evaluating priests and used-car dealers, 255–56
- judging Nixon's during the presidential debate, 239–41
- study of reactions to overpayment, 235–39

Hong Kong, 252, 260

Hooligans and Trivial Pursuit, 142, 275
Horn-honking, 4, 242–43
Horoscopes, 7, 24–25
Hospitals, superstitions and, 93–94, 96, 99–100
Hostility, 14
Hotel Meurice (Paris), 108
Hound of the Baskervilles, The (Conan Doyle), 93
Houran, James "Jim," 118, 165
Houston, Texas (level of helpfulness in), 257
Humor, 4, 168, 212–13, 216. *See also* Jokes; Laughter
    brain scans showing physical impact of, 200–203
    comedy potential of letter "K," 203–5
    creating sense of superiority, 184–91, 193, 211
Humor, *continued*
    Freud on humor, 181, 192–93, 194, 195, 196
    incongruity as a basis for, 199, 216
    national differences in, 207–8, 219–21
Hunt for Red October, The (movie), 215
Hurley, Jesse, 135
Huxley, T. H., 8

"I," use of when lying, 59, 64, 276
I Told You I Was Ill (TV show), 224
Ice House (comedy club in Pasadena), 207–8
Imagination and belief in strange phenomena, 117
Impatience and honking car horns, 242–43
Incongruity as basis for humor, 199, 216
Independence Day
    people born around, 37–38
    presidents dying on, 42
"Individualism" and caring, 262
Indonesia
    and caring communities, 262
    pace of life in, 260
Influence (Cialdini), 160
Infrasound. *See* Low-frequency sound waves
Ingersoll, Robert Green, 101–2
Initials spelling out words, 136–37
Institute of Psychiatry, 200
International Herald Tribune (newspaper), 203
Introversion, 14
    and sending greeting cards, 266
Investments and astrology, 8–12
Ireland, 253
    pace of life in, 260, 268
    superstition about hospital stays, 96
Italy, honking car horns in, 242–43
It's a Wonderful Life (movie), 161

Jack (family member named), 25
Jahoda, Gustav, 16–17
Janus, Samuel, 209
Japan, pace of life in, 260
Japanese superstition
    lucky and unlucky days, 95–96
    year of the Fire-Horse, 94–95
Jastrow, Joseph, 81–83
Jefferson, Thomas, 42
Jenkins, Rob, 154–57
Jerusalem, Israel, superstition and stress in, 104–5
Jesus, birth date of, 39
Jesus of Montreal (movie), 218
Jet lag, 27–28
Jews rating jokes, 186–87
Joel, Woolf, 89
John Fig, Inc. (company), 131–32
Johnson, Andrew, 107
Johnson, Lyndon B., 107, 155, 252
Johnson, Samuel, 90
Jokes, 143, 179, 181–225. *See also* Humor; Laughter
    age groups and joke appeal, 195–96, 224
    brain scans showing physical impact of, 200–203
    creating sense of superiority, 184–91, 193, 211
    gender differences, 189, 190, 197, 224

incongruity as a basis for, 199, 216
sample jokes, 184, 187, 189, 190, 191, 194–96, 197, 198, 199, 202, 203–4, 207–8, 210–11, 216, 219, 221–22, 225
self-disparaging jokes, 190
Jokes and Their Relation to the Unconscious (Freud), 192
Jones, Steve, 197
Jones, Terry, 223
Jorgenson, Dale, 104
Journal of Applied Psychology, 148
Journal of Personality and Social Psychology, 141
Journal of the Society for Psychical Research, 120
Judge, Timothy, 148
Juries and facial sterotyping, 158–60

"K," comedy potential of, 203–5, 276
Kabuki, 94
Kaku, Kanae, 95
Kaspar (black cat), 89–90, 107
Kassarjian, Harold, 150, 151
Keating, David, 126
Kellar, Harry, 81–82
Keltner, Dacher, 76
Kennedy, John, 107, 111, 150, 239
Ketchup as favorite food, 62–63, 64
Key, bending of, 83–84
Keyes, Ralph, 149
Kim, David, 144
King, Carole, 164–69
King, Richard, 110–11
Knees, shining a light on, 28
Knippenberg, Ad van, 142
Koko (gorilla), 47–49
Kopczuk, Wojciech, 44
Kraut, Robert, 65–66
Kroto, Harry, 197–98
Krusty the Clown, 204, 276
Kuala Lumpur (Malaysia), level of helpfulness in, 258
Kupcinet, Irv, 107–8
Kwadwo and *Kwaku*, 16–17

Labeling effecting self-image, 16–17
Labour Party, 151
Landis, Carney, 67–68
Language of lying, 58–65
LaPierre, Richard, 227–29
Large numbers, law of, 108–10
Larson, Gary, 158, 205
Las Vegas casinos, 108
Last names. *See* Surnames
Last Supper and thirteen, 97
Last Tango in Paris (movie), 161
Laugh tracks, 206
LaughLab, 181–225
Laughter, 181, 206. *See also* Humor; Jokes
health benefits of, 213–16
and "K" words, 203–5, 276
laughter plague in Tanzania, 206
Plato not a fan of, 185
and religious fundamentalism, 216–19
"Law of contagion," 105–6
Law of large numbers, 108–10
Leacock, Stephen, 219
Leaflets, sharing information via, 130
Legal proceedings and facial stereotyping, 158–60
Lehman, J. Arthur, 102
Leigh, Vivien, 54
Leno, Jay, 11
Leo (astrological sign), 14, 26
Leonardo da Vinci, 69–70, 276
Letterman, David, 186–87
Letters, studies concerning forwarding or mailing of, 90, 111–12, 113–14, 246, 252–54, 256–58, 261
Lével, Leon, 18
Levin, Mark, 99
Levine, Robert, 256–62, 270
Liberal as a trait of Democrats, 154
Liberal churches, helpfulness of, 253–54
Libra (astrological sign), 14, 26
Life decisions, surname effecting, 138–40
Life expectancy, 2, 75–76. *See also* Longevity; Mortality
and a person's initials, 136–37

Light-pull, special powers of, 86–87
Lights, impact on biological clock, 28
Lilongwe (Malawi), level of helpfulness in, 258
Lim, Megan, 232–33
Lincoln, Abraham, 107
Listening vs. looking to detect lies, 61–62, 276
Littlepage, Glenn, 61
Livingstone, Margaret, 69–70
Lodge, Oliver, 8
Loftus, Elizabeth, 77
London, pace of life in, 270
London Entertains (TV show), 224
London Zoo, 123
Longevity, 43, 75, 213
Lonides, Basil, 90
"Looking up to" someone, 147
Looking vs. listening to detect lies, 61–62, 276
Lord, Richard, 122, 124
Los Alamos, New Mexico, 231
Los Angeles, 257, 260
Lost letter test, 256–59
Lotteries, choosing lucky numbers, 97–98
Love at first sight, 173–77
"Love is blind," 176
Low-frequency sound waves, 119–26, 276
Lucky, 30–31, 91
- ambient temperature and lucky people, 33–35
- choosing lucky numbers in lotteries, 97–98
- luck and "pass the parcel" studies, 113–15
- lucky day in Japan, 95–96
- lucky numbers, 90–91, 101–2
- lucky people and birth date, 29–35, 276
- optimism and, 43, 276
- Thirteen Club (in New York), 101–2

Luke 6:21, 25, 217
"Lunacy" (Danzl), 99
Lying, 45–87, 62–64. *See also* Deception; Fake smiles
- gorillas using sign language to lie, 47–49
- listening vs. looking to detect lies, 61–62, 276
- parents lying about child's birthday, 39–41
- ways to detect lies, 51–53, 58–65

MacFarlane Burnet Institute for Medical Research (Melbourne), 232
"Mad Monk of Russia," 245
Mademoiselle (magazine), 77
Madonna (singer), 149
Magic Circle (magic club), 46
Magic tricks, 45–46
Magicians as honest deceivers, 81–83
Maio, Gregory, 187–88
Malinowski, Bronislaw, 102–3
Marksmanship, improving with subliminal messages, 134
Marriage, surname effecting choice of partner, 138–39
"Mars Effect," 39–41
Martel, Leslie, 147
Marx Brothers, 202–3
Mason, Jackie, 210
Massachusetts General Hospital, 100
Massachusetts Institute of Technology, 91
Mass-murderers, 40
- horoscopes of, 19–20, 24–25
- wearing sweater of, 106, 277

Mayo, Jeff, 14–15
Mayo School of Astrology, 15
McKinley, William, 148
Me, focus in personal ads, 170–71
Mechanism of Human Facial Expression, The (Duchenne de Boulogne), 72
Media, impact of violence in, 246–50
Medical Center (TV show), 247–49
Medical Research Associates, 250–51
Mediums and séances, 83–86
Mehinaku tribe, 148

Memories, malleability of, 77–81
Memory loss, jokes about, 195–96, 224
Memphis, Tennessee (level of helpfulness in), 257
Men. *See* Gender differences
Mendelssohn, Felix, 144
Mexico, pace of life in, 260
Michael (gorilla), 47–49
"Midas Touch: The Effects of Interpersonal Touch on Restaurant Tipping, The" (Crusco), 143
Milgram, Stanley, 110–12, 246–53, 262, 272
Miller, Michael, 214
Milligan, Sile, 225
Milligan, Spike, 209, 224, 225
"mind over matter," 83–84
Mission Impossible (TV show), 247
Mister Rogers' Neighborhood (TV show), 48
Mona Lisa (Leonardo da Vinci), 69–70, 276
Mondeville, Henri de, 213
Monet, Claude, 67
"Monogrammic Determinism?" (Morrison and Smith), 136–37
Monroe, James, 42
Monroe, Marilyn, 55, 146
Month of birth, 4. *See also* Birth dates
  and sensation seekers, 31–33
  tax benefits of December birth, 35–36
Monty Python's Flying Circus (TV show), 179, 180
Moral decline in society, 233, 235
Morris, Maxine, 46–47
Morrison, Stilian, 136–37
Mortality, 43, 95, 215. *See also* Death; Life expectancy; Longevity
Movies. *See* Hollywood movies
Mozart, Wolfgang Amadeus, 144
MRC Cognition and Brain Sciences Unit, 199–200
Mulroney, Brian, 150
Murder and boxing matches, 146
Murphy, Patricia, 27–28
Muscles and smiling, 72–73, 74
Music effecting wine purchases, 144
MythBusters (TV show), 121

Naked Gun (movie), 62, 215
Name of the Rose, The (Eco), 185
Names
  and careers, 4, 139, 140, 146
  first names, 134–35, 137–38
  initials, 136–37
  surnames, 128, 135–36, 138–40, 146
NASA (National Aeronautics and Space Administration), 119–20
Nashville, Tennessee (level of helpfulness in), 257
National Association of Broadcasters, 130, 132
National differences in humor, 219–21
National lotteries, choosing lucky numbers, 97–98
National Physical Laboratory, 122
Natural disasters and low-frequency sound waves, 120, 121
Näyhä, Simo, 94
Nazi Party, Friends of, 250–51
Negative astrological signs, 26
Neuroticism, characteristics of, 13–14
New age, study on belief in, 86–87
New Scientist (magazine), 140
New Year's Day, people born around, 37–38
New York City
  helpfulness in, 257, 258
  pace of life in, 260, 270
  treatment of abandoned used car, 263
New York Post (newspaper), 137
New York Times Magazine, 219
New Yorker (magazine), 203, 220, 221
New Zealand, 35
New Zealand Science Festival, 66
Newsweek (magazine), 213
Nicolay, Robert, 135
Nielsen, Leslie, 62–64, 65

Nixon, Richard M., 150, 155, 239–41
"Nixon effect," 239
Northern Hemisphere study of luck, 33–34
Numbers, law of large, 108–10
Numbers, lucky
  seven, 90–91
  thirteen, 90, 101–2
Numbers, unlucky, 4–5
  four, 92–93
  thirteen, 4–5, 39, 89–90, 92, 93–94, 97
Nuns, psychological study of, 75
Nurses, psychological study of, 75–76
Nyman, Andy, 83–85

Oakland Athletics, 137
Obedience to Authority (Milgram), 110
"Obedience to Authority with an Authentic Victim" (Sheridan and King), 111
Occupations
  impact of height and choice of, 147, 148
  surnames effecting choice of, 4, 139, 140, 146
Ocean's Eleven (movie), 47
Odd numbers, choosing, 230
O'Keeffe, Ciarán, 122, 124
Ola (chimpanzee), 12
Open-mindedness and caring as traits of Democrats, 157
Optimism, 14, 31, 43, 276
Orbicularis oculi muscle, 72–73, 74
Organ pipes and low-frequency sounds, 126
Oshichi, Yaoya, 94
Out of This World (TV program), 97–98
"Outrageous Okona, The" (*Star Trek: The Next Generation* episode), 204
Overpayments, people's reactions to, 235–39
Owen, Adrian, 199–200, 224

Pace of life, 259–61, 268–72
Padgett, Vernon, 103–4
Palo Alto, California (as a caring community), 263
"Pan American" smile. *See* Fake smiles
Paranormal activities. *See* Ghosts and ghostly phenomena
Parents
  lying about child's birthday, 39–41
  manipulating child's birth date to obtain tax benefits, 35–36, 44
Paris, France (pace of life in), 270
"Pass the parcel" studies, 90, 111–12, 113–14, 246
Patterson, Francine, 47–49
Patterson, New Jersey (level of helpfulness in), 257
Paulos, John Allen, 112
"Peanuts" comic strip (Schulz), 41
Pelham, Brett, 138–40
Pellegrini, Robert, 152
"Peritsi," 148
Personal ads, 4, 129, 169–73
  tips for writing, 171, 173, 276
Personality characteristics
  accuracy of astrological predictions, 14–16
  choice of greeting cards, 267
  Forer's personality test, accuracy of, 20–23
Personality Inventory, 13–14, 15
Persons, Chuck, 91
Pessimism and mortality rate, 43
Petiot, Marcel, 24–25
Petranoff, Robert, 130–32
Phenomena (journal), 15
Philip (prince), 90–91
Phillips, David, 41–43, 92–93, 136, 145–46
Photographs
  composite photographs of presidents, 155–57
  of facial expressions, 67–68
  of real and fake smiles, 68, 73–75
Physical characteristics of lying, 58
Physical response to another based on excitement, 163–64
Pick up lines, 164–69
Pillinger, Colin, 197

Pineault, Tony, 61
Pisces (astrological sign), 14
Pizza topping, choice of, 167
Plant, Robert, 144
Plato, 181, 185, 186, 191
Pogo the Clown, 19
Police Squad! (movie), 62
Polish men, height study, 147
Politics
  facial hair, impact on evaluation of candidates, 153–54
  height of candidates, 148–49, 150
  political ads, 133
  politicians and lying, 53
  surnames effecting choice of candidates, 139–40
Population density effecting helpfulness, 258–59
Positive astrological signs, 26
Positive emotions and life expectancy, 75–76
Post Offices, gauging speed at, 259–61, 268–69
Powell, Bingham, and Bingham-Powell, 107
Power of suggestion. *See* Suggestion, power of
"Practice what you preach," 254–55
Prague, Czech Republic (pace of life in), 270
Prayer and life expectancy, 2
Prejudice, 227–29, 252
Presidents
  facial analysis of, 154–57
  height of, 148–49
Pretend the World Is Funny and Forever (Fisher and Fisher), 210
Pride of the Yankees (movie), 161–62
Priests, honesty of, 255–56
"Prison study," 262
Producers, The (movie), 215
"Professional" audience members, 206
Professors and Trivial Pursuit, 142, 275
Prosocial behavior. *See* Antisocial behavior
Psychological benefits of laughter, 213
Psychology of time. *See* Chronopsychology
Punch (magazine), 220
Punch lines, 199
Puns, 200, 202
Pupil size revealing interest, 175–76

Q test for lying, xi–xii, 52–53
Quiet night in hospital jinx, 100

Racial prejudice, measuring, 227–29, 252
Railroad station experiment on time passing, 1, 268–69
Ramat Gan, Israel, superstition and stress in, 104–5
Rasputin, 245
Rat, beheading of, 4, 67–68
Reagan, Nancy, 7, 37
Reagan, Ronald, 7, 80–81, 109, 149, 155
Reanimation of the dead, 70–72
Regents Park Zoo, 120
Reiner, Carl, 214
Relaxed personality, 14, 30–31
Religion
  evaluating honesty of priests, 255–56
  helpfulness of various religious groups, 253–55
  religious fundamentalism and laughter, 216–19
Remembering, deceptive, 77–81
Republic, The (Plato), 185
Republican Party, 133, 154, 155, 156
Restaurants and tipping, 142–43, 146
Retina, 69–70
Review of Economics and Statistics (journal), 43
Rieur, 206
Rio de Janeiro (Brazil), level of helpfulness in, 258
Risk takers and month of birth, 31–33
Ritchie, Graham, 198
Rochester, New York (level of helpfulness in), 257
Rogers, Jimmie, 144

Romantic deception, 51, 57
Roosevelt, Franklin Delano, 155
Rorschach Inkblot Test, 210–11
Rotton, James, 213, 214–15
Royal Institution, 197
Rozin, Paul, 106
Rudeness in New York City, 260
Rush (music group), 144
Ruth, Babe, 137

"Sad clowns," 209, 210, 211, 213
Sagittarius (astrological sign), 14, 26
Saint, cities' names beginning with, 138
Salaries effected by height, 148
Salivary immunoglobulin A, 214
San Jose (Costa Rica), level of helpfulness in, 258
Santa Claus, size of in drawings, 4
Saroglou, Vasilis, 216–19
Saving money and decision making, 127–28
Saving Private Ryan (movie), 214
Savoy Hotel (London), 89–90, 107
Scanlon, Thomas, 93–94
School Sisters of Notre Dame, 75
Schulz, Charles, 41
Scientists, sense of humor of, 197–98
Scorpio (astrological sign), 14, 26
Scotsmen as butt of jokes, 186–87
Scottish Neolithic passage grave, 126
Scribbler, Ernest, 179, 180
Séances, 83–86. *See also* Ghosts and ghostly phenomena
Seinfeld, Jerry, 188
"Self vs. others" in personal ads, 170–71
Self-control, loss of, 216
Self-deception. *See* Deception
Self-disparaging jokes, 190
Self-esteem, levels of, 14, 134, 146
Self-identity, 23
Self-image, 16–17
Self-monitoring, 52
Self-perception, impact of superiority jokes on, 188
Sellers, Peter, 224–25
Senpu, 96
Sensation seekers and month of birth, 31–33
Sensho, 96
"Sensory overload" theory, 259, 260, 272
Serial killers. *See* Mass-murderers
Sesame Street (TV show), 48
Seven (the number), 90–91
Shakespeare, William, 109, 214
Shakku, 96
Shatner, William, 110
Shelley, Mary, 71–72
Sheridan, Charles, 110–11
Sherman, Vincent, 247
Shopping
- misuse of express lane in grocery stores, 4, 233–34
- music effecting wine purchases, 144
- "shopping mall" study, 79

"Short" on cash, 147
Shortness of description and lying, 58–59, 64
Shrinking world. *See* Small world
Siffre, Michel, 27
Simenon, Georges, 39
Similarity, psychology of, 239
- giving aid only to those with similar views, 241–42
- horn honking study, 242–43
- and similar birth dates, 244–45

Simmon, Dan, 122, 124
Simpsons, The (TV show), 204
Singapore, 252, 258, 272
Singh, Simon, 54, 197
"Six degrees of separation," 111–12
Slapstick humor, 202
Slemrod, Joel, 44
Small world, 109–10, 112–15, 246, 257. *See also* Shrinking world
- coincidences, 107–15
- "pass the parcel" studies, 90, 111–12, 113–14, 246

Smiles, 46, 65–70
- detecting real smiles vs. fake, 72–75, 276–77
- effecting sense of humor, 204–5
- of *Mona Lisa*, 69–70, 276
- people responding to, 205–6
- showing happiness, 65–66, 204

Smith, Gary, 136–37

Smith, Katie, 113
Smith, Matthew, 97–98
Smith, Stephen, 161
Sneakers, choice of color, 230
"Soapy Sam," 8
Social Register, The, 137
Social responsibility, creating, 263–64
Social status and number of jokes told, 190
Sofia, Bulgaria (pace of life in), 270
Some Like It Hot (movie), 55, 56, 59, 60
Sorrows of Young Werther, The (Goethe), 145
Sound waves, 119–26
Sour cream as favorite food, 63–64
South Park (TV show), 121
Southern Hemisphere study of luck, 34–35
Spain, honking car horns in, 242–43
Speed dating, 4, 164–69
Speeding near a school, 234
Spirits. *See* Séances
Spirituality in church and low-frequency sounds, 126
Sporting success and birth date, 28–29
Stack, Fritz, 204–5
Stack, Steven, 144–45
Star Trek: The Next Generation (TV show), 204
Stars in Their Eyes (TV show), 167
State of the World's Cities (UN), 272
Stature and Stigma (Martel and Biller), 147
Status and height, 149–51
Stereotypes, 134, 188
  and criminals, 159, 160
  effect of on behavior, 141–42
  and facial appearance, 153, 154, 157
  influence of Hollywood on stereotyping, 161–62
  national stereotypes, 220, 242
Stewart, John, 160
Stockholm, Sweden (pace of life in), 270
Stop signs, failure to stop at, 234
Stress
  and laughter, 214
  and numbers, 92–94
Student's Guide to the Seashore (Fish and Fish), 140
Study in Scarlet (Doyle), 273
Subliminal perception
  and magicians, 81–83
  subliminal messages, 128, 129–34
Suedfield, Peter, 240
Suggestion, power of, 81–87
  and false memories, 77, 77–79
Suicides
  comedians and, 209
  copycat suicides, 145–46
  and country music, 4–5, 144–45
Summer births and lucky people, 33–34, 276
Sun (newspaper), 11
Superiority as a basis for humor, 184–91, 193, 211
Supermarkets, misuse of express lines, 4, 233–34
Superstition, 4, 89–106
  growth of in perilous times, 103–5
  and hospitals, 93–94, 96, 99–100
Surely You're Joking, Mr. Feynman (Feynman), 231
Surnames, 128, 146
  and choice of residence, 138
  effecting choice of marriage partner, 138–39
  effecting choice of occupation, 4, 139, 140, 146
  effecting choice of political candidates, 139–40
  with negative connotations, 135–36
Susan (unlucky person), 30
Sweater, choosing to wear, 106
Sweden and caring communities, 262
Switzerland
  and caring communities, 262
  pace of life in, 260
Syria and caring communities, 262

Taian, 96
Tandy, Vic, 118–20, 122, 125
Tanzania, laughter plague in, 206
Taurus (astrological sign), 14, 26

Taxes
tax benefits of December birth, 35–36
tax liability influencing date of death, 43
Tea, brewing, 2–3
Teaspoons, mystery of the disappearing, 232–33
Tel Aviv, Israel, 258
superstition and stress in, 104–5
Temperature, outside
at time of birth and impact of on luck, 33–35
and time of death, 42
Teresa, Mother, 235
"Thank you" and tipping, 143
Theft
of money from collection boxes, 247–49
of teaspoons, 232–33
Thermal conductivity and firewalking, 115
"Third Reich joke courts," 187
Thirteen (the number), 89–90, 92, 93, 97
Friday the thirteenth, 4–5, 39, 93–94
Thirteen Club (in New York), 101–2
Tia (in investment study), 8–12
Tiberias, Israel, superstition and stress in, 104–5
Time (magazine), 213
Time, passage of. *See also* Chronopsychology
judging passage of time, 1, 27, 268
"Time twins" experiment, 17–19, 40–41
Times Square (New York City), 249
Tipping, 142–43, 146
Tips for writing personal ads, 171, 173
To Tell the Truth (TV show), 61–62
Todorov, Alexander, 153
Tokyo, Japan (pace of life in), 270
Tomhave, Judith, 205
Tomobiki, 96
Tomorrow's World (TV show), 53, 56, 115–16, 158–60
Tonight Show with Jay Leno (TV show), 11
Touching wood, 91, 96, 103
Tour de France race, 18
Traffic citations and bumper stickers, 243–44
"Trait Humor and Longevity: Do Comics Have the Last Laugh" (Rotton), 213
Trinkaus, John, 230–35
Trivial Pursuit (game), 142, 275
Trobriand Islanders, 103
Truman, Harry, 155
Turner, John, 150
Turner, Joseph Mallord William, 67
"2,000 Year-Old-Man" routine, 214
"Two of us" in personal ads, 170–71
Type A personality, 261

Ultrasound, 120
Unethical behavior, 233–39. *See also* Antisocial behavior; Deception; Lying
United Kingdom, 269. *See also* Britain; England
United Nations (UN), 272
United States
American sense of humor, 207–8, 220, 221–22
and caring communities, 262
Université Catholique de Louvain, 216
Unlucky
ambient temperature and unlucky people, 33–35
black cat crossing your path, 99
in Japan, 94–95, 96
luck and "pass the parcel" studies, 113–15
unlucky numbers, 4–5, 89–90, 92, 93, 97
unlucky people and birth date, 29–35
Unusual first names, benefits of, 137–38
Up the Down Staircase (movie), 162
Us, focus in personal ads, 170–71
U.S. Air Force, 130
U.S. News and World Report (magazine), 235
Used car, treatment of, 263
Used-car dealers, honesty of, 255–56

Van drivers, women, 233–35
Vanishing gloves mystery, 231–32

Vicary, James, 129, 130, 132–33
Vienna, Austria (pace of life in), 270
Violence in the media, impact of, 246–50
Virgo (astrological sign), 14, 26
Vogue (magazine), 77

Wade, Kimberley, 77–79
Walk on fire, 115–16
Walking down streets, measuring speed of, 266-8
Walking under ladders, 91, 97
Wall Street Journal (newspaper), 12
Warsaw, Poland (pace of life in), 270
Washington Park Zoo (Indiana), 46–47
Water Music (Handel), 25
Watson, Aeron, 126
Watson, Dr. (joke about), 191, 222
Watt, Caroline, 165
"We Do What We're Told (Milgram's 37)" (Gabriel), 110
"Weasel chomping" jokes, 203, 221–22
Weather forecasts, accuracy of, 230
"Wekepei," 148
Werther Effect, 145
When Harry Met Sally (movie), 214
Who Was Who, 37, 38
Who's Who, 37, 38, 137, 138
"Why did the chicken cross the road?," 182, 192
"Why Susie Sells Seashells by the Seashore: Implicit Egotism and Major Life Decisions" (Pelham), 139–40
Wilberforce, Samuel, 8
Williams, Robin, 180, 223–24
Williams, Steve, 200
"willing self to live longer," 43
Wilson, Paul, 149–50
Wilson, Woodrow, 90
Wine purchases and music, 144
Wing and a Prayer, A (movie), 80–81
Withdrawn personalities as unlucky people, 31
Wittgenstein, Ludwig, 181
Wolff, Harold, 186–87
Women, 188. *See also* Gender differences
  women van drivers acting antisocially, 233–35, 276
Worcester, Massachusetts, 251
Word of mouth, sharing information via, 130
Words vs. actions, 227–29
World in Action (TV program), 235, 255
World War II, 51
World's funniest joke, 179–225
  final result, 221–25
WTTV (Indianapolis), 131

Yahoo Internet Yellow Pages, 139
Year of the Fire-Horse, 94–95
"Yes," use of compared to other terms, 230
You, focus in personal ads, 170–71

Zaritsky, John, 207
Zimbardo, Philip, 262–63
Zodiac, signs of, 14, 26
Zweigenhaft, Richard, 137
Zygomatic major muscle, 72–73, 74